PN
1995   LAHUE   29544
.9   Continued next week
.S3
L3

Illinois Central College
Learning Resource Center

CONTINUED NEXT WEEK

A History of the Moving Picture Serial

CONTINUED
NEXT WEEK
A HISTORY
OF THE
MOVING PICTURE SERIAL

BY KALTON C. LAHUE

With a Foreword by
Kent D. Eastin

UNIVERSITY OF OKLAHOMA PRESS

NORMAN

PN
1995
.9
.S3
L3

STANDARD BOOK NUMBER: 8061–0633–6

LIBRARY OF CONGRESS CATALOG CARD NUMBER: 64–20767

Copyright 1964 by the University of Oklahoma Press, Publishing Division of the University. Manufactured in the U.S.A. First edition, December, 1964. Second printing, October, 1969.

FOREWORD

My first recollection of a movie serial is a chapter from *The Adventures of Kathlyn* which I saw presented in a small western-Iowa town sometime before World War I. The memory I have carried down the years is one of Kathlyn Williams in the middle of a ring of lions in some remote spot in the jungle. But the first serial that I recall with any degree of clarity is *Hands Up,* in which Ruth Roland starred for Pathé in 1918. This was the first "cliff-hanger" I attended on a regular weekly basis, and it made considerable impression on me. I got shortchanged on this, for the final chapters were scheduled to play the Empress Theater in Galesburg, Illinois, at what turned out to be the time of the Spanish-influenza epidemic during World War I. All theaters were closed for four weeks, and when they reopened, for some reason or other I missed the climactic final chapters.

I have varying recollections of the Eddie Polo serials made by Universal, which always played at the Empress; the ones made by Vitagraph starring Antonio Moreno, which were shown at the Princess, a block down Main Street; and *The Master Mystery,* with Houdini, and *Bride 13,* produced by Fox, both of which were exhibited at the West on Prairie Street, just off Main, where, a few years later, I made my first formal contact with the motion-picture industry by distributing handbills publicizing the attraction that would fill the theater the following week.

My memories are boyhood memories which could probably be shared today with thousands of other persons, for in the years of their box-office greatness, serials attracted everyone—boys and girls, men and women—and even matinee attendance was substantial. I have a clear memory of several evenings when I persuaded my parents to take me to see what would otherwise have been a missed chapter—of long waits in line and of adults hemming me in on all sides.

The movie serial, which, for all practical purposes, antedated the feature picture by two or three years, came about for a combination of reasons. A particular void existed in movie entertainment in 1912, as productions were limited to one or two reels and players were only beginning to be known by name. Short, unrelated films offered no opportunity to develop anything very complicated in the way of a story or to secure the association of a particular group of players with a particular set of characters. Although longer films of four and five reels were being considered, these faced the obstacle of having to break established program patterns. But a serial could accomplish the objectives of an involved and suspenseful plot, feature the same cast in the same parts over a period of weeks, and still fit into the one- or two-reel unit of programming. Thus it was during the era of the short program that the serial had its greatest success. Yet storytelling in series or serial form was not original with the movies, but, rather, was borrowed by them from fiction magazines and metropolitan newspapers of the day, virtually all of which featured serialized fiction on some regular basis.

By 1916 or 1917, feature pictures had taken over the screens of all the leading movie theaters in every city, and the serials were relegated to the position of added attractions. Although they were still potent at the box office, they had passed their peak, and by the very early 1920's, they were used more or less by the western houses or theaters in smaller towns for Friday and Saturday showings. The serials themselves hadn't changed much, although they were more elaborately produced and were better technically—but everything around them was changing, including the tastes of their once great audience.

Nowadays, silent-movie serials are somewhat of a minor legend, with very little about them accurately remembered by the public generally, and with very few of their several thousand chapters available for showing today. They are not something taken seriously where the art and technical advances of the screen are considered, so little has been done to preserve them as has been the case with most important feature pictures and the great short comedies of the silent era. Not that intent alone could have made this possible, for many of the serial producers of the silent days were firms that have long since ceased to exist. Where some continuity does exist between early producers and companies still in business, many of the original negatives have been lost over the years in vault fires or were deliberately destroyed to avoid storage costs. Today, the only remaining records of most of these productions from 1912 to the early 1920's are represented by prints in the hands of individual collectors who have 35 mm. or 28 mm. copies or 16 mm. prints that were struck thirty or more years ago.

Thus the challenge of researching serial productions for the years of the silents is a great one. When one considers that Kalton Lahue is a young man whose whole movie-going experience has been in the era of sound, one can especially appreciate the result of his labors. In recent years I have done enough in the way of research on various phases of movie history to know that, outside the major archives in New York, Washington, Rochester, and Hollywood, the digging is hard. The several years Kalton has spent in this endeavor have been devoted to running down surviving chapters of various serial productions and, in a few instances, complete copies of these early serials, which have been made available for him to view. He has been successful in reconstructing the statistics on credits and chapter titles for a rather high percentage of these chapter plays.

Over the years, many volumes have been written on various aspects of motion-picture history. Too few of them, however, have made available specific information about a segment of production from years gone by, such as Kalton has been able to provide in this volume for the silent serials, the people who made them, and their impact on the public at the time of their release.

Many of you may recall with warm affection a Friday evening or a Saturday when the notes of a piano or pianola were drowned out by the shrieks and clapping of the audience as the hero or

vii

heroine seemed about to plunge into some abyss from which he or she could hardly be expected to survive (but always did)—and the answer was a long, long week away. As for me, I'm still hoping to see one day those final chapters of *Hands Up* which for me, away back in 1918, were "Continued Next Week!"

KENT D. EASTIN
President, Eastin-Phelan Corporation

Davenport, Iowa

ACKNOWLEDGMENTS

As is always the case with a volume like this, there are more thanks to be given than space to give them. It certainly would not have been possible to put this information together without the help of many people, some of whom I wish to single out for a special reason. For the loan of material without which this project could not have been finished, many thanks should go to Ira A. Vincent, Albert B. Manski, Howard Nelson, and Tom Burkland. For their encouragement to continue when my spirits ebbed, my wife, Jeanne, along with Edgar Shew and Samuel K. Rubin, should be mentioned. With regard to particular assistance in documentation of the era, much help was given by Helen Gibson, Crane Wilbur, Francis MacDonald, Harry Benham, Grace Cunard, and Frank Leon Smith. Research, which is often a long and difficult task, was made much easier by the cheerful attitude and co-operation of Miss Cornelia Metz of the Film Library, Museum of Modern Art. Research facilities of the New York Public Library and the Kodak Library at Kodak Park, Rochester, New York, were also utilized. Miss Helen Poljacik gave up part of her vacation and carefully read the manuscript, offering constructive criticism on its final form. Finally, to the many wonderful people across the country who took time to drop an encouraging line and inquire about the progress of my work—thank you!

CONTENTS

ILLUSTRATIONS

Between pages 126 and 127

Jack Mower, Allene Ray, Larry Steers *(Ten Scars Make A Man)*——Allene Ray *(Hawk of The Hills)*——Jack Daugherty, Lola Todd *(The Scarlet Streak)*——Spencer G. Bennet, Gene Tunney, Frank Leon Smith *(The Fighting Marine)* ——Grace Cunard *(Blake of Scotland Yard)*——William Desmond, Ethlyne Clair *(The Vanishing Rider)*——Derelys Perdue, Tom London *(The Mystery Rider)*——Hayden Stevenson, Louise Lorraine *(The Diamond Master)*

INTRODUCTION

This is a work of love. What you are about to read has been compiled from original sources, carefully researched, and documented from trade papers, press books, shooting scripts, advertising posters, actual films, and many other items of the silent-movie era. Wherever there was a conflict in such sources, and there were many, I attempted to resolve the difference by resorting to information from people who were in the middle of things during those glorious days. The trade papers, such as *The Moving Picture World* and *The Motion Picture News,* although much more accurate than the fan magazines of the day, were notorious in their attempts to build a legend of glamour around the film colony, with little regard for facts. For example, so many different stories abound about the early days of Pearl White that you can take your pick. In such cases, where the star is either deceased or unavailable for comment, I have made a careful study of the conflicting stories, with a sharp eye toward corroborating facts. Documentation in the form of letters written to collectors by the star was considered when these were available.

I do not claim that *Continued Next Week* is an infallible record of the silent serial. What I do claim is that it is as careful a compilation of facts as many years of intense effort will provide. Most of the leading personalities are gone forever, their memories unrecorded; others refuse to discuss the past for reasons known only to them. And many of the actual films are lost forever to the human eye, for it was a favorite stunt of the early pioneers to use release prints, which they felt had served their purpose, for bonfires in new productions. If the company was pressed for operating funds, the prints were sold to firms which used them as a base for manufacturing varnish.

At the end of the text, in the Appendix, you'll find as complete a record of serials from 1913 to 1930 as years of probing will allow. This part of my task was made very difficult by certain tricks of the trade. It was common in the silent days to announce production of a serial and then proceed to change the working title several times before final release was made. A striking example of this was a 1920 release by Vitagraph which started out as *Moods of Evil*. This was changed to *The Black Circle*, which was, in turn, changed to *The Vanishing Mask*. Final release saw it entitled *Hidden Dangers*. From the end of World War I until the end of the silent period, state-right releases grew in popularity. A state-right release, or SR, was sold to area distributors, who, in turn, sold the exhibition rights to individual theaters or chains, whereas a regular release was distributed through the exchange system of the producing firm. The state-right release allowed many small firms to incorporate, produce a serial, sell the distribution rights, and fold up with a profit. Many fly-by-night and oddball firms popped up in the motion-picture field during the twenties. Some of these put forth serials which had little, if any, documentation in print. Therefore, you'll find that certain of these entries are somewhat vague. Their mark has been nearly erased from the pages of history, never to return. This is truer of the latter part of the period than of the early twenties.

Another point of explanation before we explore the wonderful world of the silent serial. If for some reason you find a favorite series missing from my record, it is because it is just that, a series. Here we have a fine point of differentiation between a serial and a series. I had to draw the line somewhere in order to include only what I considered to be truly a serial. Many series of films were made starring the same actor or actress but with no connection in plot. In certain cases, I accepted the term as given by the producer. Thus you'll not find Eddie Polo's series *Cyclone Smith* included. In cases of doubt, I drew this line: a serial contained the same leading figures in the cast, and it had a plot which interconnected each episode, whether these divisions were complete in themselves or were "cliff-hangers." A series, although it might contain the same cast, had no broad connecting plot between chapters. You may argue with my choices or my method.

Let me say here and now that too often the serial has been overlooked as an insignificant part of the film industry. Many people have considered it trash, not worth the time and effort. This may have been true in the sound era; I don't know, because I'm not an expert in that field. I do know that the serial was important during the period discussed in this work, and I also know that nowhere else will you find the information collected here. Very little in the way of serious film history has been done in the past sixty years, and Terry Ramsaye, Lewis Jacobs, Ben Hampton, and the few other cinema historians of note have really paid little attention to the serial as film and entertainment. I hope that the pages which follow will help fill that gap in knowledge of the motion picture and that the memories they arouse will be happy ones of less troublesome times.

CONTINUED NEXT WEEK

A History of the Moving Picture Serial

CHAPTER ONE

A BOLT FROM THE BLUE

WITH THE INTRODUCTION of the motion picture around the turn of the century, America had found a new form of entertainment. A measure of the real success of this medium of expression, which was used at first as a "chaser" by the vaudeville houses, can be found in the rapid growth of the nickelodeon from 1907 on. Actors of the legitimate stage frowned upon the movie from the beginning, and it was 1913 before their disfavor began to give way. The people took the motion picture to their hearts, much to the disgust of the rich, well-born, and intellectual.

By 1913, such pioneers such as David Wark Griffith, Adolph Zukor, and Thomas H. Ince had brought the movies out of obscurity: motion pictures were well on their way to developing styles and values of their own. Innovations in methods of filming were being brought forth, to be copied and improved upon, and the classics were being produced with increasing competence and length. "Famous Players in Famous Plays" was the byword of the day as producers climbed aboard the bandwagon. The ever increasing competition provided by foreign imports and the classics, as filmed by Zukor and Lasky, were destined to check the ascent of the older companies and eventually bring about their demise. A certain amount of resistance was to be found surrounding the heads of the older firms, a most notable instance being Biograph's refusal to market the three- and four-reel pictures that Griffith desired to produce. It was in this setting that one of the most interesting phenomena of the world of motion pictures, the American serial, was born. A buoyant baby, it was to change its form several times during the years it reigned as a top money-maker.

For the relatively short period of sixteen years, roughly 1914 to 1930, these weekly thrillers captured their audiences. People cheered the heroine on, hissed and booed the villain, and clapped loudly when the forces of right and justice triumphed over evil. The serial made no pretentious claims to immortality as an art form, as have other segments of the film industry. It had no right to recognition as such and never once pretended to. It was designed for one purpose: to entertain the masses and to show its achievement by the box-office receipts. To this end, its purpose was fulfilled, and well so. The serial began as a by-product of newspaper circulation wars and ended as the mainstay of production for two major companies in the 1920's.

By 1915, almost all of the older companies large enough to command the necessary backing had at least one serial on the market and sometimes two or three at the same time. They were not prepared to invest the sums necessary to produce the feature pictures that were becoming so popular. Their fears of shooting long, expensive pictures led them to invest in something which could be shot in a short time, at a small cost, and could be relied upon for a good return upon release. As the serial proved itself, more time and money, better plots and actresses, were devoted to the production of the product. In 1915, the list of companies turning out serials read like an honor role of the early film pioneers: American, Edison, Lubin, Kalem, Universal, Pathé, Thanhouser, Vitagraph, Reliance. The serial became a tremendous factor in their success and survival. One conspicuous absence was that of the Biograph Company, which, for reasons I've never been able to determine satisfactorily, never released a single serial. However, the firm was not to remain in business much longer, and even some of the companies which ground out serial after serial would fall by the wayside in the next few years. Failure can be traced, more than anything else, to their refusal to treat the serial in its proper perspective and release quality features at the same time.

The serial was destined to be the gravy or dessert of the motion-picture business. Periodic release of features provided the working edge necessary, and the occasional release of serials, filmed at low cost by using actors between pictures and sets which had been constructed for the higher-budget features, provided the quick financial return so smiled upon in the industry. Pathé, one of the two companies most successful with serials in the twenties, planned to make six to eight during the year; this figure varied with the market. The production of serials, however, was a minuscule portion of total production during the year. Paul Brunet of Pathé realized that one could easily overdo a good thing.

Earlier, I mentioned that newspaper circulation wars gave birth to the serial. This was not quite true in one respect. What is considered to be the forerunner of the serials, *What Happened To Mary?*, came about as the result of an arrangement between *McClure's Ladies World* and the Edison Company for a series of one-reel films which were to be released simultaneously with the publication of a group of short stories containing the same plot. The series starred one of the favorite Edison actresses, Mary Fuller, in an independent and complete film play released each month. The resulting product was actually a cross between a series, as such, and a serial. Designed to increase the number of readers of the magazine, it was important because of the impetus it created.

The opening chapter was slightly over one thousand feet in length and began with a prologue which found Mary as a baby who had been deliberately left on the doorstep of a storekeeper in a small community. Attached to her was a note directed to the storekeeper telling him that if he would raise her and marry her to one of the local boys, he would receive $1,000 in addition to the $500 which had been left with the baby in the basket. The story then jumped ahead to find Mary at sweet eighteen and wanting to leave town for the big city. In an attempt to obtain the extra money promised him, the foster father had been trying to marry her off, but she had managed to resist all of his attempts. One day, while rummaging around in the drawers of a chest, she came across the secret of her parentage and made up her mind at once that under no circumstances would she marry anyone chosen for her. A feeling of resentment came over her and she decided that her foster father had no right to keep her against her will. She

5

immediately made arrangements to leave by ship, and the reel ended with her on her way to the city after narrowly escaping the clutches of the foster father. The remaining episodes detailed her experiences in making a new life for herself.

Many of the early serials were complete episodes related to each other only by characters or a broad plot which tied together some fifteen to twenty individual subplots. Although it depended upon the company or serial, many producers had discovered by 1915 that they could work up interest in following installments by teasing the audience. The episode would devote itself to working up the tempo of action and danger to a high pitch, then suddenly the following announcement would flicker across the screen: "See The Next Episode Of This Serial At This Theatre Next ———." Financially speaking, the serial became much more successful when the "cliff-hangers" took over from the complete episodes. Many other gimmicks became standard procedure in the prewar years to increase the drawing power of the product. Among these was the practice of purposely leaving the story unfinished and so advertising it. A large prize was then offered to anyone who could submit an original and clever ending for the serial. Thanhouser offered $10,000 to the person who submitted the best 100-word solution for its *Million Dollar Mystery*. Ida Damon of St. Louis won the prize for Chapter 23 of this serial. A check for $5,000 was offered to anyone who could submit a suitable sequel for *The Diamond From The Sky*. Terry Ramsaye collected this tidy sum. Much material was thus offered to the professionals by amateurs, and although they denied it, with a bit of revision the ideas could be utilized at almost no cost or effort on the part of film writers or companies. Replies to these contests flooded in by the thousands. Money and more money was offered to entice the public and focus attention on the serials.

The year 1913 saw the actual serial form evolve. William Selig of the Selig Polyscope Company in Chicago had carefully thought through an idea, and he finally decided that it was worth trying. Newspapers and magazines had been publishing serial stories for some time and the effect was to be noticed in their increased circulation. Readers came back, week after week, to find out "What happened?" Why not the same thing with motion pictures? After all, if one could bring the same people back week after week, wouldn't it help his business? It was a matter of injecting a bit of certainty into the life of both exhibitor and producer. If he could talk a publisher into collaborating with him, both stood to profit handsomely. The stories would be read in the paper, or magazine, then viewed on the screen, or vice versa. This was basically the same idea behind *What Happened To Mary?* but Selig wanted to carry it out in a bigger manner and turn out an adventure story of sufficient interest to exploit the possibilities fully. Taking his idea to the *Chicago Tribune,* he explained it in detail. This was the same paper which had raised its voice in favor of abolishing the nickelodeons some five years before, but times were different then. Now the *Tribune* was fighting a vicious circulation battle with its six rivals, with no holds barred, and the race for readers had resulted in open warfare at times. Therefore, it was not surprising that the *Tribune*'s publishers agreed with Selig, and in December, 1913, the silent serial took form.

The fulfillment of Selig's idea was *The Adventures of Kathlyn,* and it starred a beautiful five-foot five-inch blonde, Kathlyn Williams. The story was adapted by Gilson Willets from Harold McGrath's story of the same name and was later published in book form by the Bobbs-Merrill Company of Indianapolis. Both men were to become famous in the film industry for their later work in serials. The first episode, released on December 29, 1913, in three reels, was entitled "The Unwelcome Throne." Twelve other installments followed, each of them two reels in length. Every chapter was complete in itself, although all of them were related to one another. For the most part, the film consisted of incidents that were only loosely bound together and wasn't very deep as far as the plot was concerned. It dealt with the adventures of an American girl who, under compulsion, had inherited a throne in India and her problems therewith. Both the plot and the direction were full of inconsistencies, but the photography and acting, especially on the part of Miss Williams, were excellent. Its scenes were filled with wild animals, and, as we shall see, Selig was to make this a part of his future success. The film did not prove to be smashing in its popularity, but for Selig and the *Tribune*, it was a godsend. The *Tribune* announced a 10 per cent increase in its circulation as a result.

It was E. A. McManus of the Hearst newspaper chain, however, who was to prove how successful this new type of motion picture could really be. Entering into co-operation with Pathé, he produced what proved to be the first really "big" serial and still the best remembered, *The Perils of Pauline*. An actress named Pearl White was engaged for the title role of Pauline, and with the support of Crane Wilbur and Paul Panzer, she rose to fame almost overnight. Known to her fans as "The Lady Daredevil of the Fillums," she was advertised to the trade with the slogan "Pauline Pulls People." Her popularity in the serial field was unapproachable and lasted for several years. With this example placed before it, the industry leaped upon the bandwagon. The paradox of it all is that although *The Perils of Pauline* has become a classic in the history of motion pictures, it was crudely photographed, directed, edited, and titled. In fact, when one compares it with other films of its time, it becomes an almost unbelievable farce, far behind its contemporaries.

The most unforgivable and yet humorous crime committed by those who put this serial together was the use, in the subtitles, of grammar that made even children laugh. In one episode, the subtitles inform us that the Indians are about to test the "immortal" strength of Pearl, but the word *immoral* appears instead. Many other errors in spelling and punctuation appeared throughout the subtitles, and one wonders how they ever reached the screen unnoticed. The most logical reply came from Crane Wilbur, who explained that although the subtitles were written into the original scripts, the editing of the chapters brought many changes in them. Generally speaking, those in charge of the production of this serial were French and spoke in broken English. Apparently, they wrote in the same medium. Louis Gasnier, who did much of the directing and supervised all of it, made many ridiculous mis-

8

takes in his spoken English. On one occasion, he ordered his American assistant to find the "mechanish." What he meant was the mechanic who repaired cameras. The confused assistant came back with a bottle of magnesia.

The plot of the serial was simple enough. It dealt with the attempts of Koerner, the villain, played by Paul Panzer, to steal Pauline's inheritance. Crane Wilbur, as Pauline's guardian, was unable to convince her of Koerner's complicity in the incidents which befell her until the final episode. The chapters were complete, not cliff-hangers, and Pearl fought Indians, pirates, gypsies, and many others throughout the course of the serial. Miss White came across on the screen as a genuine personality and although Panzer and Wilbur gave decent performances in their featured roles, the others involved acted on the same level as the writing and direction. As a result of *The Perils of Pauline,* Pearl's characterization created the heroine of a song, *Poor Pauline,* copyrighted in 1914 by the Broadway Music Corporation. All in all, it was much a case of the right actress in the right role at the right time. It is quite probable that even an actress of greater stature than Miss White could not have carried it off any better.

A careful study of the life of Pearl Fay White has been made most exasperating by the lack of facts and the overabundance of half-truths and fanciful myths, especially about her early years. It appears that Pearl herself actively instigated many of the false stories, which appealed to the public and which soon became accepted as fact. Even her autobiography *Just Me,* is entertainingly devoid of the truth. Much has been written about her over the years, and after comparing the many conflicting stories, one becomes increasingly aware that the absolute truth will probably never be completely known. This in itself is a great tragedy, for Pearl White was the most popular and most revered of all the "serial queens." Even her entrance into pictures is undocumented, but it seems that during an appearance in South Norwalk, Connecticut, she began visiting studios and finally signed a contract with the Powers Company at $30 per week. It is known that she worked for Powers in 1910, Lubin in 1911, and Pathé in 1912.

9

Documentation of her career began in October of 1912 when the Crystal Film Company proudly announced that she would appear exclusively in its films. Her work was competent and her name found its way into the early trade magazines at a time when many actors and actresses who were destined to become well known were still having difficulty getting their names into print. The summer of 1913 found her extremely tired mentally and physically but with $6,000 in the bank. Pearl decided to take advantage of the fact that she possessed more money than she ever imagined existed, and on Saturday, July 5, 1913, the charming star of Crystal Films left New York City on board the S.S. *Olympic* to spend six weeks in Europe. Given a send-off by her friends, she even posed for the motion-picture camera. Theater fans were treated to views of her departure when the next edition of *Animated Weekly,* a feature of the Universal program, appeared. Her avowed purpose was to visit the principal European cities, along with the studios of foreign film makers, and to study acting methods abroad. Of the seven months she spent on the Continent, the high point came at the roulette table in Monte Carlo, where she managed to win $9,000, which she promptly spent on an elaborate wardrobe.

Returning home, Pearl ran into an old acquaintance, Theodore Wharton, who was associated with Pathé Frères and who induced her to meet and talk with Louis Gasnier about a new position. Dubious of the ideas outlined by Gasnier, Pearl might have turned down the offer had it not been for a salary of about $250 per week and the promise of a great deal of publicity. She felt that the latter could not help but make her into some kind of a star. She signed, and the rest is film history. *The Perils of Pauline* went into production, and from the very beginning Pearl had many harrowing experiences which were performed for the camera but which never turned out quite the way they were supposed to. Most were filmed exactly as they happened. For one sequence, the exteriors were to be shot in Chinatown. Her director had already made arrangements for the use of a Chinese restaurant, but when the crew arrived, it was found that the proprietor had thought the matter over and decided that he would not allow his establishment to be

10

used. This was a small matter to Gasnier, who decided to go ahead anyway, refusal or no refusal. Asking Pearl if she were game, he received an affirmative reply and shooting began. The script called for a riot scene and a riot scene was what the cameras caught, but it was real and not staged. The police had to be called in to quell the disturbance and in the process, Pearl lost her cape and much of her fine gown.

After this mishap, the crew went back to the studio to film interior shots for the remainder of the day. It was then that Pearl found she was supposed to be hidden in a secret room behind a sliding panel in the wall. This was to be accomplished by the Chinese henchmen of the villain. The part called for her to be unconscious, and in order to convey this impression to the audience, she was to keep her eyes closed while being hidden. The Chinese extras who had been hired for the scene had no experience before the cameras and they were determined to make a favorable impression. Picking her up much as a mob would pick up a log to break down a door, they headed for the sliding panel. It was in this manner that Pearl found out something which no one had bothered to check: she didn't fit the opening. Her head was soundly knocked on the casing, and both arms were skinned up to the elbows by the sides of the narrow opening in the wall. A liberal application of medicinal creams and oils soon relieved the pain, and back to work she went. The next scene called for a vicious struggle between heroine and captors. Pearl was quite a husky girl and able to handle most men without too much difficulty, but she met her match with the Chinese actors. Still anxious to make a favorable impression, something that they had not accomplished in the previous scene, they broke out a repertory of jujitsu. This art of self-defense was totally unfamiliar to Pearl, and she had taken a sound beating by the end of the scene. Her reward was more of the soothing creams and oils.

On another occasion, Miss White was turned loose in a runaway balloon. The balloon was to be tied and the runaway scenes faked, but someone forgot to tie the rope properly and a heavy gust of wind pulled the balloon and Pearl free and up into the wild

11

blue yonder. Immensely enjoying the sensation, she attempted to find a way to bring the balloon down safely. This was no easy task, for she was completely at a loss with the craft. However, she soon discovered the plug in the gas bag, which, when pulled out, allowed the gas to escape and the balloon to descend. Much to her relief, she discovered that it was going to land in a vacant lot. But relief soon turned to despair. As Pearl told the story:

> By vacant, I mean the lot had no house on it, but it was densely populated as regards people. There seemed to be a million faces looking up at me as that basket finally picked out a spot to settle down on, and then it was caught by eager hands and there was hardly room allowed for it to settle on.
>
> Word went up from the back of the crowd that I was Pauline of "The Perils" and those in the back crowded forward and those forward had to push to hold their places, so they pressed up against the gas bag. I was under it and couldn't help inhaling the gas. And that's where the danger came in. The people didn't mean to be thoughtless, but with everybody pushing them, they couldn't help but push too.
>
> One man snatched my purse for a souvenir, so he said. Another man told him to return it and hit him when he refused. The friends of the first man came to his help and about ten fights ensued. Another man took out his penknife and cut a big piece off my coat; this, also, for a souvenir. Others saw him and did the same thing. There's about eight square inches of that coat that isn't there at all.
>
> And all the time, I was inhaling the gas. I knew I was losing consciousness and realized there was little hope that anybody there would see my danger and get me out. If it hadn't been for the mounted police coming to my rescue, that would have been my last peril, I feel certain of that. But they had been on the lookout for me ever since I floated away in the balloon that should have been tied, but wasn't. The water-station was the nearest place, so they took me there and I had to stay for three hours until the crowd dispersed.

Regardless of what happened to this actress, she took it in stride, knowing full well that fate might someday catch up with her. Fearing what she had to do but doing it just the same, she won the admiration and respect of her fellow workers. For the next five years, the thrills continued, although production techniques advanced sufficiently to insure that there would be fewer unplanned adventures. However, she continued to live up to her billing on the three-sheet as "Thrilling, Terrifying, Titantic, Terrific, The Death Defying Sensation, Pearl White." Her stunts were not all in films; much happened in real life. In April, 1917, she participated in the recruiting campaign in New York City. Draped in the U.S. flag, she stood on a swaying steel girder as it was lifted to the twentieth story of a building being erected on Forty-second Street near Broadway. Upon attaining this height, she dropped circulars to attract the attention of passers-by to the Recruiting Service, shouting, "I've done my bit, now do yours!" Throughout her last years, she was to suffer from the effects of a spine injury incurred while filming *The Perils of Pauline*. She never allowed the injury to be publicized, and few people knew that she lived her last days in pain. Charles W. Goddard, the scenarist for *The Perils*, told it this way:

The accident did not occur while Pearl was dropping from a plane or leaping from a train to a speeding automobile, or, in fact, doing anything dangerous at all. It happened in the course of a scene seemingly so safe that the most delicate modern star wouldn't think of asking her double to take over. In my script of "The Perils of Pauline" this scene was covered in exactly seven words:

"Panzer carries Pearl upstairs on his shoulder."

Pearl previously had been knocked out and hog-tied after a furious battle. She was supposed to be unconscious, but, to everyone's surprise, when Panzer got her half-way up the stairs, she suddenly came to life and began threshing around so vigorously that he fell backwards with her in his arms. Later I asked her why she hadn't let him carry her, as he was supposed to do, without a struggle. She replied that she guessed it was her earlier picture training asserting itself. The screen had just grown out of its "St. Vitus Dance" era, when people only went to see a picture because it moved, and the more it moved the more they felt they were getting for their money. The standard studio rule of those days was: Any actor who stops moving is fired.

So Pearl, conscience stricken at feeling herself not doing anything for the moment, automatically had tumbled herself and Panzer down

13

the stairs. Both were hurt by the fall. He was not too proud to see a doctor, but she, the unscathed victim of many a worse accident, refused.

Mr. Goddard's memory failed him on one point, however. It was Francis Carlyle, not Paul Panzer, who was carrying Pearl up the stairs when the accident occurred.

Crane Wilbur recently recalled a couple of incidents dealing with the filming of *The Perils of Pauline* which also illustrate both the ridiculous nature of the plot and the inherent dangers involved during the filming. In the case of the former, Wilbur learned that Pearl had been kidnaped and shut up in an old mill which was being flooded. Since she would surely be drowned, he sped along the beach in a car on his way to rescue her, not knowing that the villains had shot a hole in the gas tank. Of course the car eventually came to a halt, but a gale was blowing up and the purchase of a mast and small mainsail from a fisherman whose boat was pulled up on the beach solved the problem. Wilbur stuck the mast up in the car and went sailing away at high speed on dry land; Managing to reach the mill in time, he broke in and found Pearl in its flooded interior, about to drown as the water level neared the ceiling. The water was full of great rats that had presumably been driven from their holes. The rats were real, but their teeth had been cut out for the scene. They were really frightened, however, and persisted in clinging to Pearl and Crane, thus interrupting the rescue scene. Ultimately, Wilbur dived into the murky water and found a way out through a fireplace and up the chimney to safety. He returned to get Pearl, and the two escaped together.

As for the dangers involved in the filming, one of the most hair-raising came to mind when the question was put to Crane Wilbur. In one scene shot aboard a yacht off the coast of Florida, Pearl and Crane had to make an escape by diving over the side to avoid death at the hands of the villain. The yacht was owned by a millionaire who was sojourning in Florida, and it pleased him no end to have his ship used for the sequences. The cameras were on a tug a short distance from the yacht. Before the scene was taken, both Pearl and Crane were entertained at luncheon by the owner of the yacht. The ate well, but not wisely, considering that they

14

were to go overboard after lunch. When they dived into the ocean, neither heard the shouts of warning from observers on the tug. What they did not see was a school of sharks just off the starboard side; they dived right into the midst of them. Neither was aware of the danger, and, fortunately, the sudden plunge into the water frightened the sharks, and scattered them for a moment. Before the sharks had regrouped, a small boat was put off from the tug, and both Pearl and Crane were hauled out quickly. The rescue was just in the nick of time, for as Wilbur was pulled from the water, one of the great fish rubbed against him. Now sharkskin is like rough sandpaper, and one side of Wilbur's costume was torn off and his skin scraped raw.

A good example of what the successful serial meant to its producers during the prewar years can be found in the background of *The Million Dollar Mystery,* which was produced by Thanhouser in co-operation, once again, with the *Chicago Tribune.* The title came first and the stories were worked out as they were shot. The film starred Sidney Bracey, Florence LaBadie, James Cruze, and Marguerite Snow in twenty-three chapters before it was finished and played in about seven thousand theaters. The total cost of the production ran to $125,000, and it grossed almost $1,500,000 in return, giving the Thanhouser Company about a 700 per cent profit on its investment. In 1918, the Randolph Film Corporation managed to acquire all forty-six reels, reduced them to six, and re-released the film under the same title as a feature.

As the title suggests, the classic plot concerned a large sum of money belonging to the hero which was eagerly sought by his opponents. When Hargreave (Sidney Bracey) severed his connections with a secret Russian organization he had joined in his youth, the other members plotted to gain revenge. The villains learned that he had drawn a million dollars out of his bank accounts, and they set out to secure it for themselves. Countess Olga (Miss Snow) was acquainted with Hargreave's daughter, Florence (Miss LaBadie), and was able to give the thieves invaluable aid in many instances, finally gaining entrance for them at the Hargreave mansion. A search for the money began, but Hargreave had outwitted

15

them and escaped in a balloon. The gangsters, unable to locate the money, tried to get Florence in their clutches in an attempt to force her to reveal the secret hiding place of the huge sum. Frustrated time after time by Hargreave, Florence, and Jim Norton (James Cruze), the leader of the thieves, Braine (Frank Farrington), persisted in his determination to possess the million dollars until the final episode cleared matters up properly.

So successful was this particular serial that the company immediately scheduled another starring much the same cast and entitled *Zudora*. Not as successful as its predecessor, *Zudora* was changed in mid-production to *Zudora in the Twenty Million Dollar Mystery* and shortly the title *Zudora* disappeared from all advertising but remained the name of the female lead. In the first few episodes, Cruze portrayed Hassam Ali, a Hindu mystic who was also the uncle of Zudora (Miss Snow). The role required grotesque make-up, which made it fairly easy to write the character out of the story, and Cruze changed roles to become a newspaper reporter. Daniel Carson Goodman created the story and wrote the first half. Harold McGrath, who had created the phenomenally successful *Million Dollar Mystery* and who had contracted to novelize *Zudora* for the newspapers, was called upon to finish the last ten chapters. Such events as these were not to pass unnoticed, of course, and Vitagraph soon had on the screen a parody of this serial entitled *The Fates and Flora Fourflush, The Ten Billion Dollar Vitagraph Mystery Serial*. With Clara Kimball Young playing the female lead in these one-reelers, the satire produced a thrill every minute and a laugh every thrill. Incidentally, a recut, ten-episode version of *Zudora* appeared in 1919 under title of *The Demon Shadow* and was state-righted by Arrow.

Other interesting examples of the new look in motion pictures appeared during 1914. Mary Fuller followed up her success in *What Happened To Mary?* and *Who Will Marry Mary?* with *The Active Life of Dolly of The Dailies*. As a small-town reporter encouraged by her boy friend, Dolly used her ability as a satirist with excellent effects in writing a story about the local Ladies' Guild. The entire town took immediate offense because, although she was truthful,

16

she had pulled no punches. The Ladies' Guild demanded that she stop writing at once and apologize for her article. Refusing to do this, Dolly headed for the city, where she took a position with a Mrs. Yorke, a member of the fashionable set in society. Using her brains and talents, she penned a column for the *Comet,* but Mrs. Yorke drew the pay. Finally, realizing that she was being exploited, Dolly went to work at Browngrass' as a mannequin at $25 per week. She felt that the employment was only a temporary stage between her and greater things—and she was right. Receiving a note from an editor about a poem she had submitted, Dolly was so excited that she left the store without taking off the dress she had been modeling. Meeting the editor for lunch, she also had the misfortune to run into the proprietor of Browngrass', who tried to have her arrested on the spot for stealing the dress. She was saved by Rockwell Crosby of the *Comet,* who discovered that she had written the column for his paper. He gave her a job as a star reporter on the spot, and also announced that they were to be engaged. The plot continued through the remainder of the episodes, with Dolly attempting to live up to Crosby's estimation of her before she married him. This was perhaps the best of the three vehicles mentioned in which Mary Fuller worked. The plot, acting, and technical aspects of this item were far superior to the previous ones.

Mary Fuller was one of the prized possessions of the Edison Studio, but she always did her own stunt work. Miss Fuller never refused to perform a stunt, regardless of the danger involved. The fact that she did most of them for the first time only increased the risk she took. This was a time in movies when a player could not afford to allow herself the luxury of too many refusals, for there were many enterprising youngsters who would soon replace her in the public eye, if given the opportunity. Too often the stunts turned into accidents because of the inexperience of the actress or the negligence of a careless member of the crew. Miss Fuller recalled the time when she was asked to pilot a racing motorboat at top speed. A camera had been securely bound to the rear of the boat and a cameraman assigned to operate it. The fact that she had never handled such a craft before did not faze her; she was determined to do it successfully or drown in the process of trying. Before she boarded the boat, the director cautioned her not to allow the boat to swerve, but only to steer it in a straight course to the finish line. At the sound of the starting gun, she opened the throttle all the way and the boat tore off through the water like a runaway rocket. She later compared the sensation of gaining speed to that of a runaway horse, to which she was well accustomed by then. However, curious to observe her progress, she took her eyes from what she was doing to see where the other boats were and in the process, lost control of her boat. It pitched from side to side, but by a sheer stroke of luck and desperate effort on her part, she managed to gain control of the craft and bring it safely to the finish line ahead of the other boats, as the script called for. Only then was it discovered that the cameraman had almost been swamped with water as the boat swung from side to side. The violent lurching had thrown the camera out of position, and since the engine noise had drowned out the cries of the cameraman, no one realized, until it was too late, that none of the thrilling scenes had been recorded on film.

Another time, Miss Fuller was called upon to slide down a rope of knotted bed sheets from a window seven stories above the ground. This also was quite new to her. It bothered her somewhat, as there was no dramatic action occurring in the scene which would allow her to take her mind off the danger involved. Below the window from which she was to climb were concrete pavement and a sharp iron picket fence. A fall from that distance would have meant almost certain death, either from impact with the concrete or from the possibility that one of the pickets would pierce her body. But determination is a mighty thing, and determined she was. Climbing out of the window, she began to lower herself slowly with the bed-sheet rope. It was evident to all present that she was extremely nervous. All went well until she had reached the halfway mark. At this stage of the stunt, it was too late to back out and when the rope slipped a bit, she nearly let go in fright. However, since the only solution to the situation was to go down, she contin-

18

ued, but more nervous than before. When she reached the twenty-foot mark, a ripping sound reached her ears, and she looked above her to see the sheets beginning to tear. Frantically she continued down, but not fast enough. From a height of ten feet, the knotted bed sheets gave way completely and she fell, a crumpled heap on the pavement. Fortunately, she missed the fence. Her reward for the foolish danger she had challenged was a very sore body and bloody hands, but no one could say that she wasn't a trouper.

Edison produced another very good serial in 1914. *The Man Who Disappeared* starred Marc MacDermott as John Perriton. Miriam Nesbitt took the role of Mary Wales, the girl he loved. Unfortunately, Mary had a no-good brother, Nelson, who forged her name to a check and was on the verge of being discovered. If restitution were made at once, no charges would be filed, so, to protect Mary from the truth, Perriton lent the money to a pleading Nelson, whom he despised. In return, Nelson tried to steal Mary's jewels and killed the butler in the attempt. As John was the first person to appear on the scene, Nelson handed him a mask and begged him to put it on and run, thus clearing himself and giving credence to a story of a "masked bandit." John, not knowing of the dead butler, again foolishly agreed to help Nelson. Apparently, he thought a great deal of Mary. He had placed the mask over his face and was preparing to leave when Mary entered. Nelson, faithful friend, jerked the mask off his benefactor, effectively framing John for the murder. Perriton escaped and spent the nine succeeding chapters regaining his good name and the hand of Mary. Here was another excellent example of a classic plot.

Universal's first serial brought a new screen team to the fore. This was the combination of Francis Ford and Grace Cunard in a melodramatic offering full of ultramystery and abounding with action and adventure. It made them popular favorites and set the pace for the remainder of the Cunard-Ford serials. Entitled *Lucille Love, Girl of Mystery,* it began as a two-reel western with scenes set in Manila, P.I., and was expanded to a full-length serial. The plot dealt with a love triangle in a prologue which set the stage for the serial proper. Hugo, a classmate of Sumpter Love at West Point,

19

loved the woman who was to become Love's wife. Expelled from the Academy for stealing from his classmates, he acquired an everlasting hatred for Love, the principal witness against him and the winner of the girl as a result. Knowing that Love would one day be an officer in the U.S. Army, Hugo plotted his revenge carefully and became an international spy. A lapse of many years found Love in Manila with a daughter, Lucille, whose mother was now dead. Lucille loved the aide-de-camp, Lieutenant Gibson, who was entrusted with locking away top-secret defense plans. Unknown to all, the house butler was in the employ of Hugo and stole the plans after they were put away, leaving evidence to prove Gibson the culprit. When discovery of the theft was made, Gibson went to prison. A freak cross in the telephone lines allowed Lucille to overhear the butler call Hugo and she learned the dastardly plan which had framed her sweetheart. Knowing that Hugo was soon to set sail for the United States, she was determined that she would stop him and regain the vital secrets. Pursuing him by seaplane, she managed to get aboard his ship and regain possession of the plans. Hugo learned her secret, but before he could repossess the papers, the ship was racked by an explosion which forced them all overboard. The chase then led to a South Sea island, China, San Francisco, Mexico, and back to the United States before Lucille was triumphant.

The serial was filled with danger, both on and off the screen. During the first couple of episodes, which were filmed near San Diego for airship scenes, Ernest Shields fell some twenty-five feet onto a ledge of rocks and was severely injured. Miss Cunard herself suffered a bad fall, but loved doing the first of many Universal serials. She had been against playing the role at first because it was an ingénue part and not enough of the stories were already written for her to see the possibilities in the part. Strange as it seems, a role in which she was most unhappy at first made her a serial star.

Grace Cunard was born Harriet Mildred Jeffries on April 8, 1893, in Columbus, Ohio. An overambitious press agent later placed her birthplace in Paris, France. She played stock roles and entered

20

pictures around 1910 with Biograph. She also acted with Lubin, and in 1912 was sent west to the Thomas Ince Company, where she met Francis Ford for the first time. A onetime make-up artist who had played with Amelia Bingham in stock and later drifted into film making, Ford was at this time working with a number of firms as both actor and director. Because Ince was pressed for pictures to meet the demands of the exhibitors, Ford was made director of a second unit. Quite independent of mind, Ford had definite ideas of making movies, and Ince kept a close rein on his activities by screening and editing the final footage himself. Hampered by the restrictions placed upon him, it did not take too much urging from Miss Cunard to convince Ford that he should return to acting, and they both moved to Universal in 1913. At that studio, they became one of the most prolific teams in pictures: writing, directing, acting, cutting, and titling.

Ella Hall and Robert Leonard, a popular pair of players, starred in Universal's third serial, an item of unusual interest which is still fondly remembered as *The Master Key*. Scripted in a lively fashion by Calder Johnstone from the novel by John Fleming Wilson, it was an adventure story of the first order and was filled with exciting action. As the first reel opened, two prospectors, Harry Wilkerson (Harry Carter) and Tom Gallon, were trudging along in the desert, seeking a rich vein of gold rumored to be in the vicinity. Stumbling upon the ore by accident, Gallon was overcome with greed and shot his partner. Thinking Wilkerson dead, Gallon made his way to San Francisco and boarded a ship to escape the murder charge which he felt would soon catch up with him.

Once aboard the ship, Gallon found a chest in his stateroom. Inside the chest was an oriental idol, and in it, Gallon hid directions giving the location of the rich lode of ore. The ship sank off the Oregon coast, but Gallon managed to escape with the key to the chest. Upon reaching shore, he scratched the location of the sunken ship on the key.

Many years passed, and Gallon was next viewed as the semi-prosperous owner of a mediocre mine which he had fondly named "The Master Key." His daughter, Ruth (Ella Hall), was nearly eighteen, and the old man had almost resigned himself to the thought that he would never recover the lost directions. In the back of his mind was the nagging suspicion that Wilkerson was still alive, as no charge had ever been pressed against him. A young mining engineer, John Dore (Robert Leonard), had been brought in to revitalize the mine when Wilkerson suddenly appeared and blackmailed his way to the position of mine superintendent. Gallon passed on shortly, but before he died, he partially informed Dore of the key and its secret and made him Ruth's guardian.

Backed by Jean Darnell (Jean Hathaway), a tempestuous lady friend he hoped to marry, Wilkerson soon made an open bid to obtain the mine from Ruth. The scene zoomed to New York City, San Francisco, and Los Angeles as Dore and Wilkerson matched wits in a seemingly never-ending struggle for victory. Dore, aided by Charles Everett (Alfred Hickman), a financier friend, finally managed to do in the villain and secure the secret of the key for his ward. A popular item, the film was well received by avid serial fans, and although they never made another serial together, the performances of Bob Leonard and Ella Hall still evoke kind comments by those who saw *The Master Key*.

One more item of interest should be mentioned before we move on. November, 1914, saw the release of the first quasi-serial offering by Kalem. Shying away from the strict conception of a serial, Kalem produced a number of so-called "series" over the next few years and many were quite successful, but none outdistanced *The Hazards of Helen* in popularity. When it hit the screen, no one could have predicted that this railroad offering would span 119 chapters with two actresses named Helen playing the heroine. A close examination of this vehicle according to the standards I have established in the Introduction would reluctantly force me to omit it here, but because of its fabulous success, I feel it necessary to include *The Hazards* in my discussion. It was the beginning of greater fame for Helen Holmes in the serial genre, and it brought Helen Gibson into the limelight. J. P. McGowan directed these one-reel offerings and Miss Holmes originated the role of Helen, the girl telegrapher who kept the railroad running regardless of the obstacles placed in her path.

Born in 1892, Helen Holmes was working in motion pictures under contract to Mack Sennett in 1912. She first gained fame at Kalem, where she married her director, J. P. McGowan. The couple adopted a daughter, Dorothy, in 1916. Helen's specialties were railroad serials and western features, and her fans were legion. Deviation from this basic formula, among other factors, caused her to fade from the public eye in the early 1920's and she slid downhill steadily. Among her last roles before retiring from the screen in 1926 were her portrayals of female heavies in Universal serials. Her marriage to McGowan had dissolved, and she married Lloyd Saunders, a film cowboy and stunt man. Upon retirement they went into ranching at Sonora, but a succession of poor years caused them to sell out and Saunders went to the rodeo circuit to make a living. Helen was found attempting a comeback in 1936 as one of some two hundred extras in W. C. Fields's Paramount release, *Poppy*. Nothing came of this, for, as was the case with many of the older stars who wanted employment, although much was proclaimed about her earlier fame, no one offered her work. Little was heard about her until 1944, when she was discovered training dogs for the screen. Leading a quiet life in the San Fernando Valley, she was sustained by a small antique business until she succumbed to a heart attack in July, 1950. Her greatest fame had been achieved with the serials she made for Signal in 1916–17, and she would easily place among the top serial queens of the silent period. An attractive, athletic woman, Helen briefly rivaled Pearl White in popularity, but she lacked the strong direction of career which Pearl received from Pathé,

No stunt was too risky to film, and Helen Holmes went the standard threat to the heroine's life one better in *The Hazards*. In one chapter, she was tied to a locomotive piston. The villian intended that she would not leave the episode alive; her death would come as the engine picked up speed. Needless to say, she got out of the harrowing situation in the nick of time.

Kalem made the town of Lone Point famous throughout the country, and near the end of 1916 it was given a new location south of Hobart on the San Pedro, Los Angeles and Salt Lake railroad line. Spur lines were built to accommodate Kalem's train equipment and to facilitate shooting action scenes. Shortly after the first of January, 1915, Director McGowan had an accident on set and was laid up, in a plaster cast up to his waist, in Sisters' Hospital in Hollywood. Nevertheless, shooting continued, and in February the cast went to New Mexico on location with McGowan on crutches. On the first day's shooting, everything went wrong. A conductor misunderstood what was going on and a boxcar was derailed in the depot yards. After rerailing the car, the company went south into the mountains, where Miss Holmes was knocked from the side of another boxcar by a mail crane. The photography was done by attaching a car to the side of the train on another track. The engineer applied the brakes too quickly at a stop signal and dumped the camera crew on the ground. Shortly after that incident, the engine burst a flue and leaked so badly that it had to be sent back to the yards, some twenty miles away. Darkness was beginning to settle in, and the crew waited another three hours for a switcher to come out and tow in the remainder of the train. As McGowan cheerfully put it: "It's all in a day's work, anyhow."

J. P. McGowan was an Australian by birth and had tried his luck in various occupations, with little success, until the Boer War broke out. He immediately enlisted for military service and became a member of the Montmorency Scouts, winning two medals for valiant duty. The end of the conflict found him filled with wanderlust but with little currency. The next few years saw him move from Africa, where he had been a cattle buyer for the British government, to the United States, where he trained horses for the Paterson, New Jersey, police force and raised cattle in Texas. Once again lacking funds, he turned to the stage for salvation and soon entered movies with the Kalem Company. This position gave him the opportunity to visit parts of the United States, Europe, and the Middle East with the traveling Kalem troupe. Promoted to director, he made his reputation with *The Hazards of Helen* and left Kalem in midstream to join Lasky in June, 1915. Upon arriving at his new set, he was reputed to have said, "Well, where are the tracks?" Miss Holmes went to Universal shortly afterwards, and Kalem was faced with the prospects of an exceedingly popular vehicle falling flat. Fortunately, Helen Gibson was able to step in and take over the heroine's role with no difficulty. In fact, so close were the girls in appearance that many fans failed to notice the difference, and even today, when viewing segments of *The Hazards,* some film historians are prone to confuse the two.

Born Rose Helen Wenger to Swiss-German parents, Helen Gibson first saw the light of day on August 27, 1893, in Cleveland, Ohio. As a young girl she was a rider in the Miller Brothers 101 Ranch Wild West Show. The show had closed in Venice, California, in 1911, leaving the riders unemployed, when along came Thomas Ince, who signed them all to work in his pictures. So it was that Helen entered the world of make-believe. Paid the munificent sum of $8 weekly, she rode her horse daily from Venice to Topanga Canyon, where the scenes were being shot. Work with the 101 Bison Company occupied her time during 1911 and 1912. She then joined the Kalem Company, playing the sister of Ruth Roland in some films and working with Mona Darkfeather in others. The year 1913 also found her doing extra work at Selig and appearing with Tom Mix, who was beginning his rise to fame. The salary at Kalem was $50 per week—quite a difference from her days with Ince. Romance was in the air that year, and Helen married a young man who was to find fame on his own later as "Hoot" Gibson. Suddenly it was October, 1915, and Helen Holmes was on her way to Universal. The star's shoes were empty, but when Helen Gibson stepped into them, she found them an admirable fit and went on to become one of Kalem's top money-makers, carrying *The Hazards of Helen* to its end.

The trade papers gave her profuse credit as being one of the best telegraph operators who ever pounded a key, but Helen told me herself that she has never been able to operate the infernal machine. When *The Hazards of Helen* was finally brought to an end after 119 episodes, Helen moved into a second but ill-fated venture entitled *A Daughter of Daring,* another railroad epic, which didn't pan out because it was too close in theme to *The Hazards.* It was in one episode of this series that she performed what I like to think was her best stunt. Traveling at full speed on a motorcycle as she pursued a runaway freight train, she rode through a wooden gate, shattering it completely, up a station platform, and through the open doors of a boxcar on a siding, with her machine traveling through the air until it landed on a flatcar in a passing train. Of necessity, it was a case of perfect timing and underspeeding the camera. Helen's stunts did not all turn out so perfectly. In September, 1916, while riding on the back of one of a team of racing horses, she fell between them and was badly hurt. This was only one of a number of injuries which Helen received during her career, however, for they were a routine part of the life of stars who did most or all of their own stunts.

The year 1917 found her at Universal filming two-reel railroad sagas. Her salary had risen to $150 a week and there she stayed until 1920, when she joined the Capital Film Company to continue filming two-reel railroad dramas, such as *The Ghost of The Canyon.* Capital paid her $300 weekly and put her to work in the same area where she had made so many episodes of *The Hazards.* The films were made on the Salt Lake route going to San Pedro, and the Bell and Vernon stations were prominently featured, along with the famous drawbridge at San Pedro. (This is now part of the Union Pacific.) Finishing the series with Capital, she formed Helen Gibson Productions to exploit her in five- and six-reel features to be released through Associated Photoplays Corporation. She leased space at the Astra Studios in Glendale, where production began in October, 1920, on *No Man's Woman,* directed by Wayne Mack and co-starring Ed Coxen. Many stars were establishing themselves in business at this time, and where a few succeeded, many failed. Problems of financing, distribution, and exploitation dragged most of them under, and so was it with Helen's venture. Needing $1,500 to finish titling, she signed a ninety-day note for the money. A delay in shipping to New York and failure to pick up the film on time at its destination caused her to lose everything. Her marriage with "Hoot" Gibson broke up the same year. Discouraged, but undaunted, she went to work in five-reel features for Spencer Productions, drawing $450 a week. Things went along fine and the future looked rosy until a ruptured appendix in 1921 cost her the job.

Recovered from her operation, Helen worked in independent westerns until 1924, when the urge to travel led her to join the Wild West segment of the Ringling Brothers, Barnum and Bailey Circus as a trick rider. Vaudeville caught her eye in 1926–27, when she played the Keith circuit out of Boston with a Hopi Indian act. In 1927, she finally returned to the West Coast to do bit parts and extra work until 1961, appearing in features with such actors as John Wayne and Jimmy Stewart. Retirement followed, after fifty years in motion pictures. An appraisal of her contribution to the screen is somewhat difficult. She did not actually appear in a real serial, but she had all of the necessary attributes to become a top figure in chapter plays. Her ability to act cannot be questioned; it seems to have been a combination of unfortunate things which held her back from the heights she might well have attained. She was not a beautiful woman, and her rugged good looks went hand in hand with her athletic skill. Although she is rather out of place in this volume, wise career management would have made her one of the serial queens.

By 1915, serial production had moved into high gear. The success of *The Perils of Pauline* brought forth *The Exploits of Elaine,* with Miss White once again in the leading role. Pathé had learned its lesson from the production of *The Perils of Pauline. The Exploits of Elaine* was turned over to the Wharton brothers, who were to make quite a name in the serial field for quick and competent results, and this placed *The Exploits* several notches above its predecessor in all respects. This time, Creighton Hale and Arnold Daly supported Miss White, and the acting of the supporting players was quite good. Once again, the plot line was fairly thin. Elaine Dodge was searching for her father's murderer, a sinister character known only as the "Clutching Hand." In her quest for justice, Elaine was aided by a "scientific" detective, Craig Kennedy. In

this serial, however, the subplots of the chapters were more colorful and complex. Elaine managed to get into the most difficult of
situations, and Kennedy always made it on time to save her. In at
least one episode, "The Life Current," she was pronounced dead
but brought back to life by his vast knowledge of science.

It is fair to say that other than the careful attention which was
given to the subtitles, a major contribution of *The Exploits of
Elaine* was the smoother and improved narrative of the episodes,
a characteristic which became more pronounced with each succeeding serial in which Miss White starred. The combination of George
B. Seitz as producer-director and Pearl White as star soon became
a sure-fire winner. The proof of *The Exploits* was in the $1,000,000
it netted Pathé during the years it was in release. It was so popular that it brought on a continuation in *The New Exploits of Elaine,*
which was followed by *The Romance of Elaine,* for a grand total
of thirty-six chapters following the adventures of the same character. With the decision to continue the serial beyond the original
fourteen episodes came the appearance of a new menace. Ed Arwin
played the Chinese villain, Wu Fang, who confronted Elaine
throughout *The New Exploits.* Fans continued to clamor for more
of Pearl White, and had anyone doubted her drawing power in
1914, the year 1915 should have dispelled all doubts.

Immediately following *The Perils of Pauline,* Crane Wilbur
had an argument with Pathé and consequently was not in their
later serials. Instead, Lubin made an interesting offer for Wilbur's
services and he went into the cast of *The Road of Strife,* with Mary
Charleson, the petite Irish-born actress, as his female lead. She
was noted among her contemporaries for her sympathetic handling of emotional parts and was known to be a "good weeper." This
serial was written by Emmett Campbell Hall, who had written
Lubin's previous release, *The Beloved Adventurer.* He had an
excellent reputation for "keeping his finger on the public pulse,"
and the serial received good reviews. When asked recently about
the popularity of *The Road of Strife,* Crane Wilbur could only
comment: "Regret to admit that I cannot remember much about

the story except that it was cliché upon cliché. Members of the company always referred to it as 'The Load of Tripe.' "

In the town of Elmhurst, Alene (Mary Charleson) lived with Professor Gershorn; she had never been outside his home. As she grew older, an urge to satisfy the mating instinct caused her to steal out of the house, and she met Robert Dane, a young chap who took an instant liking to her. This was the "meaty" role given Wilbur. On the spot, she asked him to take her to his home and let her live with him. Thinking her demented, he took her back to the Professor's house and left her there. Wandering back inside, full of sadness because Robert had rejected her, she found the Professor on the floor. A quick examination proved him to be dead, and as she glanced up, she noticed a mysterious hand clutching the curtain. On one of the fingers of the hand was a peculiar ring, and upon seeing it, she lost her composure and ran from the house screaming. Heading straight to Dane's home, she persuaded him and a Dr. Duncan to return to the scene of the murder with her. Entering the house, they found no trace of the crime or the Professor, and Dr. Duncan, thinking her mad, took her home to live with him. It took fourteen more episodes to convince the good Doctor and Robert that she was sane and to prove that her parentage was a mystery which needed to be solved.

Cunard and Ford followed up their smashing success, *Lucille Love,* with *The Broken Coin.* When Miss Cunard first suggested doing an "imaginary principality" serial, the front office stood firm against it on the basis that it wouldn't go over. The degree of their error is now motion-picture history, and they admitted it when they wired the troupe to extend the number of chapters to twenty-two. A good cast included Eddie Polo, who had been injured doing stunts in comedies. Asked to find something for him to do, Miss Cunard put him to work making nets for a featurette she was making, *The Campbells Are Coming.* When *The Broken Coin* was started, she wrote in a part for Polo. He played a character who was always helping the heroine out of difficulty, and he soon began receiving fan mail praising his work. After a few episodes, he came on set minus the character make-up and announced that he was tired of looking that way and, because of the fan mail, was going to change his part. Needless to say, he continued production in make-up until Miss Cunard could write him out. Success had gone to his head.

The plot concerned a coin on which was a map that would lead the possessor to a great treasure. The problem which set the story in motion was the fact that the coin was in two pieces: one was worthless without the other. To Kitty Gray, a newspaperwoman, the coin meant a great story. Miss Cunard played the role to the hilt and turned in a very satisfactory performance. To King Michael, the coin meant the ability to satisfy his extravagances. However, to Count Frederick of Gretzhoffen, the broken coin signified riches beyond his wildest dreams. Unhappily for him, Kitty and the King both possessed half of the coin and the only key to the untold wealth was in the acquisition of the entire coin. The Count, therefore, had to work to gain both halves. Francis Ford played the role of Count Frederick in an exceedingly fine manner, and his direction was also of high caliber. A fast-moving, action-packed chapter play, it was full of the roustabout antics which so delighted the Cunard-Ford fans.It even contained shots, in the opening scenes, of Carl Laemmle, who portrayed the newspaper publisher who had sent Kitty Gray to Gretzhoffen in search of the story behind the coin. All in all, it was another triumph for the team of Grace Cunard and Francis Ford.

The Black Box introduced Herbert Rawlinson to the serial screen. The English-born, former Selig actor lent a certain dignity to the role of Sanford Quest, criminologist. As Quest, he portrayed a modernized Sherlock Holmes with all of the scientific equipment necessary to solve crimes. One of his inventions allowed him to see a person who was speaking over the phone. Another was a pocket wireless telephone which got him out of countless situations. He had one other thing to commend himself: great composure. For example, in one episode the master criminal spotted him standing on the doorstep and pulled a lever which dropped Quest into the cellar. Hardly ruffled at falling into this trap, Sanford brushed him-

Although she is best remembered for her role in *The Perils of Pauline* (1914), Pearl White starred in other serials. She is shown here in a characteristic pose from *The Lightning Raider* (1919).

Pursued by the police, Henry G. Sell and Pearl White talk over her troubles in a suspense-filled moment of *The Lightning Raider*.

Warner Oland and his henchmen have Pearl in their clutches in this scene
from *The Lightning Raider*. Her expression indicates that
she is already planning her escape.

Pearl White in a patriotic pose from the final chapter of *Pearl of The Army*, a "preparedness serial" released by Pathé in 1916.

Arline Pretty is neatly tied up at the end of Chapter 7 of
A Woman In Grey (1920).

Chapter 9 of *A Woman In Grey* found Arline rather speechless and wide
eyed. For the object of her concern, see the next illustration.

This is the instrument designed to dispose of Arline. Mounting suspense
is provided by the badly frayed rope.

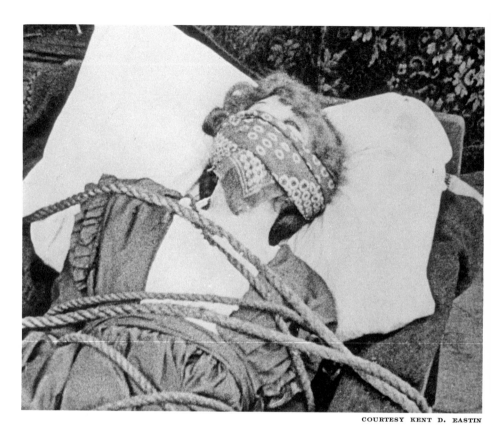

Arline seems almost resigned to her fate in this scene. Will she escape?
You bet she will—there are six more chapters to follow!

self off and put a pocket bomb made of a compact and powerful explosive against the trap door and blew himself a hole to freedom. All this and two girls to boot! The audiences ate this one up and cried for more. Universal was in the serial game for good.

In a six-episode depiction of romance, mystery and splendor of Egyptian court life, Ola Humphrey portrayed Princess Hassan. *Under The Crescent* was supposedly the adventures of Miss Humphrey when she had been married to a Prince Hassan; each chapter was asserted to have been actual happenings in her life as an Egyptian princess. The story was not particularly dramatic, nor did it contain strong action or suspense, but its strong point revolved around the well-maintained atmosphere it conveyed.

Perhaps the most interesting offering of the year was *The Diamond From The Sky,* reputed to have cost over $800,000 in production. American tried to interest Mary Pickford in the female lead, but had to settle for her sister, Lottie, who turned in an excellent performance as Esther. The twenty-three chapters were preceded by a prologue which found Sir Arthur Stanley bound hand and foot to a stake in the Virginia forest with savage Indians screaming as they danced about him. Suddenly, the screaming and dancing halted. Far above them in the sky, a great ball of fire appeared. Closer and closer it came, growing larger as it hurtled toward them. The Indians became convinced that it was an omen and had just freed Sir Arthur when the fireball crashed into the earth near by. As he left the scene, Stanley went by the meteorite which had saved his life; when he stopped to examine it, a gleam caught his eye. Bending over, he dug an imbedded diamond from it. This became a good luck charm for all of the Stanley house who possessed it throughout generations to come.

The story proper opened some 250 years later, when the Stanley family was represented by Judge Lamar Stanley and his first cousin, Colonel Arthur Stanley. The Judge coveted the power which politics and property represented, while his cousin Arthur wanted only a son and heir who would bring him into possession of the fabled diamond and the earldom in England awaiting its owner. Judge Stanley was the father of a son to whom the diamond would

31

go unless Arthur's wife bore him a male heir. The wife bore a girl and died in childbirth, but all was not lost to Arthur. On his property, a Gypsy woman bore a son the same night. Desperately, Arthur went to the physician who delivered the child and bribed him to turn over the Gypsy child; it took a bag of gold, but the doctor agreed and sent the Gypsy woman away childless. Colonel Stanley gained possession of the diamond and the earldom.

Some years later, the Gypsy returned to claim her child and broke into the mansion where Arthur Stanley and his children lived. Before she could accomplish her mission, she came face to face with the Colonel, who dropped dead from shock. The Gypsy took both the diamond and the Colonel's daughter, Esther. Changing her mind, she went to a Dr. Harding and agreed to let him retain possession of the diamond on condition that he adopt Esther. This he duly did, and soon both of the Stanley boys were enamored of her. However, the enmity had passed from father to son in both cases and when Blair, the son of the Judge, found that the diamond was in Dr. Harding's possession, he killed the Doctor and stole the gem, only to be caught by Arthur. After a fierce struggle in which he thought he had killed his cousin, Arthur took the jewel and was determined to return it, but found that he had been accused of murdering the Doctor. The remaining episodes followed the diamond as it went from hand to hand, eventually returning to its rightful owner, Esther, who married Arthur.

Close to *The Diamond From The Sky* in interest was another fine entry in 1915, a Vitagraph serial called *The Goddess*. Considering the rather quaint plot which motivated this vehicle, the main interest centered around the cast. With beautiful Anita Stewart in the lead, it was a formidable entry, and Earle Williams was on hand as insurance. They were the first-line heart-throb team which was keeping Vitagraph on top at the time. Anita played the role of Celestia, a beautiful girl who had been raised by three millionaires to believe that she had been sent from Heaven to reform the world. She began her work in the Pennsylvania coal fields, where a huge strike was in progress. The relationship between Celestia and young Tommy Barclay (Mr. Williams) pro-

32

vided the love interest. Tommy, the son of one of the men who had raised Celestia, was also a reformer. Celestia fell into the hands of Stilleter, who was handy with hypnotism and wished to use her to his own advantage. Until Stilleter died from snake bite, he was able to play one side against the other for his benefit. Upon his death, however, Celestia was released from the spell and saw everything in its proper perspective. She confessed all to the workers, who, whipped to a frenzy by a rabble-rouser, decided to kill the rich men. The end saw the millionaires and the mob leaders all dead and Celestia married to Tommy on Gull Isle, happy, because "time heals all wounds." Good acting and skillful photography raised this serial far and away above its plot line, which Vitagraph advertising claimed rivaled the works of Charles Dickens. The comparison left a bit to be desired.

An unusual offering of 1915 and one which prompted a song of the same title to appear in connection with its release was *Runaway June*. Produced by Reliance, this serial based its adventures on a wife who left her husband on their wedding trip and fell into evil hands. It seemed that she was oversensitive on the subject of having to ask her new husband for money. This was a rather ridiculous theme, as *The Moving Picture World* commented when it appeared. The reviewer, Margaret I. MacDonald, changed her mind as succeeding episodes were viewed. It was well staged and after a rocky beginning, started to prove itself. The only real fault was the excessive use of subtitles. Even the scenery was real; Episode 10 was done on board the steamer which took the crew to Bermuda to film a couple of chapters.

A map, lost treasure, two evil soldiers of fortune, and Neal Hardin (William Courtleigh, Jr.) made up the plot of *Neal of The Navy*. Lillian Lorraine's friends thought her daft when she announced that she was leaving the New York stage to play the part of Annette. After perusing the plot and success of this number, I guess they were right.

The year 1915 saw the appearance of the first authentic serial made by Ruth Roland, whose popularity was to become second only to Pearl White in the chapter-play field. Screening episodes from her serials today, one can easily see why her work was so much in demand both here and abroad. Her particular talents were well displayed in the type of stories she used for the more popular of her serial vehicles. Good supporting casts and the best in writing and directing talents helped to put across her style of acting and gave her the reputation in the 1920's as the "Queen of the Thriller Serials." Unquestionably a beautiful woman with a trim, lithe figure, she possessed thick, auburn-tinged hair and violet eyes. Although her face was a bit wide, her profile was exciting. Frank Leon Smith claimed that she had one of the best complexions in Hollywood, since she never had to wear heavy makeup. She walked with grace and pride in every step. Her low, clear voice carried itself with a touch of authority, but she was known to work for weeks without speaking to her director. She believed in living for the future, and her caution extended on set, where her later stunts were done by doubles, most notably Robert Rose.

Born in San Francisco on August 26, 1892, Miss Roland played in both stock and vaudeville engagements at the age of two as "Baby Ruth." At the turn of the century her mother died, and Ruth went to Los Angeles to live with an aunt and attend school. At sixteen she returned to the stage and played ingénue roles in stock and vaudeville engagements. She posed for Harrison Fisher, a noted New York artist, and succeeded in landing a job in moving pictures with the Kalem Company in Santa Monica. Her salary was $35 weekly, and she first appeared as leading lady in a one-reel western called *A Chance Shot,* released on July 24, 1911. Working for Kalem for three and one-half years, she turned out more than two hundred one-reel and split-reel films of all varieties: westerns, melodramas, and comedies. By 1912, she had attracted a considerable following, and Kalem released *Ruth Roland, The Kalem Girl,* which allowed her to display fancy diving from a high platform. Her salary at Kalem had gradually risen to $50 per week, and when Mack Sennett offered her work on the strength of a recommendation by Mabel Normand, Kalem raised her salary to $95 in order to keep her. With this increase in wages, Ruth felt herself

34

too valuable to waste as a custard-pie comedienne and demanded that Kalem give her dramatic roles.

Placed in *The Girl Detectives* series as the lead, she left Kalem after seven episodes were in the can and signed with Balboa to star in *Who Pays?*, a series of twelve two-reel dramas produced for Pathé release. The audience enjoyed its role as jury, and the success of this series made Pathé realize that it now had a one-two punch in the Ruth Roland–Pearl White releases. Ruth was rushed into her first Pathé serial, *The Red Circle*. This found her playing a wealthy girl reformer who was cursed with a family taint causing her to commit crimes against which her better self revolted. A crimson circle on the back of her right hand was the only visible sign of the curse. In order to wipe out the red-circle birthmark of crime, Jim Borden had killed his son and committed suicide. Detective Lamar (Frank Mayo) saw another red circle on a hand in a passing car and pursued the automobile, which he thought was connected with the robbery of a loan shark. The veiled woman inside, June Travis (Ruth), escaped, and Lamar was baffled. June's old nurse, Mary, told her that she was the daughter of Jim Borden and explained that at a camp in the West, Mrs. Travis gave birth to a son at the same time a girl was born to Borden's wife. During the melee created when outlaws attacked the town, both Mr. Travis and Mrs. Borden were killed and Jim left town, taking the Travis boy by error. The boy grew up as Borden's son and June grew up as Mrs. Travis' daughter. With this mix-up out of the way, all that remained was for Lamar to capture June and cure her of the terrible birthright.

In an attempt to cash in on the popularity of *Who Pays?*, Pathe quickly put Ruth and Frank Mayo into another series entitled *Who Wins?*. Shelved for two years, it was not released until January, 1918, and then only eight chapters were marketed under the title *Price of Folly*.

Joe Brandt, then general manager of Universal, who was always looking for a new slant and fresh ideas, conceived the proposition of a serial written by fifteen authors. Briefly, the idea put forth by Brandt was this: fifteen of the nation's leading fiction writers would be the authors of a continued picture. One would prepare the two-part opening chapter and the next in line would pick up the plot where it had been left and carry on as he felt best. This would go on until all fifteen had handled a chapter in their own manner. Corresponding with the screen episodes was a fiction version written by Hugh Weir for newspaper publication. This was the background of *Graft,* in which Hobart Henley played the leading role of the young attorney in the first three chapters. He was replaced by Harry Carey, who finished off the remaining seventeen (the serial had been extended to twenty chapters).

With the close of 1915, the serial had reached a level of maturity. In most cases, technically speaking, the productions were on a par with the features of the period. Some were less perfect than others, of course, but all took advantage of the still-developing techniques of the cinema. The plots were somewhat antiquated or farfetched, but they were fairly strong on story and satisfied the public desire for escape. From a moral viewpoint, the serials were no better/no worse than any of the other products of the film industry. They had developed their own peculiar type of actor and actress. Some players were already high in the public favor and a few were able to make the transition from serials to features and back again, but many were destined to rise to fame as serial stars only to fall from favor quickly when they appeared in other types of productions. Each serial had plenty of stunts for both the male and female leads, and in most cases, they were looked upon as capable of performing the feats as a normal part of their duties. Crane Wilbur once said: "In those days the director said, 'Of course, I can get a stunt man to do it if you're afraid.' It took a brave guy to say, 'I am afraid.' The more cowardly way was to do the thing yourself." As for the popularity of the serial at this time, Wilbur also came very close to the truth when he stated that "in his secret heart, every man is an embryo hero and every girl a heroine in danger." In the early serials, the heroine saved the hero's life nearly as many times as he rescued her. A man and woman in the audience could easily project and identify with the screen images, consciously or unconsciously. Some film historians have decried the idea of identification with the hero or heroine, but I can only point out that they never really enjoyed their movies. Growth in the proper direction in order to retain its audience throughout the silent period was about all that remained for the serial at the close of 1915, and, as we shall see, it did just that.

CHAPTER TWO

FOR THE FLAG

THE YEAR 1916 was to see more care and thought expended on plots, direction, and technical achievement. More money was spent on both production and advertising, for serials had proved to be a very profitable business. During the 1916 season alone, Pathé claimed to have spent some $500,000 in just newspaper and billboard advertising in behalf of its six serial releases. This meant that the cost of advertising a serial very often exceeded the cost of producing it. Generally speaking, producers tried to keep the cost of each episode in the $3,000–$6,000 bracket, but this procedure was to change radically in the coming years.

The big news of 1916 was a trend away from the blood-and-thunder epics of the previous year toward a strange new form of screen entertainment, the "preparedness serial." America had managed to keep out of the conflict which had raged in Europe since 1914, but was finding each day that aloofness from affairs abroad was becoming more difficult. In a manner of speaking, the new form of serial served a dual purpose: it brought fresh material of a current and often sensational nature to the screen and it also sought to prepare the American public for the possibility of entry into the war.

American scored first in this field with its release through Mutual of a fifteen-episode thriller entitled *The Secret of The Submarine*. This entry served to introduce Juanita Hansen, whose meteoric career was beset with tragedy. Born in Des Moines, Iowa, in 1897, the strikingly beautiful blonde went to work in pictures immediately upon graduation from a Los Angeles high school. She learned quickly, and popularity came her way. Before joining

American, she had made a rather nice living doing stints with Famous Players (opposite Jack Pickford) and with Fine Arts. Her life at this time gave no hint of the disasters ahead. *The Secret of The Submarine* revolved around an idea perfected by Dr. Ralph Burke. His invention would allow a submarine to remain underwater indefinitely without relying upon the compressed air which the craft stored. This was done by means of an apparatus which operated like the gills of a fish, no less! Lieutenant Jarvis Hope (Tom Chatterton) was sent from Washington as naval representative to view the first test of the machine, and he fell in love at once with Cleo Burke (Miss Hansen). Before the serial was finished, agents of Japan and Russia and even an unprincipled American had attempted to obtain the secret of the device after killing the inventor in the early episodes. Naturally, they were foiled by the end of the last chapter and the secret was safely turned over to the Navy Department in Washington by Jarvis and Cleo. It was a thrilling chapter play, and every episode left the principal characters in extreme danger. Excited audiences could hardly wait for the following episodes, even though the means used to extricate the actors from danger were sometimes a bit farfetched.

Universal came in next with *Liberty, A Daughter of The U.S.A.* Liberty was a young girl of seventeen whose father died at his hacienda in Mexico and left a vast estate. His will specified two of his closest friends as trustees of his estate and made them both guardians of his daughter. She was not to marry until she became twenty-one, unless both guardians agreed unequivocally to give their consent. Señor Juan López, played by G. Raymond Nye, was a Mexican who secretly plotted to have Liberty (Marie Walcamp) abducted and held for ransom in order to obtain funds to finance a revolution against the legal government of Mexico. This was accomplished in the early episodes, but she was rescued by a captain of the Texas Rangers, Jack Holt, who immediately fell in love with her. This means of obtaining the fortune foiled, another one was tried. One guardian, Major Winston (Neal Hart), had gambled heavily with funds belonging to the estate, and the other, José León (L. M. Wells), was sympathetic to the rebels.

The major object of José León, however, was the marriage of Liberty to his son, Manuel. By blackmailing Winston, consent was gained and the choice put to Liberty: marriage or the exposure of Winston. Liberty, a long-time friend of the Major, agreed to the marriage to prevent the disgrace of Winston but told Manuel that she would be a wife in name only. This "saved" her, in the eyes of the audience, for her later affair with the Ranger.

Meanwhile, Manuel had sold his soul to the rebels for a commission in their army and soon found himself engaging the Texas Rangers in battle. The fighting was terrific, especially in Episode 6, until the Rangers and U.S. troops were held up at the border because of "diplomatic negotiations" in Washington. The serial made a great point of American blood being shed in border raids while the "striped-pants" talked of peace and friendship. As a serial, the preparedness theme was interesting and hit home hard, but the chapters dragged because of the lack of action throughout, which was necessary to keep the story alive and moving. Marie Walcamp made an appealing heroine and projected the role of Liberty with plenty of verve. Born in Denison, Ohio, in 1894, she had first gained attention in musical comedy with Weber and Fields, Kolb and Dill, and De Wolf Hopper before entering pictures. A striking blonde with dark-blue eyes, she was to make several serials and many short-length westerns for Universal.

Next in line came a sixteen-episode thriller from the Serial Film Company. A state-right release through Unity Sales, *The Yellow Menace* brought forth the fanatical and mysterious Mongolian, Ali Singh. A scientist who was also a brutal zealot of his cause, Ali Singh would have stopped at nothing to exalt the yellow race at the expense of the whites. After convincing the audience of the inherent danger in this man by showing blood baths brought on by an upraised hand, the serial allowed his arrival in the United States to lead his followers in their efforts to overcome the supremacy of the whites. The plot was fully introduced when Mr. Bronson, a banker of international importance, backed a bill to exclude all nonwhites from American shores. Ali Singh took it upon himself to warn Bronson to drop his support of the bill and to help defeat

40

it, but the Secret Service entered the picture at this point and battled the Mongolian to defeat and death, thus proving the supremacy of right and white. The serial was interesting, but dwelt more strongly on the race issue than preparedness in the later chapters; it also suffered from overacting which today appears a bit ludicrous to viewers. The important aspect concerning *The Yellow Menace* was that it formed another link in the chain leading to other serials which warned the public of the dangers of neutrality and apathy over what might well be going on inside the borders of the United States at the very moment they were watching their theater screens.

December saw the release of the last preparedness serial of the year, *Pearl of The Army*. Written and partly directed by George B. Seitz, there were thrills in every foot. By now the name of Pearl White on a serial was a guarantee of the highest quality, and this one lacked none of the essentials. With a dramatic story of love, mystery, and adventure and an all-star cast supporting her, she achieved one of the greatest successes of her career up to that point. A strong love interest developed almost immediately in the early episodes and carried through to the conclusion. The plot concerned the attempts of the mysterious "Silent Menace" to steal the secret plans of the defense of the Panama Canal. A train wreck in the early episodes gave the enemy possession of the plans, and Pearl fought chapter after chapter, recovering the plans and foiling the Silent Menace at every turn. The high point of patriotism came on a rooftop as the shadowy figure of the Menace attempted to lower the Stars and Stripes, a signal to his followers to begin the uprising. Pearl fought bitterly to keep the flag waving and won, knocking the Menace off the building. Her efforts cleared Major Brent (Theodore Friebus) of all suspicion, and he rejoined his loved one, Bertha. Pearl was honored at the end by a full dress parade of American troops.

A very patriotic serial, *Pearl of The Army* was recut into ten chapters in later years and re-released under the same title, although not by Pathé. When originally released, it was so popular that the Family Theatre in Des Moines, Iowa, charged a dime to

41

see the serial alone. According to the local Pathé exchange, this serial did more business than any other previously done in Des Moines. Perhaps an exaggeration, but I'm inclined to believe it.

Pearl's prior release, *The Iron Claw,* was one of the best serials she ever made. Very popular with the fans, it was extended in production and received rave notices wherever it played. At the very beginning, Pearl was seen as a young woman about to embark on a career of crime under the tutelage of Legar, the Iron Claw (played by Sheldon Lewis). Flashbacks then told the audience how she had been placed in this position. It seemed that as a young man, Legar made love to his employer's wife in order to gain entrance to the plantation home. He sought to steal her jewels, but blackmail was easier, and after threatening to expose the unfaithful wife, he received the jewelry.

Unfortunately, the husband discovered his wife's infidelity and evicted her from house and home. Turning to Legar, he had the young man seized, and proceeded to cut off his arm as punishment. Seeking revenge for the horrible mutilation, Legar opened the dikes near by and flooded the plantation, carrying off the young daughter. The girl grew up in a den of thieves, and when the proper time arrived, the Claw decided to start her career of crime as a final humiliation to her father, now a millionaire. At this point, "The Laughing Mask," nemesis of all criminals, stepped in and returned her to her father safely. She became romantically involved with his secretary (Creighton Hale), and the usual torn map was worked into the plot to provide a basis for the struggle between evil and righteousness. Each chapter ended by asking "Who is The Laughing Mask?" and Harry Fraser's identity was well kept to the very end. Fraser still muses today about the sudden popularity which descended upon him as a result of his role.

There were many other items of interest released during 1916. Cunard and Ford made their last two serials together. *The Adventures of Peg O' The Ring* utilized a circus background and cast Miss Cunard in a dual role, first as a mother who had been clawed by an angry lion prior to the birth of her daughter, then as the daughter. Because of prenatal influence, the daughter became subject to mad impulses at intervals, when she would scratch and tear at everything in sight. Francis Ford portrayed her half-brother (both shared the same father), who fell in love with her without knowing her history or the fact that they were related.

Problems arose in April which caused both Ford and Cunard to drop production and go East to confer with Carl Laemmle. The first rumor had Ruth Stonehouse and Eddie Polo finishing the serial in the lead roles. A short time later, a really wild rumor circulated to the effect that Dorothy Gish would finish the job on loan-out. There was more truth to the former story. Difficulties had arisen between the stars and the supporting actors, but Laemmle was too wily to lose a good thing. A settlement was reached, allowing Ford to announce that Polo and Stonehouse would be written out of the production entirely. This was Polo's second bounce from a Cunard-Ford serial.

An amusing thing happened on set when they were using three lions. The set, enclosed in an iron cage, was on a huge stage with crossbeams some ten to twelve feet apart on the walls. Use was made of many extras, and Miss Cunard did not recall whether one of the lions really got loose or whether someone just said such, but in no time at all there were extras hanging all over the crossbeams. She still wonders how they ever got up there.

She greatly enjoyed making *Peg O' The Ring,* as it was a good role and the serial was very well received by the public. Any serial the Ford-Cunard team made was full of slam-bang action which moved at a rapid pace and brought the audience back week after week for more of the same. No production in which Ford had a hand was complete without numerous and varied knock-down, drag-out fights, and this one was up to par in that respect.

For that matter, so was their last effort, *The Purple Mask,* which was perhaps the worst of their collaborations in the chapter-play field. I say "perhaps" because this is an individual and subjective analysis and others might not agree with me. However, Miss Cunard was in accord with my judgment in the matter. The picture was made at the old studio on Sunset Boulevard for Laemmle's nephews, the Stern brothers. Trouble arose with the studio manager and Ford had to argue the contract with the Stern's, for they constantly interfered with production. Arguing and bickering went on until Miss Cunard lost all interest in the role and only looked forward to the day when the final chapter was in the can. (It showed on the screen, too.) Both Cunard and Ford lacked the normal zest which they put into their roles.

The first episode introduced Miss Cunard as Patricia Montez, a young girl high in Parisian society who was also a tomboy. You knew this to be true because she punched a gentleman friend in the face almost at once. Snubbed by Phil Kelly, a noted American detective known as the "Sphinx," she was determined to get even with this man of stone. With this in mind, she stole her own aunt's jewels in an effort to baffle him. The jewels were stolen, in turn, by a house servant and handed over to a band of crooks. In tracing them, Pat joined the band and was soon made "Queen of the Apaches." The robberies that followed were so daring and puzzling that the police of the Continent were completely at a loss. Kelly was put on the case to discover the identity of the thief who made victims of the wealthy and turned over part of the spoils to the poor. After each robbery, there appeared a purple mask, the mystery element of the story. Kelly caught Pat and retribution was made in the end, but it was an exciting venture full of fights, escapes, and stunts marred only by the stars' lack of interest in their roles. The scenes were laid in Paris, and with the exception of an automobile with a San Francisco license plate, the atmosphere was carried through with a fair amount of attention to detail.

By the time *The Purple Mask* was finished, Miss Cunard had tired of the frenzied activity which went into the making of serials; she much preferred the slower pace associated with feature production and two-reel short subjects. She had reached the financial peak of her career during 1916 with a unique salary arrangement that paid her $450 per week plus 25¢ a foot over 1,500 feet per week plus 10 per cent of the profits. The demise of the Cunard-Ford team was a great loss to the silent serial.

The Mysteries of Myra appeared from the Wharton Studio in 1916. Based largely upon occult phenomena, it was very dependent on weird camera effects, lighting, and superior technical work. Dissolves, double exposures, and fades were abundant, as was a two-color treatment in many scenes, which served to intensify the mood of mysticism. The story placed John Maynard as a member of the "Black Order," an occult group which held sway over its members by means of strange powers. Prior to his death, he had willed his wealth to the group if, by chance, all three of his daughters should die before reaching age eighteen. The two older girls had committed suicide before attaining eighteen, and Mrs. Maynard feared for the life of her youngest daughter, having some inkling of her husband's unnatural connection with the group. Art Varney (Allen Murnane) loved Myra (Jean Sothern), but as a member of the Black Order, he had been assigned to help her die. Dr. Payson Alden (Howard Estabrook), an authority on the occult, was investigating the case when he was suddenly warned to desist. The remainder of the chapters found Alden busy keeping Myra alive, against her apparent will, and he ran wild making "thought images" gained by placing photographic plates to her forehead in an attempt to find out what was going on. Naturally, all ended well, with the group vanquished and Myra in love with Alden. An out-of-the-ordinary offering, the serial was up to the high standard of quality which the Whartons could be depended upon to turn out.

Essanay released its first and only serial in 1916, *The Strange Case of Mary Page*. The plot centered about the murder of David Pollock, a young millionaire theatrical magnate who forced his attentions on Mary Page (Edna Mayo), a young stage star. A large part of the story concerned his attempts to force her to marry him, even though she loved Phil Langdon (H. B. Walthall), and was told in flashbacks. The murder occurred in the first episode, which ended as Mary was found by the body with a revolver in hand, crumpled on the floor in a faint. In fact, fainting played a considerable role, for Chapter 2 concerned the beginning of the trial and ended with Mary fainting on the stand. The complicated story was not helped a great deal by the method of telling it, but there were two redeeming points: the solution was held back until the last two hundred feet of the final reel, and Essanay did not follow it with a sequel.

Having mentioned sequels, I feel that this is the proper place to note *The Sequel to The Diamond From The Sky*, written in four chapters by Terry Ramsaye. It opened with Arthur and Esther Stanley happily married and living in their Virginia home with their small son. Things had gone well for them over the years, and they decided to take a trip to Europe. Unfortunately, the train on which they chose to travel was wrecked and they were killed. Quabba, a Gypsy who played a rather minor role in the original serial, was on hand to witness the wreck and to see the diamond stolen from the baby. And away we go for the other three episodes! The most notable thing about this sequel was the fact that Lottie Pickford was not among the cast. Rhea Mitchell played the role of Esther, which perhaps explains her early demise in the first episode. The film was released in two versions: as an eight-reel feature or a four-episode serial, depending upon the wishes of the exhibitor.

Newspaper reporting furnished the background for *Perils of Our Girl Reporters*. Each chapter dealt with an incident from the life of a reporter and was complete in itself. The story was told from the reporter's point of view and depicted in detail the manner in which front-page story material was collected. Many of the stories were based on supposedly real facts, but this is open to conjecture, considering that in the serial, girl reporters exposed the evils of the underworld, secured confessions from crooks, aided the government in capturing counterfeiters and blackmailers, ferreted out strange crimes, and, in general, foiled evil plots. Helen Green and Zena Keefe played the lead female roles.

It is difficult to argue with the premise that newspaper life can be quite fascinating. The whole world is before the eyes of star reporters: they delve into all that is queer and unusual, they mingle with the best and worst of society. If you agree with this premise, and make the reporter a girl, you double the interest of the situations. Tell the stories from the "inside" and you again increase the fascination. This was the thinking of the Niagara Film Studio when it released *Perils of Our Girl Reporters,* which was up to the average in most respects.

A few other items merit our attention before we leave 1916. Arrangements were made with Flo Ziegfeld to allow Billie Burke to appear in a Klein production, *Gloria's Romance.* Nothing was too good for Miss Burke, and the filming was done on a lavish scale, including the use of real mahogany panels on the sets. Klein salesmen sold pre-release bookings of the serial to the tune of $850,000. It flopped.

Pathé released *The Shielding Shadow,* with Grace Darmond and Leon Bary. The acting came off well and suspense was held at a high pitch throughout the entire serial, but following the plot was something of a headache. Boiled down to where it makes sense, it simply dealt with a mantle of invisibility and a box of black pellets which maintained the power of the mantle. The action came from the theft of the cloak by a group of thieves and the attempts of the hero to retrieve it.

Pathé also released *The Grip of Evil,* starring Jackie Saunders and Roland Bottomley. It followed the adventures of a poor man who inherited a fortune and set out to discover whether humanity was in "the grip of evil." The story was not clearly defined from chapter to chapter, and the lack of strong characterizations on the part of the cast detracted from an otherwise interesting possibility.

In December, the Unicorn Film Service Corporation went to court to restrain Monmouth Film Company from releasing the serial *Jimmy Dale Alias The Grey Seal* through any firm other than Unicorn. It seemed that in October the two companies had signed a contract giving exclusive rights to Unicorn, which promptly spent some $10,000 in advertising and was prepared to spend another $25,000. Monmouth was supposed to spend some $75,000 for advertising on its part, but placed only one advertisement in a New York daily. The first episode was booked for release on November 27, but the prints were not delivered. After a conference between the two firms, the release date was extended to December 4, and Monmouth agreed to keep its part of the bargain concerning the advertising. On December 8, Unicorn was informed that the contract had been canceled, as other firms were anxious to perform the release service. Ike Schlank of Unicorn immediately went to court, seeking an injunction on the basis that not only had Monmouth failed to live up to a valid contract, but it had also attempted to force him out of 35 per cent of the gross receipts and had injured the prestige of his exchanges with exhibitors. The legal procedure held up release for another three months, and Monmouth won the right to release the serial through the Mutual Exchange as Mutual featurettes. Interestingly enough, early 1917 found Unicorn deep in bankruptcy.

Thus the book was closed on the year, and as the serial looked forward to 1917, it did so with a feeling that it had grown and matured. Technically, it had kept pace with other forms of screen entertainment and in scattered cases, it had jumped ahead. Many of the stories had been brought closer to reality, and as the public continued to clamor for escape, the serial provided an avenue. Pearl White had won new friends, Ruth Roland was on her way up, and the only dim spot was the end of the Cunard-Ford thrillers.

The year 1917 opened auspiciously with a sneak preview of the Pathé preparedness serial, *Patria,* on New Year's Day. Irene Castle, who had reached the pinnacle of fame in another profession as the dancing partner of Vernon Castle, played the lead role and was billed as "the best known woman in America today." The concept behind *Patria* was to show the United States attacked by an imaginary enemy, and the heroine was to save the nation—after much suspense. However, the ultimate powers behind the film's production happened to be the Hearst enterprises, and it was too good a proposition to let pass by as it was. The Hearst papers had taken many belligerent slaps at the Japanese, Mexicans, and other sundry items related to American defense efforts over the previous few years. As the possibility that President Wilson would not be able to keep the United States out of war became more apparent, the urgency to put *Patria* on the screen grew. In a not-too-subtle way, it was to prepare the American public for the worst, and William Randolph Hearst personally took an active interest in its preparation and filming. Thus heroine *Patria* went before the cameras to face an allied army of Japanese and Mexicans. Naturally, the two nations most displeased with the results were Japan and Mexico. Pressure built up here and there, and the film was banned from the screen in various sections of the country. The final blow came to Hearst when President Wilson asked that certain alterations, such as the elimination of scenes showing actual Mexican and Japanese flags, be made in the serial. After the cuts had been made and the prints recirculated, the serial never did pick up the necessary steam to become the hit which Hearst had envisioned. Reviews ranged from good to bad. *Photoplay* did not care for it, the *New York Telegraph* enjoyed it, the *Detroit News-Tribune* was patronizing, and Hearst's *Los Angeles Examiner* was enthusiastic. So much for $90,000.

As the last of the "Fighting Channings," Patria became owner of the largest munitions factory in the United States and heir to a vast sum of money saved by generations of the Channing family for the express purpose of supplying this country with munitions at the time of its direst need. Baron Huroki and Juan de Lima, representatives of the Japanese and Mexican governments, respectively, were working against the peace of the United States by endeavoring to force the Channings to supply munitions secretly to the Mexicans. The secret trust fund was discovered by Patria and Donald Parr (Milton Sills), a Secret Service agent, but was likewise discovered by the hirelings of Huroki. While Patria arranged for the transfer of the money to a safe place, Huroki stole it and placed it on board a ship bound for Japan. He was followed by Parr, who was captured aboard ship, but not until he had forced the wireless operator to send a message to Patria. She overtook the ship in her racing launch and upon discovering the predicament Parr was in, escaped the clutches of Huroki to seek the help of a U.S. revenue cutter. Huroki ordered the ship scuttled and got away in a small boat, leaving Parr to be rescued in the nick of time by Patria. The serial went on to blame the Japanese and Mexican agents for numerous heinous crimes, including the Black Tom disaster. It was produced at a time when we were having difficulties with the Mexicans, and Hearst was certain that they would be bought by the Germans into attacking our borders, thus provoking war in this hemisphere. The degree of his belief was evident in the fact that the serial pulled no punches in actually placing blame on the doorsteps of Mexico and Japan.

It is somewhat difficult to assess the performance of Miss Castle in this serial. Frank Leon Smith considered her to be attractive, interesting, and talented, but limited in her range of acting. Since he was quite close to her, working on the same lot, his estimate is probably the most accurate and dispassionate to be had. The Hearst interests were naturally prejudiced, and plainly showed it in their exuberance over her portrayal. Opinions ran the gamut from this point downward. However, not too long ago, Miss Castle commented on both her role and that of Mr. Sills.

> My only ally was Captain Donald Parr of the U.S. Secret Service, who kissed my hand when he felt affectionate, pounded assorted villains into jelly when he felt belligerent and looked painfully mysterious over everything anybody said. Fortunately, I wasn't called on for any acting except to look terrified occasionally, and on those occasions I didn't need to act. I was.

With the release of *The Mystery of The Double Cross*, Pathé introduced a new heroine, Mollie King, to serial fans. Leon Bary portrayed Peter Hale, whose inheritance of the family fortune depended upon marriage to the girl with the mark of the double cross. Visiting the Brewster home upon his return from Europe, he came to believe that Philippa (Mollie) was the girl he sought. The villain, Bridgey Bentley, no less, was in love with Philippa. Learning of Hale's interest in the girl, he tried everything in his power to stop Peter from getting to know her better. Each chapter found Bridgey trying his level best to do Peter in, and each time, a mysterious stranger saved Peter's life, as in Episode 3, "An Hour To Live." Captured by Bentley, Peter was in deadly peril. A clock had been set to fire a revolver and end his earthly career. Before this happened, however, the "Masked Stranger" stepped out of the clock and foiled the scheme. Near the end of the serial,

Peter was framed by Bridgey, who was on his deathbed, but a young reporter, who was also in love with Philippa, cleared his name—with the help of the ever present Masked Stranger. At last Hale found that Philippa bore the strange markings on her shoulder and they were married, to live happily ever after. William Parke did a fine job of directing the film, and the cast gave an excellent performance.

Miss King's second release of the year, *The Seven Pearls,* portrayed her as an American girl who had been brought up in Turkey. She played Ilma, the daughter of former U.S. Ambassador Honest Bey. Meeting Harry Drake, a young American (Creighton Hale), she fell hard for him, and they decided to go back to the States. He mistakenly got mixed up with a band of international thieves and stole a pearl necklace which had been entrusted to Bey by the Sultan. When the jewels disappeared, the Sultan at once demanded that Ilma either recover the necklace within six months or consent to join his harem in repayment. Honest Bey was held as hostage in order to make certain that the wishes of the Sultan were carried out. In the meantime, the pearls from the necklace had been well distributed over the face of the earth, and off went Ilma and Harry in search of them. The chief villain was Perry Mason, played by Leon Bary, who hampered their search in his efforts to obtain the pearls for himself. Of course the final chapter saw the pearls returned to the Sultan, Honest Bey freed, and Ilma married to Harry —but many exciting moments had passed before this came about. Donald MacKenzie turned out a workmanlike thriller in every respect, and acting honors went to Bary, a versatile actor who was capable of playing either hero or villain with equal ease.

Vitagraph released three serials during 1917, two with William Duncan and Carol Holloway and the other a Graustarkian romance entitled *The Secret Kingdom.* Prince Simond, prime minister to King Phillip of Alania, secretly aspired to the throne and caused the assassination of both the King and the Queen. Captain Barreto, commander of the palace guard and a loyal supporter of the King, suspected treachery afoot and rescued little Crown Prince Phillip before Simond's henchmen could kill him also. With the aid of Juan, a fisherman, an escape was made to America. Twenty years later, the rightful King of Alania, Phil Barr (Charles Richman), had grown to manhood. By a quirk of fate, he rescued Julia (Dorothy Kelly), the daughter of Simond, from danger. Neither knew of her father's complicity in obtaining the throne of Alania, and there arose a mutual affection which furnished the romantic angle for the remainder of the story. In the meantime, Phil's whereabouts had been discovered, and Madame Savatz, adventuress and spy, was sent to kill him. Juan, son of the fisherman who had helped save Phil, learned of the plot and warned him. This close-knit group of characters seemed more the invention of popular fiction writer Louis J. Vance, who was indeed their creator, than a coincidence of real life. Nevertheless, with the plot set in motion, the rest of the serial dealt with Phil's attempts to prove his birthright and stay alive. This should have been impossible, since he fell into Madame Savatz's hands in nearly every chapter, but through the generosity of the writer and the kindness of the directors, Phil managed to come out all right in the end with both throne and girl.

William Duncan, a native of Scotland, came to the United States when he was ten years old. His early career included the management and later ownership of a physical-culture health school. Interested in acting, he gave up the school for an engagement in vaudeville and joined the Forepaugh Stock Company of Philadelphia. This led to his entrance into motion pictures with the Selig Company, but his star did not begin to ascend until he joined Vitagraph. A rugged, healthy individual, he stood five feet, ten inches tall and weighed a solid 180 pounds. In *The Fighting Trail*, his first Vitagraph serial, Duncan portrayed John Gwyn, a young mining engineer and the only man who knew the location of a mine which contained unlimited amounts of rare minerals used in the preparation of a new and powerful explosive needed to carry on the war in Europe. Engaged by a number of businessmen to supply ore to their firms, he soon found that the Central Powers had placed agents on his trail to learn the secret of the mine. Ybarra, owner of the land on which the mine was located, had brought up a child, Nan (Carol Holloway), who was now a lovely young lady, and Gwyn fell hard for her, providing the romantic angle. The enemy agents attacked and killed Ybarra but obtained only a portion of the map which Gwyn had left showing the location of the secret mine. Just before Ybarra died, he told Nan that she was not his child and gave her a note telling of her origin. The plot lacked a strong climax, and in some places the story was a bit trite. Such was the case of the finale, in which the villain committed suicide, leaving a note which read: "I have lost. It is the fortune of war." Fortunately, Duncan's later serials were made of sterner stuff. The most interesting part of this one, however, was the very attractive Miss Holloway. She was of medium height, and her slender build was capped with a lovely round face, full lips, and sparkling eyes.

Take a series of inexplicable murders which followed warnings imparted by a mysterious voice on the telephone. Add a secret society, the "Black Seven," and stir in a theory called "The Living Death." Ladle the mixture into fifteen parts and serve it up by a pair who were to become top box-office stars over the next few years and you have *The Voice on The Wire*, the first of the Ben Wilson–Neva Gerber offerings. Wilson, a handsome chap who appeared in the original Edison series which started all this, *What Happened To Mary?*, was teamed with petite Neva Gerber, a pretty Chicago society girl. These two were to make a number of interesting and thrilling chapter plays and thereby take up some of the slack created by the loss of Cunard and Ford. Their serials moved fast and hard with a strong mixture of mystery and violence. *The Voice on The Wire* abounded with mystery and suspense, which intensified as the story moved toward completion. It opened with Detective John Shirley (Wilson) making repeated but futile attempts to break up a crime wave. The "Black Seven" was a psychical-research body in Paris which had been forced to hold secret meetings because of the nature of its advanced theories of life and death. Laroux, a leading member of the society, proved a theory he held by mummifying the wife of another member, Dr. Reynolds. The theory became known as "The Living Death." In the chase

53

after his archenemy, Dr. Reynolds lost an arm through snakebite and had a new one grafted on successfully. He also possessed the ability to project his body through space, but from then on, when his astral body was projected, the grafted arm showed and gave the eerie appearance of an arm without a body. The answer to the killings did not become clear to the audience or Shirley until the end, when the disembodied hand was revealed to belong to Reynolds. He had waited seventeen years for revenge, but finally managed to do away with all of the Black Seven.

Joseph Girard gave another of his fine character portrayals as Dr. Reynolds, and Miss Gerber played Polly Marion, a colleague of Shirley's—and the love interest. The high pitch of suspense made the entire production a bright beginning for the popular new team. Francis McDonald (or MacDonald) recently said of *The Voice on The Wire:* "It was a devil-may-care thing, much action and trick photography. Stunts were numerous and we did them all ourselves." His toughest was a seventy-foot jump from the top deck of the coastal steamer *Yale.*

The Mystery Ship, the second Gerber-Wilson offering of 1917, concerned a girl whose father died after leaving a key to treasure hidden on an island. With a map showing its location in her possession, she set out to recover it, taking with her a friend who was to prove to be after the wealth for himself. She was followed by Gaston (Wilson), who had a grudge against her father; he turned out to be her real friend, however, and the ending found them in love. The film had a strong and interesting story built upon a time-worn theme whose mystery element was supplied by a strangely clad man and a mysterious ship which saved Betty (Miss Gerber) several times. The acting was again topnotch, and Harry Harvey and Henry McRae did an excellent job of directing.

Marie Walcamp appeared in a thriller entitled *The Red Ace,* an adventure story set in the wild and rugged mining country of Canada. It detailed the attempts of Virginia Dixon (Miss Walcamp) to clear her father and brother of treason charges while preventing foreign agents from locating a secret platinum mine. The villains had been very successful in hijacking platinum shipments, but greed got the upper hand and they tried to take possession of the mine. Full of thrills and excitement, the story interest was sustained from chapter to chapter, and both the acting and direction were of high quality. The public gave *The Red Ace* a royal reception, and fans still remember Miss Walcamp mainly for her work therein.

Universal released another serial which followed the adventures of a master criminal, *The Gray Ghost*. Harry Carter played the title role, and the first two chapters were given over to the planning and execution of the wholesale looting of a jewelry house in broad daylight. The operation was staged on an elaborate scale, making it a most gigantic and daring criminal exploit. Some of the situations involved in bringing the audacious thief and his gang to justice were dragged out to fill in the required sixteen episodes, but the story held up for the most part, and a strong love interest with various side plots helped, as did the fine supporting cast, including Priscilla Dean as Morn Light and Eddie Polo as Marco.

The one venture of Francis X. Bushman and Beverly Bayne into the serial fold was more or less a fiasco engineered under the auspices of Louis B. Mayer. The extremely popular Essanay stars had formed their own company, Quality Pictures Corporation, and arranged for distribution through the young Metro Pictures Corporation. Mayer, eagerly seeking to establish himself in the production field, approached Quality with the idea of a serial starring the romantic team. Neither was particularly flattered by the proposal because the serial lacked a certain dignity which they felt was essential to their screen image. Bushman flatly turned down the proposal, but Mayer was persistent in his efforts and finally wore the star down.

With a pair of stars in his pocket, Mayer swung into action and, with investor friends in Boston, organized the Serial Producing Company, with Colman Levin as president. Fred de Gresac did the script, which was called *The Great Secret*. It was written around the familiar theme of a beautiful girl, a fortune she had inherited, and some villains who wished to keep her from gaining the money. Christy Cabanne directed. The serial opened in Boston in an unusual manner. Mayer managed to book it in several different theaters, and the first three or four chapters were offered to allow a patron to get well into the plot by jumping around between theaters. The promotion worked well in Boston, but national release through Metro failed to bring in the receipts Mayer had hoped for. In fact, the film brought in just a bit over its production costs, which were largely the $15,000 salary of the stars. It brought little acclaim to the reputation of either Bushman or Bayne; as a matter of fact, it became a milestone in their careers which they preferred to forget.

Jim Loughborough of the Metro staff told the following story after paying a visit to Quality Studios. He went to see Christy Cabanne, who was directing *The Great Secret*. The watchman was temporarily absent from the door, and a huge, sinister-looking Chinaman suddenly appeared and gazed inquiringly at Jim. Jim explained what he wanted and the Oriental beckoned him to follow along. Outside Cabanne's room, the Chinaman paused. "Maybe," he said, leering hideously, "you give some piece dollah, room rent me no got?" Loughborough tersely stated there was nothing doing in the panhandling line and walked into Cabanne's presence. "Who," demanded Jim of the director, "is that grafting, yellow dope fiend that hangs around here?" Cabanne smiled as the pseudo-Oriental glided forward and stood grinning fantastically. "This," he said, "is your old friend, Francis X. Bushman, disguised for his role in the eighth episode." Loughborough had a rough time living that one down.

In 1917, Paramount brought forth the one and only serial it ever produced. *Who Is Number One?* was a story of revenge. Because he had scorned her, Camille Arnot sought to ruin the famous inventor Graham Hale. She believed that the most effective method would be for him to lose his most beloved possessions one by one, the process culminating with the loss of his son. Camille felt that this would destroy Hale's mind. In the midst of all this hate stood Aimée Villon (Kathleen Clifford), who loved young Tommy Hale. She fought to save the Hale family from the mysterious "Number One," who seemed determined to destroy their happiness. Actually,

56

it took the final chapter to clear it all up, for Camille was, in reality, the estranged wife of Graham Hale, Tommy was his son by another woman, and Aimée was the daughter of Graham and Camille. Under a spell at times, Aimée had really been Number One all along and had been stationed with her father for the purpose of revenging her mother. "All's well that ends well," but suffice it to note that Paramount shied away from this field of motion-picture entertainment thereafter.

Helen Holmes made *The Lost Express,* which, although it added little to her fame, did not cause her to lose box-office popularity or her many fans. An example of this appeal was her late 1915 release, *The Girl and The Game,* which by this time had drawn well over $2,250,000 in admissions. Since her departure from Kalem, her railroad serials had all been made in the same vein, but the fans continued to support her faithfully. The early episodes of *The Lost Express* related the disappearance of a train carrying the contents of a safe belonging to Helen Thurston's father. Destined for a bank vault in a near-by town for safekeeping, the most precious possession was a formula for the manufacture of granulated gasoline. Fourteen chapters were devoted to regaining the valued formula and solving the mystery of the disappearing express. Tom Lingham played the double-dyed villain, and L. D. Maloney gave fine support in a "man of mystery" role. The story was full of action—and also full of holes and inconsistencies. Nevertheless, it was interesting and moved so rapidly that it held the audience in suspense throughout, not allowing time for logic to be applied to the plot. The ridiculous nature of some of the material Frederick Bennett supplied can be seen in Chapter 2, "The Destroyed Document," which found Helen creeping along the top of a moving train with a magnifying glass. It seemed that Harelip the criminal was at that very moment examining a page from the formula, and Helen, with her trusty glass, managed to focus the rays of the sun onto the paper. This, of course, instantly destroyed it before Harelip could read the writing. All this on a moving train and far from being logical or convincing. J. P. McGowan rose above the script, however, in his direction of the final episode. The spectacular climax saw an entire town destroyed by fire. After learning the secret hiding place of the missing express from a member of the gang who was dying, Helen drove her high-powered car into the mine and engaged the two remaining members of the syndicate in a desperate fight. At the successful conclusion of the struggle, she was able to back the iron monster out of the mine and thus end the mystery. Fade-out.

Pathé's two top serial stars appeared in only one vehicle each during the year. Ruth Roland had made a few society dramas for Balboa which did not go over too well with critics or fans. She then made *The Neglected Wife,* which was more or less a love triangle in fifteen chapters, playing "the other woman," who tried to break up the home of a successful lawyer and his wife. Roland Bottomley and Corrine Grant co-starred in these roles. *The Neglected Wife* was not as successful as it might have been, for the thrills and adventure which fans expected were lacking. At its conclusion, Ruth married Lionel T. Kent, a Los Angeles auto salesman, and left Balboa for Astra, which also released through the Pathé banner. This brought on a suit for breach of contract by Balboa, but the settlement was in Ruth's favor. It was with Astra that she was to skyrocket to fame everlasting in the serial realm.

Pearl White made the most of her role in *The Fatal Ring* and added fresh laurels to her reputation. As Pearl Standish, she portrayed a rich girl who had so much money that she didn't appreciate what it could do for her. She was bored with life until a man named Nicholas Knox made a demand on her at the point of a gun. He wished to acquire the violet diamond which he claimed her father had bought after it had been stolen from the Sacred Order of the Violet God. Knox was the eastern representative of the High Priestess, who had recently arrived in this country with her henchmen to recover the gem. In the course of affairs, Pearl won him over to her side, and together they battled to stay alive and retain the precious jewel. The serial was well made and the role was perfectly suited to Miss White's talents. As usual, a fine supporting cast backed her up.

Toward the end of 1917, the serial found itself in trouble. From its very beginning it had proved to be a prosperous area of screen entertainment, but this prosperity was quite deeply rooted in external conditions. The world had been at war since 1914, and many men had entered uniform when America joined the fray. Women stepped into their shoes and carried on at home, in offices, in factories, on the assembly lines. In short, women became equal with men in nearly every way. The audience during this time was composed mainly of children and the mass of the people—those in the lower socio-economic groups. The intellectuals paid little attention to the serial, dismissing such as ridiculous and foolish. The female stars of the serials faced adventure, danger, and villains week after week, all the while keeping their honor unsullied and their virtue intact. This was something for women to admire and men to respect.

With so many women and children in the work force, the wages paid were disgustingly low. It has been estimated that $7 per week was the bare subsistence level during this period, and it was not unusual to find many women drawing not more than $6 weekly. For these few paltry dollars, they worked most of their waking hours and still managed to keep body and soul together. The new machines and concepts which were destined to give the working class more leisure time were just beginning to make their presence known. Thus the serial was, to these people, a means through which they were able to inject a feeling of adventure and excitement into what would otherwise have been a hard, drab existence. In the exciting chapters of a serial, they could lose themselves for a short time, could admire the resourceful nature and common sense of the heroine. In fact, the serial could be compared to their own lives, but on a different plane. The conclusion generally reached was that although "heaven would protect the working girl," her best friend was herself. Who can tell how many took new strength from the serial, strength to continue the life they led? At the outset, then, the serial owed its popularity to the fact that it offered sheer escape.

But more than escape was needed after America's entry into the war, for movie-going became a fashionable entertainment of the growing middle class. These people were, in a word, more sophisticated and demanded subtler and more refined plots. Their standards were more critical; they were more secure in life and their interests differed from earlier audiences. The intellectuals also "discovered" the motion picture during this time, Vachel Lindsay leading the way with his investigations during 1915.

Gradually, producers recognized their public's new tastes, and photoplays became more sophisticated. This, coupled with the addition of a war tax on movie admissions and an especially severe winter in 1917–18, caused the box office to slump rather badly. The serial soon appeared to be headed toward the cheaper movie houses and rural areas, where audiences were not so critical. Some gloomy prophets even predicted the eventual disappearance of the chapter play, but the years 1918–19 found the serial format in transition, to emerge again in 1920 as a real contender at the ticket window. The years of transition were difficult for many firms, however. For example, 1918 was a particularly poor year for the continued-weekly pictures, with only thirteen releases. The war in Europe drew to a successful climax, and suddenly, war pictures or films hinging on the war effort were a drag on the market. Producers, caught short by the Armistice, were forced to shelve many films, which represented a large aggregate value. The influenza epidemic that struck during the year closed down thousands of theaters, and attendance dropped off greatly in those which remained open. Many small studios were forced to the wall and died a sudden death; others cut back drastically in an effort to weather the crisis.

This combination of circumstances, both visible and invisible, naturally caused Hollywood much concern, and it reacted in a predictable manner of self-incrimination and soul searching. Many articles published in the trade and fan magazines of that time about the future of the motion picture sound today as if they had been written very recently. Production was cut back until a new trend could be sensed, although exhibitors complained that salvation lay in more and better pictures. However, caution was the keyword of the day, and this applied to serials. With the exception of two, the scripts which were filmed for release during 1918 were done by proved performers.

A preparedness serial of the first order was made by the Whartons in their Ithaca studio and fell flat on its face. Approved by George Creel, the chairman of the Committee on Public Information, it was a first-class propaganda piece which aroused much pro and con but little coin. It was caught in general release by the end of the conflict, and since it was so wrapped up with the war situation, it lost appeal almost at once. Marcus Loew and Joseph M. Schenck had both refused to play it in their chains on the grounds that it would have ruined their business. They felt that it was "too great a contrast to the thoughts and opinions of the German patrons." As it turned out, they would have had little to worry about. William J. Flynn, retired chief of the Secret Service, bore the dubious honor of authorship. The story proper dealt with an organization called the "Criminology Club." The club convinced the U.S. Secret Service that there were hundreds of German spies loose in the United States and offered its services in unearthing them. King Baggot, in his first serial appearance, portrayed Harrison Grant, the president of the club, who took an active role in locating the spies. Marguerite Snow played Dixie Mason, a youthful and beautiful Secret Service agent dedicated to Grant and his mission. So much for *The Eagle's Eye.*

The General Film Company released a twelve-episode serial of single reels produced by the Jaxon Film Company in early 1918. William Sorelle played the role of the secret agent and Jane Vance undertook the part of a girl who was immensely interested in both radio and the war effort. *A Daughter of Uncle Sam* found them working together and trapping spies via radio.

Pearl White's release of the year bordered on the fringe of the war effort and was a brisk but well-paced item of interest. The mystery developed from the fate that hung over the House of Walden, celebrated munitions manufacturers. The family had made munitions for the highest bidder over generations past. Nature had taken the game in hand, and the present members of the family were trying to stave off the doom of heredity. In order that control of the Walden War Works would remain in family hands, Pearl's father arranged her betrothal to a cousin. Soon after, the father was put to death at the hands of assassins. Antonio (Tony) Moreno, as the young scientist Harry Gresham, was in love with Pearl, who returned his devotion, since she was not at all interested in the cousin to whom she had been promised. To cap the works, another cousin, Zelda (Peggy Shanor), was the vamp who loved Gresham and did her best to block his efforts to win Pearl and make secure the House of Walden. The "Hooded Terror" furnished the necessary spine-tingling mystery. Thus went *The House of Hate*.

Ruth Roland became world famous as a result of *Hands Up*. Written by Gilson Willets, it was a fine entry which had all the ingredients of a successful serial and was well received, winning Miss Roland a host of new fans. As a young magazine writer, Echo Delane, she was sent to a mission in southern California to get an article about a band of descendants of the ancient Incas. Mistaken by the Indians as a "Princess of Prophecy," she narrowly escaped sacrifice to the Sun God by the heathen worshipers. It soon came to light that she was believed to be the lost heiress of Strange Ranch, and the story was further complicated by her cousin, Judith, who wanted the ranch herself. The "Phantom Rider" managed to save Echo from the deadly perils in which she found herself. George Chesebro, Ruth's leading man, entered the army during the filming, and George Larkin took over for him.

During the filming of *The Lion's Claw*, Marie Walcamp was attacked by one of the beasts and bore a scar from the encounter for the rest of her life. As Beth Johnson, she was one of a party of English people caught in the African jungle during the war. She became involved in a plot conceived by the Central Powers to stir up a holy war among the natives of Mohammedan influence. The elaborate settings and jungle atmosphere reflected the excellent efforts involved in this serial. It had a lively tempo and an absorb-

James Cruze (*left*) and Sidney Bracy in a moment of concern from "The
Mystic Message of the Spotted Collar," Chapter 1 of *Zudora*
(*The Twenty Million Dollar Mystery*), a 1914 Thanhouser release.

Helen Gibson strikes a determined pose in "The Wrong Train Order,"
Chapter 58 of *The Hazards of Helen* (1914).

Marguerite Snow found herself in a perilous situation in this scene from
The Million Dollar Mystery (1914).

Earle Williams and Anita Stewart in *The Goddess* (1915),
an early Vitagraph serial.

Lillian Lorraine, the beautiful Ziegfeld Girl who portrayed Annette in Balboa's ill-fated *Neal of The Navy* (1915).

"The fight in the speeding freight car." Irving Cummings as Arthur
Stanley in a scene from Chapter 5 of
The Diamond From The Sky (1915).

Despite the efforts of William Tedmarsh (*left*), Juanita Hansen bites the
hand of George Webb in this scene from the final chapter of
The Secret of The Submarine (1916).

Carol Holloway and William Duncan, the two "big guns" in Vitagraph's
serial of romance and adventure *The Fighting Trail* (1917).

ing and dramatic plot, but was somewhat complicated to follow. Both the acting and the direction were of high caliber.

Ben Wilson directed a Universal chapter play, *The Brass Bullet*, which starred Jack Mulhall as a playwright who had been confined in a sanitarium by error. He managed to escape to Pleasure Island, where Juanita Hansen, a young heiress, was about to be kidnaped. Learning of the plot, he launched into the business of saving her and clearing her name. This was the item which started Miss Hansen up the ladder as a serial queen of note, for it led to her signing the contract offered by Colonel William Selig, as we shall see.

Eddie Polo got caught up in the Secret Service craze in *Bull's Eye*. Clayton, a prominent western ranch owner, had a beautiful daughter, Cora (Vivian Reed), who was attending college in the East. As Cody, the ranch foreman, Polo was sent to accompany her home, and trouble began while he and the girl were on the train headed back. Certain big interests desired to keep them away from the ranch for a time while her father was disposed of. The efforts to clear up the murder and resulting mystery were hampered to an extent as Cody fell in love with Cora, who loved the young Secret Service agent involved in the case. As if this were not enough, Sweeney, the outlaw chief, really complicated matters by taking a violent fancy to Cora. Suffice it to say that all turned out as you'd expect it to.

All three releases by Vitagraph were written by Albert E. Smith and Cyrus Townsend Brady. *A Woman In The Web*, the first to be issued, was built around the Russian Revolution and starred Hedda Nova as a princess and member of the Tsar's embassy in Washington D.C. Two of her staff were involved in a plot against the Tsar, and upon reporting this information, she received instructions to return to Russia. Jack Lawford (J. Frank Glendon), whose father represented the Tsar in business dealings in the United States, followed her abroad because he was in love with her and sensed that trouble would engulf her. Indeed it did, for when she arrived in Russia, the revolt broke out, and as a person of royalty, she was in extreme danger from all sides. Lawford immediately joined her, and the pair had many adventures while trying to stay alive and attempting to return to safety.

William Duncan brought forth another of his variations on a theme with *A Fight For Millions*. As Bob Hardy, he fell in love with Jean Benton (Edith Johnson). Her father had left a fortune in mining properties, and two of her distant relatives were anxious to marry her for the money. One was a western outlaw and the other an eastern dude who was a coward at heart. The will left her all of the fortune, provided that she marry one of them within a year. How Hardy circumvented the will, won the girl, and disposed of the cousins provided the action. Joe Ryan gave an admirable portrayal as the chief heavy and was soon to win stardom in Vitagraph serials for himself. *The Iron Test* starred Tony Moreno and Carol Holloway in a serial of circus life as a pair of acrobats who outwitted the "Red Mask" in his attempts to do them in.

Probably the best serial that Francis Ford was to make without Grace Cunard was *The Silent Mystery*. It was packed with melodramatic thrills and creepy doings in the best manner of Ford's productions, and his regular followers got a run for their money. The cast followed the pace he set, and the result was strict attention to putting the episodes over. It seemed that Mrs. John Graham (Elsie Van Name), traveling with her daughter Betty (Mae Gaston) in Egypt, stole the "Eye of the World" from a mummy. The theft was discovered and when the Grahams returned home because of financial difficulties, they were followed by the Priestess Kah (Rosemary Theby) and her associates. The Priestess Kah was determined to regain the jewel at any cost. Betty made a loveless marriage, and her husband was murdered on their wedding night. A great mystery soon began to gather around all who had touched the stolen gem. Betty's brother tried to sell shipping secrets to the Germans, but she prevented him from doing so and was captured in the process by Kah, who had secured German aid to regain the jewel. Betty was rescued by Phil Kelly

(Francis Ford), who discovered he loved her and was able to rescue her from the silent and almost invisible power that pursued her until the mystery was finally unraveled. Rosemary Theby made an excellent villainess from beginning to end.

CHAPTER THREE

OUT OF DEATH'S SHADOW

Sᴇʀɪᴀʟ ᴏᴜᴛᴘᴜᴛ ɴᴇᴀʀʟʏ ᴅᴏᴜʙʟᴇᴅ in 1919 over the previous year's figure; the results were interesting in many ways. This year was to see the end of an era in serial productions. George B. Seitz directed Pearl White in what was announced as her last starring serial vehicle, *The Black Secret*. Miss White had signed a contract with William Fox to appear in five-reel features, and with the exception of *Plunder,* also directed by Seitz and released by Pathé four years later, it was her last. The abdication of the "Lady Daredevil of the Fillums" left Ruth Roland as the undisputed "Queen of the Thriller Serials." Song plugging with the serials became popular again during the year. *Romantic Ruth* accompanied the release of *The Adventures of Ruth* in December, 1919, and the release of *The Fatal Fortune* by SLK Serial Corporation saw the appearance of *Pretty Helen,* written by Walter R. Hall and William A. Sullivan. Neither song ever became an all-time favorite, but they gave the exhibitors something catchy to tie up with their publicity efforts.

The Tiger's Trail, Ruth Roland's first release of the year, turned out to be one of her most popular serials. The plot began as a Gilson Willets adaptation of *The Long Arm,* a melodrama of city life written by Arthur B. Reeve of Craig Kennedy fame. Louis Gasnier, who was president of Astra (which did the filming for Pathé release), thought it would make a dandy western and proceeded to give Frank Leon Smith the task of rewriting it. In the end, Smith turned out what amounted to an original story. George Larkin was chosen as leading man and Robert Ellis took over the directoral reins. He ran into bad luck and was replaced by Paul

66

29544

C. Hurst, an old hand at the business. The plot followed the attempts of Hindu tiger worshipers and crooked cowboys to prevent Ruth from obtaining valuable mines that were rightfully hers as a result of a deal between her father and two other men.

With *The Adventures of Ruth,* another winner was chalked up for Miss Roland. She played the role of Ruth Robin, daughter of a millionaire. As the story opened, she was attending a seminary for girls. Her father, Daniel Robin, was a recluse who lived in perpetual fear of death at the hands of a criminal band known as the "Terrible Thirteen." The father had been forced into membership of the gang against his will, and his fear finally became reality. Shot in the back by La Farge, the leader of the band, Daniel Robin summoned his daughter. On his deathbed, he told her in the presence of his trusted butler, Wayman, of the "Peacock Fan," which she had to recover. It had been stolen by the Terrible Thirteen but contained a secret which affected her. He also informed her that she was to accept thirteen separate keys as they were handed to her by an unknown person and to follow the instructions in each instance. Ruth agreed to these terms, and after her father's death, she started out on the first mission. The keys and the adventures accompanying each one formed the basis of the remainder of the serial, which, quite naturally, ended with the recovery of the Peacock Fan and the capture of LaFarge.

Helen Holmes returned to the serial fold with her first release since *The Lost Express* in 1917. In *The Fatal Fortune,* she moved the locale away from railroading to an island, known as "Devil's Isle," in the South Seas, which had a fortune hidden upon it. A man had deserted his family earlier in life, amassed a fortune, buried it, and left a map before dying. News of the death and rumors of the fortune were brought back by passing sailors, and Helen, as a good reporter would, investigated the matter. Her efforts soon revealed to her that the old recluse had been, in fact, her father. She managed to secure the map, but the "Faceless Terror" took it away from her. After many problems and dangerous situations, she regained possession of half the map, and a battle of wits began between her and the desperate villain; each sought to secure the portion of the map which the other had. Lieutenant Jack Levering portrayed the handsome pilot who was always close by when she needed help. As an action serial, this one had the stuff, but her fans had closely identified Helen with railroading and they missed the old scenery. It was a state-right release by SLK, and as a consequence, the box-office potential was considerably reduced.

The return of Cleo Madison to serials marked the release of *The Great Radium Mystery*. A rather undistinguished entry in the field, it concerned the disappearance of the heirs to one of the greatest fortunes on earth. The plot was routine, but the appearance of Miss Madison helped to put it over, and it introduced a new face in the ranks of Universal's directors. Born in Port Rohen, Ontario, Robert F. Hill had started his theatrical career on the stage and worked up to stage manager of a stock company. Writing was a sideline with him, and it led to a position as scenario writer for Triangle. With the demise of that organization, he moved to Universal and very shortly began his rise to fame. Receiving credit as co-director of *The Great Radium Mystery*, he did the second-unit work in a creditable manner.

The Lion Man, adapted from *The Strange Case of Cavandish*, proved to be an interesting variation on a theme. Stella Donovan (Kathleen O'Connor) was a girl reporter sent by her newspaper to cover a society circus being given by a millionaire named Frederick Cavandish (J. Barney Sherry). The circus was an exclusive affair and reporters were not allowed, but Stella contrived to assume the role of one of the female performers. She even carried out the wire-walking act of the performer she was impersonating. While engaged in filling the role, Stella overheard a plot against Cavandish. It seemed that he had made a new will which disinherited his nephew John (Robert Walker). John and a tricky lawyer named Enright (Henry Barrows) were assisted in their plot by Celeste La Rue (Gertrude Astor), an actress. Their plan was to do away with Cavandish and then destroy the will in order to make certain that John would inherit the property. Jim Westcott (Jack Perrin), a young mining man from Arizona, came to see Frederick Cavandish on business and foolishly became involved in a quarrel with him. Shortly afterward, Westcott was accused of having killed Cavandish, who had disappeared during a fire in his home. Stella and Westcott united in an effort to recover the will. A series of dangerous incidents followed during their quest, but they were fortunate in having the able assistance of a strange being known only as the "Lion Man." Guess who?

Many other interesting serials appeared during the season. A great deal of filming was still centered around New York, with Pathé having produced many of its serials up to this time near Fort Lee, New Jersey, and Ithaca, New York. *The Great Gamble* took its players to Ausable Chasm, near Lake Champlain, for location scenes, where Charles Hutchison had ample opportunity to demonstrate his athletic ability to the fullest. Anne Luther played a dual role as twin sisters in this Joseph A. Golden production. One had been reared in wealth and luxury; the other was raised by an adventurer who secured possession of the child upon the death of her mother. The story involved an attempt to substitute the poor child for the wealthy one and Hutch's effort to fathom the mystery surrounding the daughter, whom the father believed to have been drowned as a baby. A major fault of the dual role by Miss Luther was confusion. It was impossible at times to understand which sister she was portraying, and hence the audience often could not tell whether she was for or against the villains. The titles were of little help in establishing and maintaining coherence. However, she was a decorative addition to Hutchison's stunts and at times appeared to be trying hard to imitate Pearl White.

The Terror of The Range was one of the shortest full-fledged adventure serials on record, lasting only seven episodes. The title was derived from the name of a mysterious bandit who murdered and looted as the head of a band of marauders. His identity was a secret: he always wore a wolf's head during the raids. A United States government agent, John Hardwick (George Larkin), was sent to the ranch which seemed to be the center of the bandit's activities, and he rounded up the crooks in jig time. Betty Compson provided the love interest.

Already a producer, director, business manager, and writer, George B. Seitz took on a new task with *Bound and Gagged*. Frank Leon Smith had written a ten-chapter comedy melodrama which poked fun at the heavier serials. In fact, the gags outnumbered the homicides, and Seitz was delighted with the script. When Smith mentioned Walter McGrail for the lead, Seitz shocked him by declaring that he would play the role, and play it he did—to the hilt. Both Pathé and the audiences gave the film a good reception.

One of the quaintest advertising gimmicks appeared when Vitagraph released *The Perils of Thunder Mountain,* starring Tony Moreno and Carol Holloway. Although the release date was late in May, exhibitors were exhorted to advertise fully the fact that the serial took place amidst plenty of snow, thus assuring the customers of "welcome relief from the expected heat of the coming summer."

Elmo, The Mighty brought forth Elmo Lincoln as Captain Howard Armstrong, forest ranger. The story dealt with the efforts of a syndicate to steal valuable timber lands, with Elmo setting forth to stop them. Grace Cunard appeared in this Universal production as Lucille Gray, a former Red Cross nurse who had met Armstrong on the battlefields of France and pleasantly renewed an old acquaintance in the setting of the north woods. A mysterious motorcycle rider cloaked in black, the "Phantom Menace of Mad Mountain," helped Elmo and Grace out of the tight spots.

James J. Corbett left the ring and entered motion pictures to star in the Universal serial *The Midnight Man,* where he adorned the scenery and lent the value of his fame to the marquee. Concocted with a view toward exploiting the personality and physical prowess of the former champion, it was greeted with mixed reaction. In assuming the role of the hero, Corbett was under the handicap of appearing as an older man than was usually seen in such a role. He did much to overcome this disadvantage by performing feats that would have put many younger men to shame and was assisted by a winning smile and a pleasing on-screen manner. An interesting plot was lucidly set forth, but in general construction, the serial leaned heavily toward the melodrama found in earlier productions and lacked the imaginative qualities and scenic beauty which characterized other productions of the year.

In closing out the year 1919, we should note that this was the beginning of the era of state-right releases in the serial field—the development which makes research of this period quite difficult. Little of a definite nature ever appeared in print concerning many of these serials. Casts, dates, and titles changed constantly. Firms entered the field for one or two releases and then disappeared. In many cases, release dates are impossible to ascertain, for they differed materially, depending upon the section of the country and the firm handling the release within that area. For example, *The Master Mystery,* produced by Octagon Films Incorporated, was released in the eastern United States on March 1, 1919, and in the West on May 1. With this serial, Harry Houdini began a brief and unsuccessful screen career.

Vaudeville had been feeling the effects of motion pictures for some time, and many of the old headliners were quite bitter about being replaced in many instances by the "flickers." Not so Houdini, who realized that something had to be found to replace his act as a money-maker and a means of keeping his name before the public eye. In 1919, he simply decided that he should become a movie star, and thus evolved the idea of a fifteen-episode serial. Arthur B. Reeve, creator of Craig Kennedy, collaborated with Houdini on the script, which dealt with a mysterious combine known as "International Patents, Inc." The firm was controlled by a ruthless business magnate from his castle home. The castle overlooked the sea at the beginning, but as the story progressed, the sea inexplicably became a river. Below the castle was a secret storehouse, carved from the massive rock, called the "Graveyard of Genius." That was the location of models of inventions which the combine had purchased from inventors and then stored to keep progress from destroying their profits.

Houdini portrayed Quentin Locke, a secret agent of the Justice Department, who was investigating the activities of the combine. The evil genius at its head just happened to have a beautiful daughter, Eva (Marguerite Marsh). Considerable support was

71

given to the plot at this point by the introduction of one of the suppressed inventions, which moved under its own power. This was a giant metal robot called "Q, the Automaton," which lumbered out of its hidden den for each episode. Forever defying bullets and heavy doors (which it smashed like kindling wood), the Automaton deployed a group of ruffians identified only as "The Emissaries of the Automaton" in an effort to destroy Locke and Eva. After surviving many deadly perils, including acid, barbed wire, poison fumes, "DeLuxe Dora" (Ruth Stonehouse), and the "Madagascar Strangler," Locke perfected an explosive bullet which penetrated the heavy steel body of the metal monster, only to reveal that it was controlled all along by a very human villain inside. The source of the robot's superhuman strength was never brought to light. Incidentally, Floyd Buckley played the robot in a thoroughly ludicrous manner.

Even though *The Master Mystery* was unusual and quite interesting, it was not too successful. Lack of success was to follow Houdini through a few more films before he quit pictures for good. His failure has often been attributed to a puritanical streak which inhibited the freedom of his on-screen love-making and also to the inability of the movie-going public to distinguish between the authenticity of his screen feats and the camera-fabricated miracles of the ordinary serial. It was simply a case of the public's expecting more than usual and not appreciating it when they saw it. For the record, Houdini had to sue Benjamin A. Rolfe, Harry Grossman, and Octagon Films for his 50 per cent share of the profits from *The Master Mystery*. The State Supreme Court, New York County, handed down a verdict in May, 1922, which awarded him the sum of $32,795.18 as his due through the period ending September, 1919.

Jack Hoxie made his appearance in *Lightning Bryce,* a National Film Corporation opus which was state-righted through Arrow. Playing the title role, he was supported by Ann Little as Kate Arnold. Even if nothing else could be said about this particular serial, it would be necessary to commend the fine performance given by Miss Little. The plot was a bit involved at first, but once it got under way, it became quite easily understood. It seemed that two men who had been prospecting for years finally struck it rich with a large gold deposit. One was the father of Kate; the other was the father of Bryce. They tied a string about the blade of a knife and wrote the location of the gold on the string. On their homeward journey, one was stabbed and the other was killed when Indians set upon them. The string wound up in Kate's possession, but Bryce got the knife, along with a letter explaining how the gold might be found. The villain succeeded in getting the knife away from Bryce and the race was on, with each side endeavoring to obtain both items. You know the rest.

Oliver Films state-righted *The Carter Case (The Craig Kennedy Serial)*, which starred Herbert Rawlinson as Kennedy and purported to follow the further adventures of the "scientific detective." Marguerite Marsh played the object of his affections. This entry was hailed by exhibitors for attracting many people who did not ordinarily go to serials. They attributed its drawing power to the impossible situations and wild fiction of the plot. Francis Ford took time off from his directing to star in *The Mystery of 13,* a slam-bang Ford release for Burston Productions. Supported by Rosemary Theby, he turned out a creditable Ford-type serial, but he was tiring of acting and his fans were deserting him for the newer and more subdued serial stars.

Near the end of 1919, William Duncan was asked by a New York reporter why the serials were so successful. Published in a London fan magazine, *Cinema Chats,* his reply is quoted below.

Why are the serials so successful? Because they answer the suppressed desires of every man and every woman. All of us are very elemental when you get under our skins. Nowadays, nearly everyone leads a humdrum existence bringing home the bacon. But we have all dreamt of wild adventure and winning "our girl against odds." It has developed, however, quite contrariwise. The serial "thriller" only portrays what all of us would have liked to live out—a life of deeds, not words. The girls feel the same way about it, I might add, most women do. In the good old days, a man fought for his womenfolk—very often there was coffee and pistols for two before daybreak but now it is all so dry and matter of fact. . . . Yes, the serial "thriller" is the only manifestation men and women have of the romantic life they have always wanted to live. Office boy or bank president, grand dame or sweet sixteen, they all feel the same way. The only difference is one looks hopefully forward while the other looks regretfully back.

CHAPTER FOUR

THE DELUGE

✤

As THE MOVIE INDUSTRY entered the twenties, many changes were to be seen, both in theater patronage and in the type of material shown on the screen. The idealism and patriotism which had characterized the middle of the second decade of the 1900's had disappeared, to be replaced by a period of "normalcy"—that quaint word so peculiar to President Harding. Actually, America was tired and worn out. A large war, the largest that mankind had ever seen, had been fought and won. Recession followed war prosperity and was replaced, in turn, by more prosperity. Moreover, the war had taken thousands of American men abroad, where they had ample opportunity to learn more about other nations and their people. During the course of it all, the nation had risen from a young power to one with international strength, a rather meteoric rise. America didn't quite know what to do with her strength at first; what she finally did decide to do was reflected by the defeat of the League of Nations in the United States Senate.

As we have seen, more sophisticated audiences had begun to patronize theaters. Pure slapstick of the more risqué kind promoted by the old Keystone comedies found less favor with the people and was being replaced. The more trite plots of the features had changed in character, too. Once again, Hollywood was to seek out the oracle of success, the box-office barometer, and the new high priest soon took his throne. An ample amount of sex became the prime attraction on the silent screen, and with it, the stock of Cecil B. deMille rose 1,000 per cent. The strange fact here is that within bounds, the silent serial became more respectable. In the setting of sin and salvation, which became the order of the day for the silver screen, it is twice as difficult to understand the success of many of the serials, still plodding along well-worn paths, unchanged except for the shift in emphasis of the leading role. Difficult to understand, that is, unless you remember them as "escape valves," which they continued to be. Difficult to understand, also, unless you consider that this form of entertainment had developed staunch fans who stood by during thick and thin. We will shortly witness a major shift in serial story lines which seemed at the time to be necessary for survival.

Perhaps the largest and most important change was in the starring role of the serial. As we have seen, the most popular stars before, during, and right after the war were women. In the twenties, women were to take a back seat in leading roles, yet remain to furnish feminine interest and sex appeal as male stars began to dominate the serial realm. True, Ruth Roland's fans grew with each serial, but Pearl White had left Pathé in order to make features for Fox. The twenties produced only Allene Ray as a leading feminine serial star. On the other hand, Charles Hutchison, Eddie Polo, William Desmond, William Duncan, and Jack Daugherty rose to the top as male leads. To be very frank, the serials of the later silent period did not "make" or produce top female stars as the early serials had. Pearl White, Grace Cunard, Helen Holmes, Marie Walcamp, and Ruth Roland, among others, owed their fame chiefly to serials made before 1920. The lack of top stars cannot be attributed to the serials themselves, for in the twenties, as before, some were very good, some were very bad, and the majority fell somewhere in between, depending upon the observer. Perhaps no sound, conclusive answer will ever be found to explain why the serial was so popular in the later silent period and yet failed to produce female stars of the first magnitude.

More attention than ever was given to the plot and settings. Serial companies began to leave for the East and the West on location. Universal sent Eddie Polo to Europe to work on a serial which never materialized and Marie Walcamp to the Orient, where she starred in *The Dragon's Net* and married her leading man, Harlan Tucker. Upon her return, she retired from the screen for nearly seven years, returning in mid–1927 with a role in the FBO production *In A Moment of Temptation.* Polo had left New York in June, 1920, and upon arriving in the British Isles, set about shooting scenes for *The Broken Idol.* Soon after, the title was changed to *The 13th Hour,* and very shortly, Polo and the entire company returned to the United States. Some of the scenes shot abroad were incorporated in other productions, and he took a few weeks' vacation before setting to work in Universal's West Coast studio on his 1921 releases, which utilized the remainder of the foreign scenes as background. By this time, the serial had become a staple item in the production rosters of Pathé, Universal, and some of the state-right releasing companies, such as Arrow. It was also in 1920 that William Fox committed himself to produce his first serial. One notable fact is that First National, United Artists, and Goldwyn never produced or released a serial at all. Paramount, which had one domestic production to its credit, did import a few foreign serials—to its everlasting regret. One example was a four-chapter serial in five-reel episodes. Entitled *Mistress of The World,* it received discouraging reviews from all quarters, disparaging remarks from patrons, and screams of agony from exhibitors, who booked it on the strength of the Paramount trade-mark of 1922. Many exhibitors learned their lesson with this one, and bookings fell on subsequent imports until Paramount realized that the public was against them.

The year 1920 was to see the entry of Jack Dempsey into the serial world in an attempt to cash in on his popularity in the ring. Surprisingly enough, Dempsey carried it off in grand style, and his acting in *Daredevil Jack* wasn't too bad. He played the part of Jack Derry, a college athlete who assisted Josie Sedgwick in her quest for information leading to a secret oil basin found by her dead father. Probably much of the credit belonged to Director W. S. Van Dyke, who was to gain a reputation for fast, skillful work of a not too inventive nature. Some credit should also go to a fine supporting cast which included such up-and-coming craftsmen as Lon Chaney.

Van Dyke also directed another serial released in 1920 which was quite interesting in some respects. It was produced by Burston Films for state-right release and starred King Baggot in his second and last serial role. Baggot, nearing the end of a long career in films as an actor, was given the opportunity to maintain his reputation in the matter of multitudinous roles, appearing in ten different characterizations. As Sheldon Steele, a scientific criminologist and man of wealth who found fascination in the pursuit of crooks, he was called upon to assist two daughters who were being frustrated in their attempts to gain a fortune left them by their murdered father. Unknown to them, the murderer, known only as "The Hawk," was the man whom they supposed to be their uncle and who, as their guardian, had sole control of the fortune. Naturally, the efforts of the hero led him into many different sections of the underworld, and this gave Baggot a chance to assume as disguises the characterizations of a Chinese, a longshoreman, a miner, a waiter, an East Indian swami, a stoker, the head of a detective bureau, and, when in the service of the sisters, an employee of the same agency. This gem was known as *The Hawk's Trail*.

The Lost City, state-righted by Warner Brothers and produced by Colonel William Selig, starred Juanita Hansen and a host of wild animals. Selig seemed to be rather good at this sort of thing. Miss Hansen had made a nice living at Universal, Fox, and with Sennett, moving with each opportunity to better herself financially. She had already proved, at Universal, that she could carry a serial as the star, and Selig was in need of such a person for his jungle epic. Juanita talked her way into the lead role. Production had barely started when the director, E. A. Martin, was taken ill and confined to his bed. After some six weeks had passed, he was suddenly notified that his star had signed a contract with Pathé, effective January 1, 1920. With twelve episodes left to film and only ten weeks to complete them, Martin left his sickbed and went back to work. He rewrote the chapters, segregated Juanita's scenes, lumped them into a continuous schedule, and finished shooting them all by December 22, 1919. The remainder of the episodes were shot after Christmas, and Juanita left on schedule to fulfill her Pathé contract. *The Lost City* was revamped into a seven-reel feature which Celebrated Players Film Corporation released as *A Jungle Princess* in November, 1920.

Moving to the East, Miss Hansen swapped homes with Texas Guinan, who had gone to Hollywood to make a series of pictures for the Bulls Eye Film Corporation. Her first release under the Pathé banner, *The Phantom Foe,* was a spooky serial which Bertram Millhauser turned out. George B. Seitz had been scheduled to direct, but he was tied up with the production of another of Frank Leon Smith's comedy melodramas, *Pirate Gold,* in which he co-starred with Marguerite Courtot. A young man who had been around Pathé for a number of years received his first experience as second-unit director under Millhauser; Spencer Gordon Bennet served in the same capacity on Miss Hansen's next Pathé serial and then advanced to the position of assistant to Seitz. His career took fire in the twenties.

In *The Phantom Foe,* William N. Bailey portrayed the hero and veteran Harry Semels was the villain in a story of the strange disappearance of Janet Dale, her father, and her aunt. A masked stranger in a long fur coat roamed the house at will: no one seemed able to capture him. It was typical material in which one would have expected to find the lovely Miss Hansen emoting and was an interesting and entertaining number. Pathé had fond hopes of boosting this girl into the place left vacant by the departure of Pearl White and there is some indication that she might have made the jump, but at this point her career took on the aspects of a tragic melodrama. Her salary, status, and mode of living had changed overnight when she signed with Pathé. Her salary went to a reputed $65,000 yearly, she received star billing with the other Pathé serial greats, and she sold her soul to the Devil.

To this point, Juanita's career had the brilliance of a shooting star on a hot summer night. Only in films a few years, she had reached the pinnacle of success. Now the long descent was to begin. Working day and night, she finished two serials for Pathé. During this time, she had reached the point where she could no longer sleep and arise refreshed for the day of hazardous shooting ahead of her. She went to parties on her free evenings and worked the rest of the time. The world was spinning, and she was living hard and fast. She drove her white Mercer racer as hard as she drove herself. The saying made the rounds: "You step in and you look out." Traffic laws and Juanita were friendly, but not on speaking terms. Near the point of being physically worn out, she first discovered the effects of drugs at a Hollywood party. After snuffing her first pinch of cocaine, she felt rested almost at once. For the first time in many months, her worn nerves felt at ease and her entire body relaxed. Even her mind felt calm, but clear. Instantly, she decided that cocaine was exactly what she needed to keep up with the pace of her work and play.

For a time, the drug did not appear to harm her and she failed to realize that she was becoming an addict. Waking one morning, she found herself out of cocaine, but neglected to pick up a fresh supply on her way to work. By midmorning she was in the middle of an agonizing experience, for her body told her how much she craved the drug. A friend who was also on the stuff saw how terrible she looked, drew her aside, and provided the necessary relief from his own supply. Nonetheless, she had been severely frightened and visited a doctor, who suggested a change of scenery. From this time on until 1928, she was in and out of sanitariums, taking cure after cure. After completing *The Yellow Arm* for Pathé, she left the fold to form her own company, but things never materialized as she expected. First arrested in January, 1923, on a charge of possessing narcotics, she protested that she had been cured the previous June. In and out of jail, on and off the stuff, she dragged on agonizingly until 1928. At this stage of her life, fate stepped in.

Successful in musical comedy on the Broadway stage, she had effected what she hoped to be a permanent cure. Returning to her hotel on a warm summer day, she stepped into the shower and turned on the water. Instead of a refreshing stream of cold water, she was greeted by a scalding blast of steam and boiling water. For the only time in her life, Juanita Hansen screamed and fainted. The scalding water continued to pour over her limp form, and had it not been for her companion, she most certainly would have been scalded to death. As it was, more than half of her body was burned

80

and the doctors didn't give her a chance. She finally regained consciousness and refused to allow them to give her a pain-relieving shot. Holding out for several days, she astonished all who knew her with her firm grip on life. However, she was only human, and the agony finally forced her to give in. She received a shot every day until she was well, and by that time, she was once again a confirmed addict.

Bringing suit against the hotel, she charged that her fame had been snuffed out by the jet of boiling water, which ruined her near-classic beauty and left one side of her body an ugly mass of scar tissue. A jury awarded her $118,000 of the $250,000 she asked, and nearly all of this was spent on plastic surgery. The remainder went for drugs, since by this time she had reached the addiction level of morphine and heroin. Unable to get a job either in films or on the stage, she went to one sanitarium after another. In 1934, she took what was to be her last cure in Oakland, California, and went to work for the WPA Theatre Project at $94 per month. In 1936, she was again picked up as a known addict and a hypodermic syringe and drugs were found on her. Her highly unlikely story of helping an addicted friend proved to be true and the court set her free. She then went on a lecture tour across the country, seeking to educate youngsters with a playlet illustrating the dangers of addiction and attempting to collect enough money to open a sanitarium similar to the one in Oakland, which she claimed had worked such a miraculous cure on her. She dropped into obscurity and spent her last few years working as a train-order clerk for the Southern Pacific Railway.

Found dead in her Hollywood apartment on September 26, 1961, Juanita Hansen was the victim of a heart attack. Although she had earned an estimated $1,000,000 between 1914 and 1922, her money was gone, fame had left her, and she had no known survivors. She could have remained a popular favorite over the rest of the silent years, whether or not she filled the shoes of Pearl White, for there was something fascinating about watching this lovely woman weave her charm and athletic prowess through the episodes of her serials. After all, not too many of the serial queens were beautiful women, but watching her perform gave the viewer the feeling that she was saying, "Damn the good looks, full speed ahead." She came across on the screen as a fresh, wholesome personality, but the public was robbed of her full measure because she was never fully able to conquer the terrible craving she had acquired so early in life. The Devil took his due.

Pathé had announced *The Crooked Dagger* for release on September 19, 1920, but it never saw the light of day. Wharton Studios had completely cast it and placed Helen Ferguson in support of the leading man, who never arrived. The slot had been held open for a vaudeville hoofer and song writer, Jack Norworth, who was better known for his association with Nora Bayes earlier in his career. His vaudeville engagements left him with June and July free, and Wharton Studios planned to wrap it up in the can in eight weeks, but contract problems between Pathé and Norworth did the serial in.

Upon being graduated from high school in Paris, Illinois, Jean Paige had gone east to college, where she specialized in elocution for two years. In 1917, she accepted employment with Vitagraph to play in the "O. Henry" series being made at its Brooklyn studio. Her career did not move very rapidly, and she soon found herself playing the female heavy in serials. She and Joe Ryan reached stardom together. Ryan had portrayed the male heavy in numerous Vitagraph serials, and it was decided to star him with Miss Paige in a serial to see what they could do. After completing *Hidden Dangers,* Jean was abruptly moved over to starring roles in Vitagraph features, where an extensive effort was made to boost her stock with the public. It seems that she had married Albert E. Smith, president of Vitagraph, in December, 1920.

Bride 13, the first serial produced by Fox, disclosed the navy's role in protecting American shores against a band of Tripolitan pirates who descended upon the coast and kidnaped thirteen wealthy brides, holding them for millions of dollars in ransom money. The navy, asked for help by the girls' families, gave generous aid. We should note that Fox did not embrace serials very warmly thereafter.

To my mind, the most humorous production of 1920 was *The Screaming Shadow,* produced by Hallmark Pictures Corporation and starring Ben Wilson and Neva Gerber. The advertising for this serial centered around the following theme quoted from Hallmark advertising: "Founded upon the scientific discovery that substitutes of monkey glands prolong human life. See this serial and learn to live forever." I have often wondered if this chapter play had any connection with the soon to appear goat-gland craze. At any rate, you must give the exploitation theme an *A* for effort.

Wealthy old Dr. Horatio Scraggs had converted his fortune to gold and named four babies as his heirs. The children were branded at birth with mysterious marks which were to appear when they had reached young womanhood. When the marks were decoded, by use of Scraggs' diary, the hiding place of the gold hoard would be revealed. After hiding the gold, the old man was struck by lightning. When his lawyer read the will, he became extremely angry because nothing had been left to him. Stumbling onto the diary which revealed the secret, he was discovered by a house servant, and during the scuffle which ensued, a dog wandered off with the book. In the meantime, Marion Leonard (Neva Gerber), who had been adopted from a foundling asylum by the wealthy Leonard family, celebrated her twenty-first birthday. The lawyer tried to kidnap her but failed, and she met A. B. C. Drake (Ben Wilson), better known as "Alphabet" Drake, a criminologist who helped her unravel the secret of *The Branded Four,* a Select release which helped to maintain the reputation Wilson and Gerber had built up among serial fans.

With the influence that science and science fiction were to have in the twenties on the plot of the serial, one of the earliest and best of its kind was a state-right release done by Frohman Amusement Corporation under the title *The Invisible Ray.* The action opened at an easy gait, distinctly defining the origin of the plot and leading to thrills that grew as the chapters progressed. The villains of the story were after the "invisible ray," which was contained in a metal box. There were two keys to the box, one of which was suspended from the neck of Mystery, played by Ruth Clifford, a girl of about twenty who had grown up at the Hope Foundling Home and was loved by all who knew her. She had been left at the door of the institution in a basket when she was a baby, and with her was a note stating that the key must never be taken from her neck and also telling of a meteor mine where wonderful rays of light had been found by her father. If concentrated, the rays would have produced an atom of light energy powerful enough to destroy the world. The second key and the box containing the material which could produce the rays of light were in unknown hands at the beginning of the serial.

Jack Stone, played dynamically by Jack Sherrill (son of Frohman's president), was in love with Mystery and had planned an elopement which, according to arrangement, was to be carried out at 10:00 P.M. on a certain night. On the same night, she was mysteriously kidnaped and taken to a secret underground chamber, where torture was applied to force her to give up the key. Unknown to her captors, the key had fallen from her neck at the door as she was carried away. In the meantime, Stone and a man named John Haldane visited a crystal-gazer who revealed the whereabouts of Mystery. A chase through underground passages followed, and Mystery was finally rescued, only to fall into the hands of the enemy once more. Haldane, by the way, while posing as a friend to Jack, was in reality a secretary associated with a band of kidnapers known as "The Crime Creators." The upshot of the fifteen chapters proved the crystal-gazer to be Mystery's mother, who was presumed drowned in a steamship accident. Jean Deaux, a shadowy character constantly in pursuit of the key, was frequently on hand to rescue Mystery from danger. He turned out to be her father. The story was sufficiently logical, as such, to base the episodes on, but at times there were rather gaping holes which a careful observer would question. Nonetheless, it provided the necessary scientific interest as a background for the love scenes and adventure. All told, it was successful for a state-right release and rather prophetic in a way. Remember, this was 1920 and the theory that isolation of the atom would produce energy of untold force when unleashed underlies the action.

As a part of his new contract with Canyon Pictures, Franklyn Farnum starred in an exciting western serial. The plot laid the opening scenes in the house of an industrial magnate, Stilwell, who had gained his fortune by ruthless business methods. He had called many of his victims and invited them to be his house guests. Most accepted and had arrived, but were apprehensive over the reason for their presence in his mansion. Shortly, he entered their midst and announced that he intended to retire at once and told them the details of the disposal of all his holdings into "one lump" to be given away. He then left the room to get the "one lump," which was in the library safe. As the startled house guests began to recover from their shock, they discussed the odd turn of events. For months they had concentrated their efforts on his ruination, and now he was about to destroy the reason for their revenge.

As Stilwell took his treasure from the safe, strange forms struck down his guards outside the house and an eye peered through the curtains. A shot rang out and Stilwell slumped to the floor, dead. When the guests rushed in, they found the safe and desk rifled and the treasure nowhere to be found. The scene changed to the mysterious hill where Steve Durant (Duke Lee) ruled his inner circle of crafty, strong, and fearless men. The name given this eerie place was "The Land of Vanishing Trails." In an earlier day, Durant would have been a feudal lord; as it was, however, he ruled over a sort of no man's land. Enter Silent Joe, played by Farnum, who was saved from death by the daughter of Durant (Mary Anderson), and we have the two antagonists face to face. Durant sought the fortune which belonged to Stilwell, and Silent Joe attempted to prevent his acquiring it. Here we have the beginnings of a fine mystery serial with thirteen more episodes to go before the solution is finally resolved. The fortunes varied, with first one side and then the other gaining the advantage, only to lose it shortly. Filled with hard riding and fighting, magnificent gallops over the boundless mesa, dashes down inclines which must have taxed the horses, bodies hurtling down ravines, leaps over chasms, explosives, and the like, *Vanishing Trails* was another very good production from Colonel Selig.

Universal reworked a familiar theme in *The Flaming Disc*, casting Elmo Lincoln in the dual role of hero and villain. This was somewhat of a switch, as it was usually the poor heroine who had to suffer through double exposures. The plot started off with a bang. Professor Wade (Lee Kohlmar) had perfected a lens of great power which was capable of reducing iron and steel to ashes. Rodney Stanton (Roy Watson), master criminal, wanted it badly for his own devious purposes. Elmo Gray, the inevitable Secret Service man, was watching both Stanton and Professor Wade. Stanton obtained the lens and the Professor's daughter (Louise Lorraine) early in the story, and Elmo was opposed at every turn by his brother (which he also played), who was under the hypnotic influence of Stanton and thus was a member of the gang.

Born at Stillwater, Oklahoma Territory, in 1890, Art Acord performed his first professional stunting in 1910 with the Dick Stanley Wild West Show. In 1911, he was working with the Buffalo Bill Wild West Show. His all-round versatility in stunting and riding soon led him into motion pictures, where he quickly found fame as Buck Parvin in a series of films for American. While competing in a rodeo in Salt Lake City during July, 1913, he married Edythe Sterling, an actress. They settled in Glendale, California, near Helen and Hoot Gibson, who became their close friends. Acord moved on with different companies, but after his wife divorced him in 1916, he left pictures to enter military service in 1917 and saw combat action in France. Released from the army in 1919, he returned to Universal, where he was given the starring role in his first serial, *The Moon Riders*. Throughout the twenties, he starred in numerous serials and many features, which were generally well received by his fans.

The arrival of sound was more than Acord could cope with, and, depressed a great deal about it, he took an act into Mexico in 1930. Making a decent living at this, he soon gambled away what he earned, and in early January of 1931, he was found dead. The *New York Times* reported that his body contained enough cyanide to kill several men. However, Helen Gibson has reason to believe to this day that Acord met with foul play. She says:

There are no records any place; as to Art's death, all I can say is I saw the letter M. K. Wilson [her leading man at Universal in the twenties] received through the American Legion. He has passed on and so has Art's wife and everything has been destroyed. Art loved life too much to do that. He was a tough fellow who would fight at the drop of a hat and he always won. He just ran into some bad ones in Mexico.

Grossman Pictures released *The $1,000,000 Reward* on a state-right basis and covered the nation with "wanted" posters offering a million dollars for information leading to the return of the girl on the poster, Lillian Walker. It was a clever advertising gimmick which opened many eyes. In the story, Betty Thorndyke (Miss Walker) was the daughter of the richest diamond-mine owner in South Africa and the victim of two simultaneous plots against her person. Carefully and secretly reared in California, she suddenly became the object of a large reward offered for her whereabouts by the stockholders of the mine. Her father had died and the stockholders were anxious to have the property divided among them. Crooks read of the offer and decided to win the reward, preferably by foul means. At the same time, Betty's welfare was endangered by one of the stockholders, who hoped to gain a larger share in the mines by disposing of her. The plot was not new, but the carefully planned and executed advertising campaign gave a certain distinction to Director George A. Lessey's efforts.

Speaking of advertising, *The Mystery Mind* was preceded by a barrage of syndicated publicity which included articles by J. Robert Pauline on "Auto Suggestion in Every Day Life." Pauline suggested that the principles of hypnotism were applied unconsciously by millions of people in their relations with others and attempted to prove that a mother influenced her child by suggestion, although unaware of it. He also tried to demonstrate how suggestion tended to make for success or failure in marriage, business, personal relations, and other areas. The articles were designed to arouse wide interest in hypnotism and psychic forces, and especially to entrench the name of J. Robert Pauline in the minds of millions to whom he was already familiar as a former hypnotist and headline vaudeville artist. The ultimate objective was to warm the audiences up to him as he played the lead role. He never made another serial.

Tarzan made his first of many serial appearances in the National Film Corporation release *Son of Tarzan*. Directed by Harry Revier, who had a speaking acquaintance with Tarzan (he had previously turned out the Goldwyn feature *Return of Tarzan*), and Arthur J. Flaven, this fifteen-episode thriller concentrated on the adventures of Tarzan's son. P. Dempsey Tabler appeared as Tarzan and Karla Schram portrayed Jane. Kamuela C. Searle, who played the role of the son as a young man, was killed during the filming of this serial. Tied to a stake, he was supposed to have been rescued by an elephant. After carrying the stake and Searle away to a point of safety where it was to lower both to the ground gently, the animal rewrote the script by heaving both to earth violently. The stake broke in half, and Searle died as a result of the injuries he suffered.

Under the auspices of Warner Brothers, Helen Holmes formed the Holmes Producing Corporation and completed her next-to-last starring serial role, but not without a measure of difficulty. Upon her entering into the agreement with Warner Brothers, it was announced that she would star in *The Danger Trail*, with Gilbert P. Hamilton directing. The Warners, however, needed money badly and *The Danger Trail* became a feature which they hoped would finance further production. Shooting then started on *The Tiger Band*, which immediately ran into production problems. In order to put the serial in the can, Helen found it necessary to advance $5,000 to Warner Brothers; it was agreed that repayment was to be made at the rate of $500 per week. Claiming that she had received only four payments, she was forced to file suit against the firm in an effort to regain the remaining $3,000. The resulting litigation tied up matters so firmly that release of *The Tiger Band* went onto the state-right market almost unnoticed.

Before we leave 1920, let's look at one more action serial. Joseph A. Golden, who had produced *The Great Gamble* with Charles Hutchison, once again starred him in a chapter play for the Allgood Picture Corporation. In *The Whirlwind,* Hutchison was given full opportunity to prove himself a master of the motor-cycle. He played Charles Darrell, who had just returned from France after winning the title "The Whirlwind," among other war-time honors. Darrell met Helen Grayson (Edith Thornton) in a rescue scene when her horse bolted and threatened to throw her. He later became involved in an attempt to catch a band of crooks which had for its leader a man named Carnley (Richard Neil). In addition to holding a high social position, Carnley was also the fiancé of Helen. Covering his villainies, he managed to carry on his double life with success. Darrell pursued the criminal through a series of hair-raising events, including long-distance dives, taking his chances with the shell of a burning building, and scaling many stories of a brick apartment house with the assurance of a pro-fessional acrobat.

During the year, the serial received its fair share of criticism and attack. The best exchange of opinion came when G. A. Atkin-son, a cinema correspondent writing in the *London Daily Express* attacked the American serial as follows:

> We all know that the serial film is a compound of artificial thrills of the most bloodthirsty and adventurous kind. It is largely a screen convention, like serial fiction, having no relation whatever to real life or ordinary human experience, and it is accepted as such by cinema audiences in western countries. . . . In most serial films, the heroine is in distress to almost the last palpitating second. Frequently, she is rough-handled, not always by white men. The prestige of white women in India is totally inconsistent with the adventures of white women in serial films. Still more important in this connection is the fact that in many serial films the villains are black, yellow or brown men whose villainy at the expense of the whites is glorified throughout the film, although they are brought to book at the finish; but it may be doubted whether the moral of the eleventh hour vindication of virtue is fully seized by the exultant natives, who have witnessed the triumphs of their colored kind through so many long drawn out previous episodes.

Arthur E. Rousseau, export manager for Pathé Exchanges, Inc., discounted this attack with the theory that native audiences in the

Orient had become sufficiently sophisticated to understand that fiction, not fact, was being pictured and to accept the performance for its entertainment value only. He further countered with the recollection of many Pathé serials as examples which did not exploit in any emphatic way the villainy of black, yellow, or brown men at the expense of the whites.

The reception of most of the year's production by the audience proved beyond doubt that, providing it met certain standards of construction, there could hardly be a question of the success of any serial. A prime requisite was good casting, directing, and acting. The method of presentation had to be more or less a formal one: a simple plot, clear complications of events, and swift movements strung along at intervals, with a thrilling climax for each chapter and a plausible opening for each succeeding chapter. The plot had to leave sufficient room to build upon for following chapters, and it was desirable that there be no awkward breaks in the continuity. A love story, although secondary to the plot, was usually present and was utilized both for emotional relief from the thrills and as a thread by which to hang the plot.

90

CHAPTER FIVE

BACK TO THE PRIMITIVE

A S AN ENTERTAINMENT MEDIUM, the serial was beginning to undergo a radical change by 1921. Criticism and complaints had been directed toward this story form in previous years, but the scandals which came out of Hollywood in the early twenties started to rock the nation and had a more lasting impact. Local citizens' groups across the country began to apply pressure either to cease the exhibition of serials or to close the theaters. Some groups, such as the Woman's Picture Committee in Buffalo, New York, led by Mrs. Thomas E. Tynes, requested that the city's exhibitors stop showing serials as Saturday matinees. The other extreme was represented by Mayor Fred Bater of Superior, Wisconsin, who banned all serials on January 1, 1921; he attributed his attitude to the belief that a sudden wave of petty banditry and crime among juveniles in the city was largely caused by the sensational crime episodes appearing in serial chapters. In many states during 1921, censors ruled against the serial in its form at the time, prohibiting holdups, the liberal use of weapons, torturing of the heroine, and, in particular, the method of handling the female characters of the story. Some censors refused to permit even the laying of a hand upon a woman.

Since the serial had been a potent source of revenue to the producing companies, they were not favorable to the suggestion that it be discontinued and consequently, the story form began to undergo a basic transformation. In previous years, some attempts had been made to base the stories on historical grounds; Universal had been a leader in this direction. Instead of tortures, holdups, criminal conspiracies, and the like, natural thrills and hazards such as might really have occurred during historical adventures proved to be a happy compromise, and it was discovered that romance and thrills could be nearly as abundant—and perhaps more convincing—when natural perils were depended upon. By "natural perils," I mean dangers encountered with wild animals, desert treks, storms, and other things. What this amounted to was growth in the sophistication of the serial plot and dropping some of the trite, overworked clichés which the serial formula had called for up to this time.

Several difficulties faced the producers. Such historical adventures as *Winners of The West* had to cover a lot of territory and pad quite a bit to run the story out to the roughly 36,000 feet of release footage required. Art Acord played the part of a young hunter and trapper in a continuity which spread from the attempts of John C. Frémont to blaze a westward trail, through the California gold rush, and finally to San Francisco in pre–Civil War days. Twisting through this historical path was the familiar lost cave of gold dating back to an expedition of Sir Francis Drake, complete with a map. As Arthur Standish, Acord sought the map, which the villain had tricked from him. Naturally, love and romance were on the same trail, and by the time he had reached the end of his journey, Acord had both gold and girl. He did have one large problem, though. The foreign market was more interested in a larger dose of mystery, thrills, and adventure with a shorter dose of education. The Wigwam Theatre in Oberlin, Kansas, put it this way: "These thrills from history are not what you might think. Too much history and not enough thrills."

On the other hand, *The White Horseman* had starred Art as Wayne Allen, a young westerner who had been willed a piece of apparently worthless land occupied by two brothers, both of them squatters. One day the two were out foraging and found an ancient bracelet which had a line of picture writing engraved on it. Translated, the writing directed them to the base of a mountain, where they discovered a system of underground mines which had belonged to a long-extinct tribe of Indians. Inside, they found a chest full of blue opals. A violent argument soon broke out between

92

them: one wished to tell Allen of the discovery and the other wished to keep the treasure unknown to anyone but themselves. The latter chose his opportunity and shoved his honest brother over a cliff in order to silence him. On his way from the mine, he was captured by a roving band of outlaws, the "White Spiders," who soon became determined to possess the secret of the mine for themselves. Into this situation rode the mysterious "White Horseman" to set matters straight.

With *Hurricane Hutch,* Pathé proved to its own satisfaction that the success of a serial was not entirely dependent upon gunplay or a homicide in every episode. A paper mill, mortgage, and the struggle to obtain a lost formula for making paper from seaweed occupied Charles Hutchison, who was given ample opportunity to introduce many daredevil stunts. Thus, despite many grumbles from exhibitors and some patrons, the blood-and-thunder epics of earlier days were, for the most part, relegated to history, and fast-moving stories, often with historical background and many thrills and stunts, took their place.

Hutchison's previous number for Pathé during the year was *Double Adventure,* which was held up some two months when the star broke both wrists in a rather nasty fall filmed for the closing sequences. After this accident, Hutchison relied a great deal more on a double to stunt for him. In *Double Adventure,* he portrayed Bob Cross, a young newspaper reporter who was trailing the notorious crook "Painter Paul." In the course of his investigations, he came across a plot to abduct Martha Steadman (Josie Sedgwick), the grandniece of a millionaire named Biddle. As Cross arrived at the Biddle estate to warn Martha of the devious plot against her, he discovered the body of old Mr. Biddle. Jules Fernol (Carl Stockdale), a business associate, had disposed of him, for the elder Biddle had discovered that Fernol had embezzled Martha's fortune. Bob was a ringer for the dead man's son, Dick Biddle, and the crime was charged to him. Realizing that a mistake had been made, Cross allowed himself to be arrested and sent to jail. After satisfying the police as to his true identity, he gained their help in staging an escape and began his efforts to rescue Martha from danger and locate the real murderer. Hutch, of course, played both roles with his usual zest.

Juanita Hansen's last serial was *The Yellow Arm,* directed by Bertram Millhauser, an excellent production in every respect. The story was unusually mystifying and thrilling, and Miss Hansen gave an unforgettable performance. Three half-caste Chinese sought to revenge themselves on a man whose father had married a Chinese princess and brought her to the United States. John Baird (Warner Oland) returned home after an unexplained absence of five years, and promptly, attempts were made to dispose of him and kidnap his children. Around this basis, the action revolved. William Bailey and Juanita, as travelers who had been forced to seek refuge in the Baird home by a terrible storm, were mistaken by the Chinese for members of the family and the race was on.

The Avenging Arrow cast Ruth Roland as Anita Delgado, daughter of a fine old Spanish family in southern California. On her twenty-first birthday, Ralph Troy (Ed Hearn), was very much attracted to her. A mysterious arrow shot over the wall brought an end to the festivities and renewed the traditional threat to daughters of the Delgado family. Her female ancestors had all been killed on their twenty-first birthday. Anita and Ralph joined together to unravel the mystery surrounding her family and thwarted the efforts of the secret enemies who had sought to exterminate her. The film added little to her professional status but made the cash register ring pleasantly.

George B. Seitz directed and starred in another serial written by Frank Leon Smith. Originally titled *The Man Who Stole The Moon,* the story's leading characters had been Martians, but Pathé decided to remove the extreme fantasy from the plot and retitled it *The Sky Ranger.* A kind of prologue opened the first chapter by showing a man clinging desperately to a huge globe which was being rapidly hurled through space while other heavenly bodies came perilously near. Showing this to be but the dream of a man, the serial then plunged at once into snappy action that was humorous and at times resembled a farce comedy. Smith was excellent

Marie Walcamp and "friend" during the filming of *The Lion's Claw* in
1918. One of the beasts later attacked her, and she bore a scar
from the encounter for the rest of her life.

A tense moment for Ruth Roland in *The Tiger's Trail* (1919). She had earlier won box-office acclaim as Echo Delane, a young magazine writer, in *Hands Up* (1918).

Eddie Polo (*center*) in a scene from the 1920 Universal serial *King of The Circus*. He also starred in *The Vanishing Dagger*, which was released earlier the same year.

In this scene from *Captain Kidd* (1922), Polo expresses
himself in no uncertain terms.

Ruth Royce makes a point that Jack Mower will well remember in Universal's 1923 chapter play *In The Days of Daniel Boone*.

Neva Gerber rewards Jack Perrin with a coy "thank you" after an
exciting rescue in *The Santa Fé Trail* (1923).

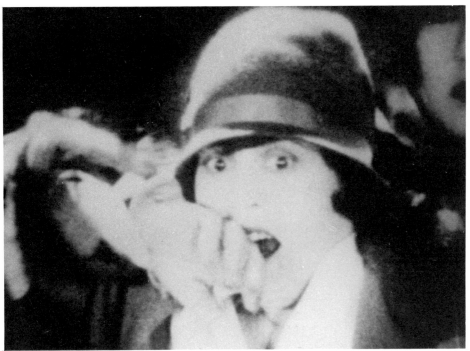

Neva Gerber effectively registers horror at the sight of "The Frog" in
Officer 444, a 1926 release.

William Desmond assures Eileen Sedgwick that he will protect her
in this scene from Universal's 1924 hit *The Riddle Rider*.

in putting together this type of material. The story hinged on the existence of a powerful light invented by the heroine's father. June Caprice portrayed the female lead. Naturally, crooks conspired to obtain the light. Weird effects were introduced through the person of a mysterious man who appeared in a plane and became one of the conspirators. The inventor of the plane, which had incredible speed and a silent motor, was a former stage magician who used hypnotic powers and was played by none other than Harry Semels.

Breaking Through introduced Carmel Myers to serial fans. A Vitagraph entry, this western story centered about a fight to put through a single railroad track from a mine in Alaska to the coast. If it was not completed within a specified time, the heroine (Miss Myers) would lose her title to the property. Wallace Mac-Donald, as the young engineer, aided in her successful fight.

Joe Ryan's first starring role in Vitagraph serials had been in *Hidden Dangers,* a 1920 release. He was quickly cast in another for 1921, *The Purple Riders,* and was an excellent choice for the lead. It started off with a punch and immediately informed the audience that there was no love lost between two of the principal characters. Their hatred for each other culminated in murder, of which the victim's drunken son was accused. The audience was shown the guilty party at once and knew him to be a partner of the victim and also "The Purple Shadow" (Joseph Rixon), leader of a band of outlaws who continually defied justice. Subsequent chapters dealt with the efforts of the sheriff (Ryan), who was in love with the dead man's daughter (Elinor Field), to clear her brother and catch the real murderer. The chief criticism of the film was that the time-worn plot, although it never dragged, was repetitious because the chapters overlapped and covered the same ground too often.

Ann Little appeared in a serial state-righted by Arrow and entitled *The Blue Fox.* She gave a very good performance, and the entire chapter play was well produced. Delving into the past, the opening episode explained that an Eskimo tribe had become so enraged at a white man for marrying one of its young girls that he was killed for his troubles. The Eskimo wife died of grief and left a baby girl who was brought to the United States and raised. Some eighteen years later, grown to a beautiful young lady, the girl (Miss Little) was determined to wreak vengeance upon the tribe which had destroyed her family. This and the discovery of a blue fox skin which disclosed, via Indian signs, the location of a rich mine furnished the action. Of course the skin was torn into separate halves in the early episodes, which further stirred up the plot.

Francis Ford directed and starred in his last major serial role with a dual portrayal in *The Great Reward*. Ella Hall returned to serials to co-star in this Burston Films production. This one hardly made the grade, for it was a below-average example of direction and although it contained the usual amount of slam-bang Ford action, it was unusually inconsistent. Without a doubt, it was the poorest serial Ford was ever connected with. His star was on the wane, and before long, he was to fade out of the serial picture, reappearing at intervals only as director. Trick photography and double exposure played an important role in this Graustarkian plot. The action centered around a mythical kingdom, Lyria, where two young Americans managed to get mixed up in a plot to depose its king, who at times lost his reason completely. Ford, it turned out, was the living image of the King and found himself forced by the monarch's friends to masquerade in his stead. This led to an increasing number of complications, all of which were smoothed out by the last reel, much to the amazement of the spectators. It hardly seemed possible that even Francis Ford could have solved this mélange.

Warner Brothers started somewhat of a cycle in continued plays with its July state-right release of *Miracles of The Jungle*. A no-star cast appeared in this serial directed by E. A. Martin and James Conway, with Ben Hagerty and Wilbur Higby filling the lead roles of two Secret Service men who were sent to Africa to find a man suspected of murder. Early in the story, the supernatural was introduced by the appearance of "The See'er of All" (John George), who was able to conjure up visions by means of a magic pool. In this manner he was able to see what was presently going on or what might have gone on in the past, anywhere in the

96

world. This device was used as a flashback of fifteen years in the past to show the murder suspect in a sympathetic role. It also served to introduce the villainous "Red Fox" (Al Ferguson), who had stolen the suspect's two daughters (Irene Wallace and Genevieve Burte). They escaped from his clutches and went to the See'er soon after the Secret Service men arrived. Subsequent action saw the Red Fox, with the aid of natives, trying to recapture the girls. The villains were no match for the ladies, however, as the Secret Service men and a giant Zulu, played by Frederic Peters, came to their aid. Together, they captured the Red Fox and cleared the girls' father of the charges wrongly laid upon him. Plenty of action was provided by the lions, while the comedy relief was furnished by a multitude of monkeys.

As I mentioned above, this began a cycle of jungle pictures in serial form. True, an occasional jungle serial had appeared on the silver screen, but in the next ten months, five were to appear, thus assuring that anyone who wanted animal thrills could find them without looking too hard. December saw the Weiss Brothers –Numa Picture Corporation with *The Adventures of Tarzan* in hand. Directed by Robert F. Hill, who was to make quite a name for himself in the serial field during the twenties, it starred Elmo Lincoln and Louise Lorraine (who celebrated her sixteenth birthday during the filming) in fifteen episodes of typical Tarzan material. Lincoln had played the title role in the 1918 feature *Tarzan of The Apes,* which had been very successful. The early producers had discovered what their successors confirmed: Tarzan was potent box-office material regardless of any other factor. In the beginning reels, Lincoln played the role with a bare chest but soon covered it up. He claimed that this inconsistency was due to censors who insisted on "good taste." Early in the serial, Frank Merrill (who years later would fill the role) began doubling the star in acrobatic scenes, and his athletic skill heightened the thrills inherent in the plot. Lincoln later insisted that continuation of the stunts would have endangered his insurance. The serial was recut and re-released in 1928 in a shortened length with sound effects by Weiss Brothers Artclass.

By 1922, the production of serials required a larger expenditure of money, for both costs and salaries were spiraling upward. The minimum sum spent neared $90,000, and many serials went above $200,000 prior to release. There were several reasons for the relatively high cost. Each chapter had to be complete within itself, with a beginning, a plot, and a climax. Since the subplots had to dovetail neatly in order to give the finished product the necessary polish, more time and money was spent on the preparation of the story. The cast had to be above average in ability if it was to continue through the separate stories without being inconsistent in characterization or otherwise displeasing. The directors and stars had to be the best because the emotions portrayed, of necessity, ran the gamut in nearly every chapter and only the skillful could carry it off successfully. Last but not least, the total footage of release more than equaled that of five features combined, giving credit for the overlapping scenes. By this time, Pathé had become deeply entrenched in its attitude toward the fifteen-episode serial with the first chapter in three reels; Universal and most of the other producing firms showed a market preference for the two-reel, eighteen-episode serial. The exhibitors, however, were beginning to call for shorter serials, and the two-reel, ten- or twelve-episode serial was just around the corner. Many of them felt that the producers were padding and dragging out their product in order to obtain better rentals over a longer period of time than the product merited.

Such was the case with *The Adventures of Robinson Crusoe,* a Universal release. A number of exhibitors complained because the serial left the original story after the second episode and was extended in length after release. The management of the Wigwam Theatre in Oberlin, Kansas, put it nicely in a letter to the *Motion Picture Herald* summing up the general complaint:

Played 11th episode and the next should be the last, but Universal could not break away from the old habit of making 18 episodes, so they prolonged the agony six more. They run out of story in the second chapter. All they do is show Myers with Gillette-shaven face chase the cave girl and savages around the island or get lost in a swamp full of toy alligators. Biggest frost in years.

Other exhibitors complained that the first twelve chapters stalled and that the remaining six were padded.

Eddie Polo had caused much consternation in the Universal ranks when, after being announced as the star of the forthcoming Robinson Crusoe epic, he refused to sign a new contract and went into business for himself. The Star Serial Corporation was established, with Joe Brandt at the helm, and, using the Peerless Studios in Fort Lee, New Jersey, Polo went to work filming a serial script. Carl Laemmle felt it necessary to take ads in the trade papers (a favorite device of his throughout the years) to announce that although the parting was amicable, Polo intended to produce a similar serial. Thus Laemmle warned the exhibitors to wait for Universal's "superior version" to appear. After a barrage of well-worded and carefully phrased charges and countercharges, Polo announced that his first serial would not deal with Crusoe but with Captain Kidd, the famous buccaneer.

As the story opened, the heir of a wealthy old English family was summoned to the side of his grandmother, who was near death. When young Edward Davis arrived, he found that his cousin, Phillip Raleigh, was also present. Raleigh was sent from the room and left in a huff. He hated his cousin, not only because Ed was the favorite of the old woman, but also because of Ed's relationship with Louise Bradley. The dying woman began to tell Ed a story concerning one of his ancestors of the same name, and the story drifted back to the seventeenth century, when Edward Davis, a penniless young chap, was competing with Lord Bellamy for the hand of Janice Sanderson. Against her father's wishes, Ed spirited the girl away and they were married. In the meantime, the old fellow died and Bellamy charged Ed with murder. In an attempt to escape, Ed was shanghaied. Shortly after the *Albatross* put to sea, it was taken by pirates and Ed came face to face with the notorious Captain Kidd. In an effort to save a friend, Davis joined the pirate band.

Back at Sanderson Hall, Bellamy had pressed his case with Janice, who could stand him no longer. After converting her fortune to gold, she set sail from England. Learning what was in the wind, Bellamy booked passage on the same ship and when the vessel was taken by the pirates, saved his life by telling Captain Kidd of the treasure. The chests were taken ashore, buried, and a map made of their location. Eddie managed to get the map, the girl, and himself off the ship. The scene then returned to the present day, and young Ed Davis was charged with the mission of locating the treasure. His cousin, Phillip, did not make the task easy. This was to have been the first of a series of six independent serials by Polo's firm, but he was reputed to have committed over $350,000 in production costs on a state-right vehicle which flopped, and he dropped out of the serial fold forever.

Universal continued its policy of historical serials with a premium on hard, fast action and clean-cut plots with *In The Days of Buffalo Bill,* which was written from a title. The sales division of the company appreciated the value of the name *Buffalo Bill* and also realized that it was a name known over the world. His life was studied, the history of his times was carefully gone over, and the result was a popular chapter play which dealt with the building of the Union Pacific Railroad and the last days of Abraham Lincoln, weaving in the career of the world-famous scout and Indian fighter. More than the usual attention was paid to historical correctness, but the usual amount of wild fiction was added. The popularity of this offering can be attributed to the western background and the acting of Art Acord and Dorothy Woods.

William Desmond's only release of 1922, *Perils of The Yukon,* was a story set against the backdrop of the transfer of Alaska from Russia to the United States. The action evolved from the love affair of an American, Jack Merrill (Desmond), for Olga Basanof (Laura La Plante), the daughter of a wealthy Russian trader. The villain, Petroff, also loved her and did his best to do away with Merrill in order to have a clear field with the lady.

Ben Wilson, who knew serial construction and production from start to finish, duplicated his past thrillers with *Nan of The*

North, an Arrow state-right entry. Duke Worne, also a veteran of serial action, directed the episodes, which were of the "shoot 'em up" variety, and the serial as a whole was above the average of the year's releases. The exteriors were filmed at Yellowstone National Park, and, believe it or not, there were precipices, gulches, forests, snow-clad mountains, and rushing streams enough to go around for the fifteen chapters and then some. It also marked the fourth stellar serial performance by Ann Little, who seems to have been one of the most underrated heroines in the serial business. The action centered around a gang who sought to obtain from a fallen meteorite the powerful substance known as "Titano." Whoever possessed this fabulous element would have in his clutches a source of unlimited energy which could be put to good or evil uses, for it was supposed to have been more powerful than the combined forces of radium, electricity, steam, and gasoline. Opposing the gang was Leonard Clapham, who portrayed a member of the Royal Canadian Mounted Police. Miss Little furnished the love interest as a cultured girl who lived in seclusion in the forest with her foster father. The presence of Joseph Girard as the polished villain with a female associate added crosscurrents in the scheme of romance and skulduggery.

The jungle cycle continued in 1922 with the January release of the Universal historical offering *With Stanley In Africa.* George Walsh and Louise Lorraine co-starred in this picturization of the search for the lost Dr. Livingstone. The plot kept to the facts as closely as possible, but in order to produce eighteen full episodes and give viewers the adventure and thrills which they expected from a serial, it was necessary to intersperse plenty of fiction with the truth. There had to be a logical reason for Miss Lorraine's presence and the serial had to keep moving rapidly, so Universal wove in a subplot which dealt with an attempt to revive the slave trade. The end result was a production which could have been taken as fiction with a correct historical background or as fact embellished to make it more tasty to the serial-hungry public.

February saw the release of the next Warner Brothers offering in the jungle field. An immense zoo and Mrs. Josephine Hill were hired to complement the work of Grace Darmond and Philo McCullough in *A Dangerous Adventure*. The difficulties encountered in filming this type of story began early and plagued Sam Warner to the last reel. Near the start of filming, Miss Darmond fell from an elephant's back and was confined to a hospital bed for over a week. In a letter to his brother Harry, Sam told of the difficulties he had encountered and of the efforts necessary to keep the insurance company paying off at the rate of one claim per day of shooting. Some of his problems were detailed most specifically:

> Mrs. Hill was attacked by one of her leopards and bitten in the neck and leg. An artist we had working insisted on shaking hands with a lion. He is still in the hospital, having nearly lost his hand. Another trainer got in the way of a tiger and landed in the hospital but is now out nursing 22 wounds. A negro tried to put out a flaming torch in some gasoline and almost burned the place down.

The final result of Warner's headaches was a pretty fair adventure story in all respects, but after all these years, I still question Philo McCullough's shiny and well-combed hair after his bitter encounters with the wild denizens of the jungle. The thirty-one reels were recut into a seven-reel feature and released as such in the autumn of 1922, presumably to appeal to the nonserial public.

The high point of the cycle was reached in the offering that ended it. The Export-Import Film Company contracted to state-right Colonel William Selig's latest entry, *The Jungle Goddess*. Directed by James Conway, who had previously worked on the Warners' initial jungle picture, this serial was far more elaborate in production values, more daring in presentation, and more expensive than any of Selig's earlier ventures. Access was gained to the use of more than 470 wild animals, which were constantly on call for scenes. Among the many spectacular stunts was one staged on a large jungle-god set that took a reputed two months to build. The stone god housed twenty lions which were involved in a hair-raising rescue of the heroine. The climax came when a large elephant swung his trunk about a trapped lion and threw it viciously to the ground, snuffing out its life. Said *Film Daily:* "Selig has made an animal serial which has enough thrills produced from animal sequences to make even the hardest-boiled fan admit it is there." The serial also had the distinction of having three different villains. As fast as one was killed off, another took his place.

The story concerned the daughter of an English lord who was kidnaped and thrown into the basket of a balloon. Accidentally cut loose, the balloon drifted until it was shot down days later in the darkest reaches of Africa by flaming arrows from native bows. The young lass, well portrayed by Vonda Phelps, was immediately offered up as a sacrifice to the lions, but miraculously escaped. Because of this, she was adopted by the tribe and accepted as a white goddess. Years later, the goddess was grown up and Elinor Field took over the role. At this time, her playmate of childhood days in merry old England (Truman Van Dyke) decided to hunt for her. Many adventures stood in his path before he finally managed to locate her, but once reunited, they began an effort to reach civilization together safely and the path home took them through Africa, India, and China.

A summation of this serial would have to pay tribute to both the fine acting by the entire cast and the quality direction by Conway, but the lion's share of homage would have to go to the old master showman, Colonel Selig, who was adept at turning out good animal pictures. His experience went back through the years and was studded with many pictures made by the old Selig Company, which maintained its own zoo. In fact, as you will recall, animals played a large role in Selig's initial serial bow, *The Adventures of Kathlyn*.

The release of *The Radio King* in October, 1922, marked the appearance of the first ten-episode serial from Universal's studios. It dealt, as the title suggests, with the then recent invention of radio and contained scientific and instructive material interwoven with romance and adventure. Brad Lane (played by Roy Stewart) was involved in assisting and protecting a government radio expert, John Leyden, in his experiments. Marnée, an electrical wizard and leader of a group of international radicals, sought to steal Leyden's invention and overthrow the government. The conflict between the

103

two forces formed the basis of action, and Louise Lorraine provided the love interest.

Charles Hutchison made his last two Pathé serials in 1922, both low-budget items directed by George B. Seitz. His final entry and the more interesting of the two, *Speed,* wound up his lengthy serial career in much the same manner as it had started: with lots of action. He was to make one more effort in 1926 for Arrow, but it was not a comeback in any respect. As "Speed" Stansbury, Hutchison was accused of taking money from a bank and attempted murder. The man who could prove his alibi had fled to South America; he was a tool of the man responsible for placing Speed in a false light. A chase to bring him back included hairbreadth escapes and adventures on land, sea, and in the air. Fights with a man-eating alligator and a shark, plus a leap from an airplane to a fast-moving train, were among the highlights, with Speed finally winning out.

Analysis of Ruth Roland's two serials for Hal Roach, which Pathé released, closes the year. Her first was *White Eagle,* reminiscent of the plot of *Hands Up.* W. S. Van Dyke and Fred Jackman co-directed. Although Ruth and Van Dyke didn't get along together, he was able to inject some fine action sequences. Miss Roland played a girl who learned that she was to decide which tribe of Indians was to gain possession of an inexhaustible pool of molten gold. This singularly dubious honor alighted on her lovely shoulders because of the tattooed trident on the palm of her left hand. Insofar as the Indians were concerned, she was Princess White Eagle. Fortunately for Ruth, a mysterious "White Rider" appeared in times of direst need to rescue her.

Ruth's other release of the year is often mentioned as one of her best vehicles and contained one of the finest stunt-suspense sequences in all of serial history. Fred Jackman directed, and his handling of the runaway boxcar scene was a superb and masterful job, making it a thrilling experience to view even today. The boxcar, towed by a wire, was photographed on level ground with the cameras inclined and undersped in order to make the car appear to fly down the mountain grades and defy the treacherous curves.

Bertram Millhauser's adaptation didn't allow the action to bear too close scrutiny from the standpoint of logic or consistency, but the excitement generated from Jackman's handling of the subject allowed the viewer to overlook logic in this instance. The plot placed Ruth as heiress to a vast timberland and detailed her efforts to retain the title, which was coveted by the timber trust. The background was set in the high Sierras, Alaska, and Argentina. Bruce Gordon provided a virile leading man who kept close track of Ruth in *The Timber Queen.*

A look at 1922 in retrospect points up the heavy pressure which those who advocated censorship of the movies brought to bear against the silent serial. Especially bitter, but quite typical, was the attitude of a former member of the Pennsylvania State Board of Censors, Ellis Paxon Oberholtzer. In his *Morals of the Movie,* published by the Penn Publishing Company in 1922, he denounced the serial in the following fashion:

> It is meant for the most ignorant classes of the population with the grossest tastes and it principally flourishes in the picture halls in mill villages and in the thickly settled tenement house and low foreign-speaking neighborhoods in the large cities.

He went on to chide the producers in a most chastening manner:

> Not a producer, I believe, but is ashamed of such an output, and yet not more than one or two of the large manufacturing companies have had the courage to repel the temptation thus to swell their balances at the end of the fiscal year.

105

FACING THE CRISIS

PEARL WHITE'S CONTRACT with Fox expired in 1922, and this gave her an opportunity to tour the Continent. Her live performances were as thrilling as her celluloid ones, as is attested by an event of April 25, 1922. Pearl had just finished her performance at the Theatre Casino de Paris in the gay capital of France. The act consisted of swinging out over the audience from a rope attached to an airplane suspended from the ceiling. At the end of it, both she and the plane were lowered to the stage. Bowing to the loud cheers of the audience, she just missed death when a fifty-pound weight fell from the catwalk above her. It did succeed in tearing a wing off the plane, and thoroughly shocked the audience, as well as Pearl, but she did not lose her nerve. Thanking the people for their interest and applause, she hurried from the scene of near-death as the next act appeared. Her self-control was supreme, but the fright had shown in her voice.

When she got back home later that year, Pearl decided to return to the screen in an attempt to regain some of her former fame and glory. Wisely, she planned to use the serial as her path to the top again, and Pathé was eager to oblige. After all, the name *Pearl White* meant coin at the box office and Pathé seldom passed up that kind of opportunity. Teaming her with George B. Seitz, who had directed so many of her previously successful serials, they put her to work. She had divorced Wally McCutcheon in 1921, and in her loneliness she plunged completely into her work. Her timing was off and her eyesight was somewhat impaired by many years under bright studio lights. The old back injuries from the days of *The Perils of Pauline* were bothering her again. She decided to use a double for some of the more dangerous sequences, and on the morning of August 11, 1922, Pearl finally realized that the odds were closing in on her.

A 38-year-old New Yorker, John Stevenson, had volunteered to double for her in a hazardous stunt. The script called for the heroine to leap from the top of a moving bus to the steel girder of a bridge under which the bus was to pass. On the screen, this was to appear as an attempt to escape the clutches of the pursuing villain. Donning the clothes of a woman, complete with blonde wig, Stevenson received his briefing from Seitz. People began to gather near the scene as word spread that Pearl White was to perform one of her famous death-defying stunts. Stevenson, in his female garb and wig, appeared to most of the bystanders to be Miss White. They were completely taken in by the double and remained so until his body was removed from the scene. Standing on top of the bus as it started off, the actor attempted the stunt and to the surprise of all concerned, failed. He was thrown some twenty-five feet before landing. The closest that anyone could come to offering an explanation was that possibly his fingers had slipped on the girder because of accumulated dust and he had lost his grip. A few hours later, he died in Roosevelt Hospital from a fractured skull and cerebral concussion. Pathé, which had Miss White under exclusive contract, stoutly maintained the fiction that no doubles were ever used for her and referred all questions to the Seitz studio. Seitz refused to discuss the matter and Pearl could not be found for comment. The serial was quickly finished, and Pearl went into hasty retirement.

The theme of *Plunder* concerned a skyscraper in the Wall Street area of New York City. A treasure of fabulous wealth had been hidden underneath the building many years before when pirates and Indians carried on warfare at the foot of Manhattan Island. A villainous gentleman who knew of the secret hoard attempted to secure all of the stock in the building by fair or foul means. Pearl portrayed a leading stockholder and, with the help of a mysterious "Mr. Jones," sought to beat the villain at his own game and reach the bottom of the mystery. The serial received good reviews, but it was far from the best of Pearl White.

Haunted Valley was the last of the Ruth Roland serials, although it was released prior to *Ruth of the Range*. While the serial was being filmed, Ruth informed Pathé that she would not renew her contract but did not give a reason for quitting. The story of a gigantic engineering project, with Ruth as its dominating spirit, was done by Frank Leon Smith. Because of the villainy of a presumed friend, the project was about to fail. From him she borrowed $1,000,000, giving Haunted Valley as security. True to her generous nature, Ruth felt this to be inadequate security for the loan, so she pledged to marry him unless she met her obligation on time. Naturally, the villain desired both her and the valley, and every obstacle was placed in her path to prevent repayment of the loan. George Marshall directed and Jack Daugherty co-starred in this excellent vehicle.

Ruth of The Range was an average serial plot which gave rise to good entertainment, plenty of action, and suspense. The dilemma around which the story revolved was that of a young girl, Ruth, who attempted to free her father (Ernest C. Warde) from a group bent on stealing his discovery of "Fuelite," a substitute for coal. The action was obvious and entertained without too much mental exertion because there was a vitality in the theme which made it an unusually strong attraction. All this is really surprising when you consider that Smith came onto the scene after the serial had been started by Gilson Willets. Willets had died with the script in his head, and no one else knew what the riddle was to be or where to go next. On top of that, Ruth demanded that Bruce Gordon, her dynamic co-star, be replaced. On this point, Smith was adamant and Gordon stayed on, although not on speaking terms with his female lead. Ernest Warde, who directed in addition to playing the part of Ruth's father, catered to Ruth and shot many close-ups of her, neglecting the action, which soon bogged down. W. S. Van Dyke was hired to rectify the situation, and Ruth raised the roof. She didn't care very much for Van Dyke, and numerous problems arose from this situation. He did manage to get the serial moving again and staged some excellent and realistic Indian attacks. Some critics have complained that this serial was "a stinker," but when you consider the behind-the-screen story with what appeared on the screen, it was not as bad as it might well have been. Let's just go on record as saying that Miss Roland had done better.

Pathé also put forth a rather unusual release, *Her Dangerous Path,* with Edna Murphy in the lead role. She was called upon to interpret several different types of heroines in an attempt to illustrate various dangerous paths which fate might call upon a girl to pursue. Each episode had a variation in story, but they were definitely linked into an effective serial package with thrills, adventure, suspense, love, and romance as the dominating factors.

Universal released three more of its historical serials in 1923, beginning with *Around The World in 18 Days,* an updated version of Jules Verne's novel. The story was more acceptable than the usual historical plot, probably because it was changed in content to conform with modern society. The variety of settings used for this globe-trotting tale of intrigue and adventure added an extra dimension to the acting of William Desmond and Laura La Plante. Desmond, as Phineas Fogg III, who was supposed to be the grandson of Verne's famed circumnavigator, pledged to circle the globe in order to visit various stockholders of a large international fuel concern. His mission was to obtain their proxies for use in an election to determine company policy. The president of the firm was deeply involved in an attempt to manufacture synthetic fuel to be used to benefit the poor, but, opposed by the vice-president, he was forced to submit his project for approval. Miss La Plante, as his daughter, furnished the inspiration for the trip and accompanied Fogg on his venture. He made use of the latest inventions of the time, including planes, express trains, speed boats, and even submarines, meeting with adventure at every crossroad as a result of the obstacles placed in his way by the henchmen of the villain. It goes without saying, of course, that he finished the trip on time and all ended in favor of justice.

Next came *The Oregon Trail,* built around Dr. Marcus Whitman's journey from New York to Oregon to carry the Word of God to the Northwest Indians. Filled with patriotic verve, it contained scenes of Washington and Jefferson planning the Louisiana Purchase, the closing of the deal with Napoleon, the Lewis and Clark expedition into the Far West, and Eli Whitney inventing the cotton gin. Art Acord, a trapper who was successful in his fight against a vicious syndicate, had Louise Lorraine to console and inspire him. What more could a man ask for?

Jack Mower and Eileen Sedgwick were the stars of *In The Days of Daniel Boone*. This time the Tories and Indians were the villains as Boone attempted to establish a colony on the frontier prior to the Revolutionary War. The most outstanding scenes in this chapter play contained a spectacular duplication of General Braddock's campaign and defeat during the French and Indian War.

Having left Vitagraph in early 1923 for Universal, William Duncan made his first appearance under the new banner in *The Steel Trail*. Cast as a construction engineer, he fell in love with the daughter of a disabled businessman who was building a railroad. To inspire realism, much of the action was filmed on and near the site of actual tracklaying. It was standard Duncan material which continued to please his fans.

Universal also released a real sleeper in April with a newcomer who displayed a pleasing personality and natural manner of acting on the screen. His name: Fred Thomson. But once again, the show belonged to that fine trouper, Ann Little. She scored another success in a slam-bang, action-packed entry reminiscent of earlier days. Duke Worne directed *The Eagle's Talons* and made good use of Al Wilson, an accomplished stunt flyer, for aviation played a large role in the plot. Things began moving at a rapid pace in the very first episode as Miss Little, hanging onto the wing of a rapidly climbing plane, fell to a moving automobile. Recovering quickly, she leaped from the car to another plane and transferred in mid-air to the first one. The story dealt with an unscrupulous gang with great wealth who sought to corner the wheat market, thereby enriching themselves still more. Had they been successful, the poor would have suffered much misery, but a financier who held an incriminating document over the head of the gang furnished the opposition. His mysterious disappearance just as the gang sought to capture him removed him from the possibility of falling into their clutches, and they turned to his daughter (Miss Little) in an attempt to force him to terms. At this point, Thomson stepped in and brought things to a favorable climax. Greater fame came to him later as a western star for F.B.O.

Francis Ford directed a fast-action dual-role item with a well-worn plot, *The Fighting Skipper,* for Arrow release. The action turned around property left to "Skipper," as Peggy O'Day was known. After the death of her mother, her seafaring father had amassed a fabulous fortune in pearls. Having spent much of his life in acquiring the wealth, he buried it on Thunder Island. While there, he married again, and when he left to return to the United States, he left behind a half-sister to Skipper, an identical double for her. Shortly after his return, he died, and the papers proving his ownership of the island, along with the location of the treasure, disappeared. Jack Perrin as the male lead assisted Miss O'Day in her attempt to gain possession of her rightful inheritance.

A more interesting theme was provided for *The Social Buccaneer,* which starred Jack Mulhall and Margaret Livingston. The script placed the action in both New York City and an imaginary central European kingdom. The Princess (Miss Livingston) was faced with a financial crisis brought on by schemers who wished to usurp her throne. Mulhall, a young New York clubman, was determined to help her and in doing so, made good use of the fact that before the war he had been quite a fop in New York social circles. The war had made a man of him, but his ability to assume the role of his previous character stood him in good stead while he secretly worked in favor of the Princess. All ended well, as one might guess, but it was a novel twist to a plot which might have degenerated into a rather routine item save for the fine character delineation by Mulhall. Robert F. Hill, fast becoming one of Universal's best and most dependable serial directors, did the honors.

As the year 1924 approached, independent showmen were apprehensive about the serial market. The established companies

111

were turning out a regular schedule of continued pictures, but the independent market had been floundering since late 1921. Of thirteen releases in 1922, only four were state-righted. Of fifteen releases in 1923, only two were independent. Of these six serials, three had been released by Arrow, a firm which had long dominated state-right production and which was, at first, well able to compete with the stronger establishments, such as Pathé and Universal. Eddie Polo's firm had crashed shortly after being launched, and even Vitagraph, one of the old pioneer companies, had dropped serial production after losing William Duncan to Universal in 1923. To independent showmen, the signs were discouraging. They appeared to be losing strength in a period of industry growth. For example, using 1911 as a base year, total annual admissions had risen from $102,000,000 to an excess of $600,000,000. The investment in the industry had grown from $100,000,000 to well over $1,500,000,000. Naturally a portion of these figures represented rising costs, but since the estimated weekly attendance had gone from 28,000,000 to more than 50,000,000, a market clearly existed. Even with the disappearance of many small nickelodeons over the years, the number of theaters had grown from approximately 13,000 to more than 16,000 over the thirteen-year span. Spokesmen for the major firms continually assured the motion-picture industry that the public still wanted good serials, and the trade papers exhorted the independents to patch up their differences and concentrate on the market. It is worth noting, however, that in spite of their cheerful pronouncements, both Pathé and Universal were soon to announce new policies. The truth of the matter was, the serial had begun to lose favor with fans. Chapter plays were no longer providing the lucrative coin which cheered the front office. To regain lost audiences, producers were turning in ever increasing numbers to the western story line, which always seemed to be able to hold its own at the box office. The success of James Cruze's *The Covered Wagon* appeared to give a basis to their thinking. After the introduction of the historical serial and the dropping of the old fashioned thriller-chiller plot at the turn of the decade, few serials had been really successful in bringing in the receipts which had come to be expected of them.

Pathé put forth a new policy beginning with *Way Of A Man* (released on January 20, 1924), which saw a feature version released simultaneously with the serial. In November, 1923, Pathé had let it be known that a nine-reel feature of this production would appear in order to attract those customers who did not ordinarily care for chapter plays. Release saw it reduced to seven reels, and it proved to be a tightly constructed entry with no waste footage. Universal followed in mid-1924 with a trade announcement that serial production for the 1924–25 season would be cut in half, from eight serials to four per year, ostensibly to improve the quality of each release.

Strength began to return to the state-right field when Rayart began serial production. The firm was organized by W. Ray Johnston in July, 1924, and lost little time in entering the continued-picture market. *Battling Brewster,* its initial release and an average serial which did not attract very much attention except from Rayart, was the subject of an unusual switch. Announced to the trade in September, 1924, for release on October 15, it was to have been directed by Paul C. Hurst, with Bruce Gordon in the leading role. Complications developed in the contract between Rayart and Dell Henderson Productions, which was to film the serial, and a complete change in the line-up occurred. Henderson took over as director and cast Franklyn Farnum in the lead. Looking about for a female co-lead, he finally settled on Helen Holmes to play the role, her final leading part in serials. Rayart was pleased enough with its reception to announce immediately the start of another serial, but exhibitors did not generally share this enthusiasm.

Arrow, which was losing interest in serials, did put Jacques Jaccard to work on two entries. *Days of '49* dealt with the discovery of gold at Sutter's Mill and the wresting of the great territory of California from the grip of Mexico and its annexation to the United States. The film began with the colorful life of John Sutter (Charles Brinley), portrayed as a very conscientious person who let his human emotions overrule his dreams of empire. Neva Gerber played Sonora Cardosa, who had been granted a large tract of land in California by the Mexican government. The grant interfered with Sutter's plans, but he graciously faded out of the picture. The villainous Marsdon (Wilbur McGaugh) and his equally villainous female companion, Arabella Ryan (Ruth Royce), tried to obtain the grant for themselves—by fair or foul means, of course. Their evil machinations were finally halted by "Cal" Coleman (Edmund Cobb), who aligned himself with Sonora Cardosa. Filled with action and good acting by the chief performers, the serial was well received. A minor criticism would be that bull's-eyes were continually scored at long ranges from wildly careening wagons and madly galloping horses, but everyone knows what remarkable marksmen our early frontiersmen were. *Riders of The Plains*, Jaccard's other effort, starred Jack Perrin and Marilyn Mills in an otherwise undistinguished fifteen-chapter western.

Pathé hit the jackpot in 1924 with the release of Allene Ray's first serial. She starred in four releases during the year, and her reputation increased with each succeeding one. One of seven children, she was born Allene Burch on January 2, 1901. This five-foot three-inch, 114-pound golden blonde had attended San Antonio and Fort Worth schools before going into musical comedy. A crack swimmer, golfer, tennis player, and horsewoman, she was called to the attention of Harry Myers, who had gone to San Antonio in 1919 to make a series of two-reel westerns. She worked for Myers, Sawyer-Lubin, and Western Pictures Corporation before landing a contract with Pathé in 1923. In January, 1920, her stock had been boosted considerably when she became one of the finalists in the "Fame and Fortune Contest" sponsored by *Motion Picture Classic*. She was an immediate hit with serial fans, and once teamed with Walter Miller, she was to regain for the serial much of the prestige lost when Pearl White and Ruth Roland retired.

Way Of A Man was a western, as was typical of the serials of this period. It was staged on the old frontier, *circa* 1848. After the death of his father, John Cowles (Harold Miller) went west to seek his fortune. On the way he met and fell in love with Ellen

114

Meriweather (Miss Ray), the daughter of an army colonel who was a friend of the Cowles family. They continued their hazardous journey together, and the wagon train they were accompanying was nearly wiped out by an Indian attack arranged by a treacherous white renegade, Gordon Orme (Bud Osborne). After many trials and tribulations, John and Ellen eventually wound up in a California gold-rush camp, where Orme was finally defeated and John was free to marry Ellen. The serial was filled with whizzing action from beginning to end and combined with colorful backgrounds which were well chosen and photographed with skill. *Way Of A Man* was one of the best of the year. Under the careful direction of George B. Seitz, Allene Ray gave a sparkling performance which emphasized her natural charm, athletic ability, and beauty. The result was remarkably free from the overacting so characteristic of the period. Miller portrayed the hero with customary dash and gallantry, and fine support was given to the stars by the remainder of the cast. Advertising for this entry played heavily on the fact that the story was done by Emerson Hough, author of *The Covered Wagon* and *North of 36*.

Pathé quickly rushed Miss Ray into another serial which had been announced several years before for Charles Hutchison but had been shelved. The scene changed from West to East for *The Fortieth Door*. In reality, Aimée (Miss Ray) was a French girl, but she had been reared by a group of Mohammedans. She was bethrothed to one when along came a young American scientist (Bruce Gordon) who swept her off her feet, and they fell madly in love. Learning of her French background, he tried to help her escape from her palace prison. Hamid Bey, played by that grand old villain, Frank Lackteen, the prospective bridegroom, worked all kinds of plans to prevent her escape from his clutches. All of his efforts were to no avail, however, for Gordon succeeded in bringing French troops in the nick of time to rescue her from the wedding and all ended happily. Also released as a 6,000-foot feature, *The Fortieth Door* added lustre to Allene's rapidly ascending reputation. She appeared to be the hottest property that Pathé had come across for a long time.

This led to *Ten Scars Make A Man,* which had a rather complicated plot in that the subplot conflicted with the main theme for viewer interest. It opened with scenes of two girls, played by Rose Burdick and Allene, who were at a boarding school in the East. It then switched to their family home in the West, where trickery was implied in connection with the ranch, involving western cattlemen and eastern financiers. A fencing master entered as the first of the villains who had designs on the girls. Jack Mower, the hero, proposed to Allene, the younger sister, and was told that he must acquire ten scars before winning her hand. His first came almost at once as he was blackjacked from behind in attempting to rescue Allene from the clutches of the fencing master. Through a sinister connection, both girls were threatened with expulsion from school and disgrace unless they paid a large sum to the villain. They wrote to their uncle, who owned the ranch, for the needed money, but he had mysteriously disappeared while searching for buried treasure in California. It was up to Mower to solve their problems. Coupled with this situation was the strange background of the elder sister, Miss Burdick, who believed that she was the direct descendent of a beautiful Spanish countess who had carried on a series of flirtations which had resulted in pitting men and nations in mortal combat for her favor. Believing that she possessed the same fatal power of attraction, Miss Burdick attempted to emulate her ancestor, and the arduous task of keeping her sister's love affairs from ending disastrously fell to Allene. The serial lacked action in the opening episodes, but the pace quickened as the chapters passed and it was another winner at the box office.

Galloping Hoofs followed the general outline of successful serial construction with action, villainy, melodrama, heroism, and climatic endings in each chapter. In short, it was an old-time Seitz production. The action hinged upon the possession of a treasure box that was to be opened at a designated time. Miss Ray was the rightful owner, but two crooks endeavored to obtain it from her. She had inherited a stock farm and race horses, but her father's death had left her in bad financial shape. Johnnie Walker was on hand to help her and the final episode found the box back in her possession. When opened, it provided the happy ending, for it contained an oil grant in the country of Innerwady. Thus Allene Ray established, in just one year, a sterling reputation which was to grow with each following release over the next few years.

Pathé also kept Edna Murphy busy during the year. *Leatherstocking* was an adaptation of James Fenimore Cooper's forest tales of frontier America. *Into The Net* was woven around the workings of the New York City Police Department. Filmed there with the co-operation of the police, it concerned the efforts of a metropolitan police force in solving the disappearance of twenty beautiful young heiresses who had been abducted and held for $1,000,000 ransom by a well-organized band of criminals. Good acting and streaking action helped maintain the suspense in entirety. The story, supposedly written by Richard Enright, police commissioner of New York City, was actually done by Frank Leon Smith. Smith recently told an amusing anecdote about the Commissioner's gratitude:

> After it was over, several of us were taken to Police Headquarters to meet the Commissioner. I was introduced as "the young man who wrote the scenario" and I put out my hand. Enright took my hand, pulled me forward a little; big smile—and I thought he was going to say something. Nuts. Not a word for the guy who'd ghosted a 10 episode serial for him. He was pulling me ahead and out of the way so he could greet Miss Edna Murphy, who was in line behind me.

Universal led off with William Duncan in *The Fast Express,* but his second entry of the year was by far the more interesting. *Wolves of The North* was a vigorous melodrama of the great outdoors involving a fight between a giant fur syndicate and individual traders. Duncan, a small trader, became manager of a smaller rival concern and took on the syndicate. The plot was further complicated by the villainous activities of fur pirates, who preyed on both sides. The romantic angle was furnished by the love affair between Duncan and Edith Johnson, the daughter of the manager of the syndicate trading post. In the opening stanzas, she resisted all of Duncan's efforts to aid her, although fate and

117

the script continued to place her in positions where she had to accept his help in escaping various perils. Duncan left all of the usual mechanical devices behind and came up with a genuine thriller in what was to be his last serial. The settings, photography, and direction were worthy of many feature productions. The story was human and well told, but a clever little actress named Esther Ralston stole the acting honors with an exceptional performance. Duncan and his wife retired in 1925 to devote more time to their three children and traveled around the country until he became ill. Confined to their home, they remained devoted to each other until his death in 1961.

Lucien Albertini, the European daredevil, lived up to his reputation in full measure in *The Iron Man,* a serial which was very slight on plot. This is really a generous summation of a story that hinged on a kidnaping in Paris with a scene change to a motion-picture studio in Hollywood. The entire affair revolved around Albertini's ability to evade death successfully. Everything, including logic, was sacrificed for speed and thrills, but the use of elaborate settings helped to put the story across. Director Jay Marchant made no bones about it; what he wanted and what he turned out was a thrill product which did not beat around the bush but did what it was intended to do: sustain interest at a high level. Fights in an airplane in mid-air, a race between an automobile and a motorcycle, a collision between a racing car and a truck loaded with high explosives—they all aided in helping to overlook an impossible story. An interesting performance was turned in by Joe Bonomo, who, working for Pathé and Universal, had gained a reputation as a stunt man who would do almost anything, provided he had the time to prepare properly. Stardom was to arrive shortly for this 22-year-old athlete from Coney Island.

The Riddle Rider concerned a mysterious figure in a western oil field who avenged the wrongs inflicted upon the less fortunate members of the community by a group of oil barons and land grabbers. In reality, "The Riddle Rider" was the editor of the local paper, who was crusading to drive out the undesirable element that was exploiting its fellow men. William Desmond handled the dual role nicely, and Eileen Sedgwick furnished the love interest as a young heiress who was trying desperately to hold onto her land in spite of the attempts of unscrupulous scavengers to wrest it from her. From the standpoint of the central character, the serial was interesting enough to merit a well-done sequel in 1927.

Early in 1924, in conjunction with Tod Browning, Ruth Roland launched her own production organization to produce a series of features. After a couple of undistinguished releases, the firm was disbanded, and except for a small part in a 1927 picture, Ruth was no longer seen on the silent screen. In 1929, she was married for the second time (to Ben Bard), and in 1930, she tried a comeback in a sound film, *Reno*, a society picture which was well publicized but poorly patronized. She often spoke of returning to the screen in what she termed an "old-fashioned serial," but instead did radio commercials, singing tours, and a film in Canada. On September 22, 1937, cancer claimed the 44-year-old actress, thus ending the career of the Queen of the Thriller Serials.

CHAPTER SEVEN

FLYING SQUADRON—TO THE RESCUE

J OE BONOMO, THE STUNTMAN from Coney Island, was elevated to serial stardom by Universal in 1925. *The Great Circus Mystery* placed him in the proper background to perform his feats of strength, and Louise Lorraine provided the love interest. His second vehicle, *Perils of The Wild,* an adaptation of *Swiss Family Robinson,* was directed by Francis Ford with that director's customary slam-bang action, but it didn't quite come off. In an effort to play down to the children in the audience, Ford crowded views of animals into the scenes wherever he could. The conflict which served as a pivot for the story was between Frederic Robinson (Bonomo) and Sir Charles Leicester (Jack Mower) for the love of Emily Montrose (Margaret Quimby). Originally announced as a ten-episode serial, it was extended for no good reason while still in production. Bonomo put on a fine display of the prodigious feats for which he was well known, but his histrionic range was rather limited. Mower proved to be a handsome villain. A few of Bonomo's stunts taxed the imagination to the limit, but the most jarring note in the whole item was the fact that his natty striped shirt seemed impervious to dirt or water.

Some years prior to the opening sequences of *Fighting Ranger,* a prosperous cattleman, John Marshall (William Welsh), shot an influential politician in self-defense. Fearing for his life, he took his small daughter and fled into the mountains that were a part of his immense ranch. Unfortunately, the only person he chose to trust was "Topez" Taggart (Bud Osborne), his ranch foreman. Topez managed the spread for many years, but when he discovered valuable wealth on it, he turned against his employer. At this point in the story an airplane flying over the mountains suddenly developed engine trouble. As it plunged toward earth, a parachute blossomed in the sky and forest ranger Terrence O'Rourke (Jack Daugherty) made good his escape from the doomed craft. Injured upon landing, he was nursed back to health by Mary Marshall (Eileen Sedgwick). O'Rourke had been sent by his superiors to aid Marshall, and as soon as he recovered, he took an active role in bringing about an acceptable solution to the difficulties.

Ace of Spades concerned the favorite device of a group of villains who terrified their victims by sending the black card as a warning. Strangely enough, this was a western which placed the story in 1889 and used the Oklahoma land rush as a backdrop. The plot hinged on a desperate fight for possession of a French survey map made in the time of Napoleon. The map gave the location of mineral deposits to be found in the area which France sold to the United States as the Louisiana Purchase. The script writers went all the way overboard on this one by beginning the first chapter with an introduction which went back in time to the year 1803 and brought in many famous Americans. William Desmond and Mary McAllister starred and Henry McRae turned in his usual fine job of directing, in spite of the story.

Pathé, which was showing signs of sliding downhill in story quality, released *Wild West,* which depicted the race for homesteads in the Cherokee Strip in 1893 and involved medicine shows, a circus, and a search for a lost father. *Idaho* told the story of a family which sought wealth in the western mining country of the late 1800's. The son was killed and just as the goal was about to be reached, the father was murdered. Vivian Rich, as the daughter, donned her brother's clothes in an attempt to wreak vengeance for her family's death. Only a dispatch rider (Mahlon Hamilton) and a frightened doctor who refused to help her knew her secret. A good pace was established at the start, and it accelerated as the story progressed. Miss Rich was quite effective in the role of a man. She was able to appear very feminine in women's clothing or masculine in men's clothes. Neither vehicle showed the ability of Robert F. Hill, who had moved over from Universal, for both were weak scripts but he did his best to save them.

Davis Distributing Division turned out a pair of interesting state-right items which Vital Exchanges released. Ben Wilson was given production control over both and co-starred with Neva Gerber in both efforts. In a western setting *The Mystery Box* dealt with a box given to Dolly Hampton (Miss Gerber) with instructions to guard it with her very life. Her sweetheart, Jack Harvey (Ben Wilson), was accused of murder but managed to escape the posse. Mysterious forces tried to gain possession of the box, which brought ill fortune to many of its seekers, but they were unsuccessful in their efforts. The second of the two serials, *The Power God,* was the more interesting and the better received. Wilson directed this one with a touch that revealed the old fire and turned out a fine production. An elderly inventor had perfected a marvelous new engine which generated power but used no fuel. The implications of this invention led a giant power and fuel syndicate to attempt to suppress and destroy it. Anticipating such a move, the inventor had cleverly built the engine in such a manner as to hide its secret. Even when the parts were assembled, the secret of assembly had to be known in advance in order to carry out the one step which would insure the operation of the device. This safeguard was given only to his daughter, Miss Gerber. Not even his most trusted assistant (Wilson) was informed of the secret. He died unexpectedly, however, and the girl was sought by the syndicate in an effort to extract the needed information, but she lost her memory in an accident. Had it not been for Wilson, the villains would have accomplished their evil plan: he managed to rescue the girl before the secret could be wrested from her. Final defeat of the syndicate was made in a thrilling, no-holds-barred, last-minute race to register the patent in Washington. It was a well-made affair which still showed many of the flashes of Wilson-Gerber magic that had endeared them to many fans.

Rayart continued its serial program, and the most interesting release was *The Flame Fighter.* Although it moved rather slowly a great deal of the time, each episode contained two or three exciting moments which placed the audience nearer to the edge of their seats. Such was the case in Chapter 3, "The Silent Alarm," with Jack Sparks (Herbert Rawlinson) doing an exciting dive from a Los Angeles fireboat chugging at top speed across the bay in an attempt to reach a burning yacht. Sparks felt that he could get to the yacht faster by using a seaplane anchored near by. Getting into a rowboat containing the plane's girl pilot, he took the oars and quickly reached the plane, which was soon air borne. Circling the yacht, he came to the conclusion that the only way in was by parachute. Strapping one on, he attached it to the leading edge of the wing and jumped. The rotten chute tore loose as the episode concluded.

Rawlinson, who did his own stunts in this serial, was a natural for the role of the young fireman, Sparks. His wavy hair and sugary smile, plus his ability to kid the role a bit, helped him put it over in good fashion. Brenda Lane, as the feminine interest, was a cute youngster with the bobbed hair common to the period, and did her best. Perhaps the greatest complaint would concern the numerous fight scenes between the firemen and the thugs. If anything, the manner in which Robert Dillon staged them proved not only that firemen can't fight, but that the crooks were worse in their ability to use their fists.

Allene Ray really hit her stride when Pathé teamed her with Walter Miller to begin a long and fruitful association. They differed from earlier serial teams in one important respect. Together, they projected the ideal of American romance in a positive manner. Her natural beauty, coupled with a trim, lithe figure and graceful movement, made her the perfect heroine. Her willing, co-operative nature and extreme modesty won the respect and admiration of her fellow workers. Courageous in carrying through with the script in order to put the scene on film, she soon became a favorite of her director. In short, she was a professional in the true sense of the word, although her background contained no theatrical experience or tradition. She was married to Larry Wheeler, and they studiously avoided the party circuit, preferring to stay home and live like ordinary people. Frank Leon Smith remembered her as "a good little housewife and a splendid hostess."

Miller was a Dayton, Ohio, boy who had been raised in Atlanta and educated in Brooklyn. A member of the original Biograph Company, he had been in films for many years when he was tapped to play the lead to Miss Ray in a serial based on *Black Caesar's Clan*. Frank Leon Smith did the screen play, entitled *Sunken Silver*. It had imagination, mystery, thrills, and romance—in short, all the necessary ingredients of a successful serial. This isn't really surprising, since it was directed by George B. Seitz, who paid more than the usual attention to continuity and character development. After the final reel was in the can, he left Pathé to do westerns for Paramount. His assistant, Spencer G. Bennet, was a most remarkable young chap who had come up the ladder the hard way: stunt man and minor acting roles. Bennet was to direct the remainder of the Ray-Miller epics, but received the initial assignment only after numerous pleas to the front office were made by Frank Leon Smith. A stanch believer in Bennet, Smith found out that Pathé wished to replace Seitz with a "name" director and went to work in behalf of his friend. Pointing out the experience to which Bennet could lay claim under the tutelage of Seitz, Smith drove home the fact that the firm should pay more attention to the talent within its own ranks.

The idea behind *Sunken Silver* related to a factual incident of 1804 in which a ship burdened with gold was lured to the Florida coast, where pirates set upon it and demolished the vessel. In the course of these events, the treasure was lost, and modern times found a group searching for it. They were successfully opposed by a Secret Service agent (Miller) and the descendents of the original pirates, who formed the third corner of the triangular struggle. As Doris Sutton, sister of the villain, Miss Ray furnished the love interest for Miller. Frank Lackteen turned in another very creditable performance as the chief villain.

Sunken Silver was an immediate success, and the Ray-Miller team was put to work on *Play Ball*, a plot involving America's national pastime, baseball. A rather complicated plot done by

Frank Leon Smith revolved around the romance of a millionaire's daughter (Miss Ray) and a rookie ballplayer (Miller) who was the disowned son of an influential senator. The Senator was investigating the business affairs of Miss Ray's father, who was being heavily influenced by an exiled count. The Count was attempting to get the necessary money for a revolt in his native land. This led to one of the best Ray-Miller vehicles and one of the finest serials ever constructed.

Edgar Wallace's novel *The Green Archer* was bought by Pathé, and Smith adapted it from an English locale to an American setting. Several castles in the Hudson River Valley were used for location scenes, and a replica was built in Pathé's Long Island studio. Earl B. Powell, a professional archer, was retained to supervise the archery sequences. Bennet turned in an excellent production which did not go overboard on stunts but sought—and obtained—a highly skillful development of the story. Basically, it concerned a self-made millionaire (Burr McIntosh) who was obviously guarding a deep, dark, and devious secret. Miss Ray, the heroine, believed that the key to the secret was to be found in the disappearance of a girl whom she sought. For entirely different reasons, a reporter and a captain of the state police (Miller) sought to solve the mystery of Bellamy Castle. In doing so, they were brought face to face with an even greater mystery at crucial moments: the identity and nature of a mysterious masked figure dressed in green whose every appearance signified death or near-death of someone who seemed to be getting near the heart of the mystery. The story was built up so that the finger of suspicion pointed conclusively at first one character, then another. The motives of the "Green Archer" defied solution until the final chapter, for he attacked friend and foe alike.

During the filming of the sixth episode, Pathé threw a huge party for Miss Ray. It was staged on the set of Bellamy Castle in the Long Island studio. Guests who arrived at the studio followed green arrows and lights as they ascended the stairway to the baronial dining hall of the castle. Miss Ray received the guests and poured tea. Many who were present tried their hand at archery in the studio-annex gallery while the others danced to lively music. The height of the festivities was the coronation of Allene as the "Queen of Serials." Burr McIntosh explained to those present why she merited the title, and Bennet placed a small coronet, symbolic of the honor, on her head. She was to live up to the title in both studio advertising and her on-screen performances.

By 1926, Pathé had become firmly entrenched as "The House of Serials." A systematic layout of work under Production Manager Willard Reineck allowed the serial units to bring in the finished product within 8 per cent of the original cost estimate, 4 per cent of the allotted time schedule (not considering inclement weather), and 20 per cent of the estimated footage. The company's serials cost an average $125,000 each, and it was believed that they reached about 40 per cent of the 20,000 theaters then in existence across the land. Second-run houses largely comprised the 40 per cent figure. In fact, Pathé executives felt that this represented about two-thirds of all second-run theaters in the nation.

William Lord Wright, the head of West Coast serial production for Universal, declared early in the season that the serial was again returning to favor in the public eye and announced that six to eight entries would be made by Universal for the 1926 season. However, the firm was clearly placing more emphasis on the longer and more expensive features known as "Universal Jewels." Short subjects had begun to lose appeal as more and more theaters turned away from them in favor of a double-bill.

Its best was the first release of the year, *The Scarlet Streak*. Bob Evans (Jack Daugherty), star reporter of the *Times*, was assigned to a story of international implication which he accepted gladly. At the same time, Richard Crawford and his daughter, Mary (Lola Todd), were putting a new machine through its tests. The machine was so terrible in its power potential that the inventor felt it might prove to be the end of warfare forever. Near by was the "House of the Closed Shutters," which foreign agents had made their headquarters. The leader, "Monk," kidnaped Crawford, and Mary quickly appealed to Bob to follow the kidnapers. Evans jumped into his car, and as he drew near to the speeding

Jack Mower (*left*), Allene Ray, and Larry Steers in a scene from Chapter
10 of *Ten Scars Make A Man*, one of four serials in which
Miss Ray starred in 1924.

"HAWK of the HILLS"

Mary's presence is dangerous to the Hawk's gold-stealing plans.

WITH
ALLENE RAY
and
WALTER MILLER

Pathéserial

CHAPTER ONE "THE OUTLAWS"

Trouble is about to begin for Mary Selby (Allene Ray) in Chapter 1 of
Hawk of The Hills (1927). Directed by Spencer G. Bennet, this fine
chapter play featured Frank Lackteen as Hawk and Walter Miller
as Laramie, a villain who becomes the hero.

Jack Daugherty and Lola Todd discuss the missing contents of the safe in *The Scarlet Streak* (1926).

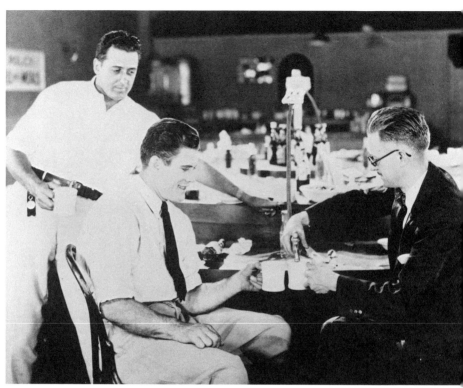

Left to right: Spencer G. Bennet, Gene Tunney, and Frank Leon Smith at the Turntable Cafe, a set used in *The Fighting Marine* (1926). The serial was filmed just before Tunney began training for his fight with Jack Dempsey.

Grace Cunard, one of the real pioneers of the motion-picture industry, as she appeared in Universal's *Blake of Scotland Yard* (1927).

William Desmond and Ethlyne Clair face a moment of decision in
The Vanishing Rider, a 1928 release.

Derelys Perdue is menaced by "The Claw" (Tom London) in this scene
from Universal's *The Mystery Rider* (1928).

"You may trust me, Doris. I think you know that." Hayden Stevenson and Louise Lorraine in a scene from *The Diamond Master* (1929), a remake of the 1921 chapter play *The Diamond Queen*.

auto containing the abducted Crawford, he gave the wheel to Mary and leaped across into the villain's vehicle. As Bob engaged Monk, the frightened Crawford jumped out and was picked up by the girl; Bob and Monk continued their struggle. The car finally went out of control, and they both jumped to safety just in time as an oncoming train rammed the driverless automobile. In the confusion that followed, Monk escaped.

That night, at a ball in Crawford's home, Monk and an accomplice stole into the house in disguise, attacked the host, and spirited Mary away. Hearing of this, Bob volunteered his help and was given full details of "The Scarlet Ray," the story to which he had been assigned. Learning about the awesome weapon, he destroyed his story and struck out to find Mary. Through the remaining chapters, the tide swayed from side to side until the end. The criminals were brought to justice, the machine was destroyed forever, and, of course, Bob and Mary lived happily ever after. The cast turned in an excellent performance in this exceedingly melodramatic serial. Logic was sacrificed to provide the necessary situations for thrills, but the action proceeded at a rapid pace and if the viewer was not too critical, it all fitted together quite well.

Francis Ford directed a western which opened with the villain killing one man and framing another in an attempt to secure possession of a small image of "The Winking Idol." The image was the key to a hidden gold cache that had belonged to a group of Indians. Years later, the son of the murdered man (William Desmond) and the daughter of the imprisoned man (Eileen Sedgwick) took up the quest to recover the idol. Plenty of action and stunts were found in *The Winking Idol*, as in all which Ford megaphoned. After making one more release for 1926, Desmond and his wife, Mary MacIvor, went on a very successful vaudeville tour before returning to the screen the following year.

The Radio Detective brought the character Craig Kennedy back to the screen—as a friend of the hero, Eastern Evans (Jack Daugherty), this time. Evans, in addition to holding the secret of a marvelous invention which would revolutionize the field of radio, was a Boy Scout leader. Naturally, an unscrupulous syndicate wanted the invention, known as "Evansite," and tried many scurrilous tricks to obtain possession of it. Jack Mower, as Craig Kennedy, and a group of Boy Scouts banded together to help Evans foil the criminals. The serial appealed mainly to two groups: radio addicts and Boy Scouts.

Fighting With Buffalo Bill was a rather confusing adaptation of William F. Cody's story *The Great West That Was*. The action was built around numerous characters who were traveling in a wagon train at the outset. A prosperous but highly unprincipled lawyer (Robert E. Homans), his equally unprincipled son (Cuyler Supplee), and a young female ward of the lawyer (Elsa Benham) and her sweetheart (Wallace MacDonald) constituted the immediate members of the plot. The lawyer had successfully convinced his ward that her father had died some years before. He managed to intercept all letters from the father in order to keep up the deception. Money had been enclosed in each letter and the lawyer had quietly pocketed it. A recent letter had described a rich gold mine, and the object of the trip was to reach it before the girl's father was able to return. The lawyer's son and MacDonald were in keen competition for her favor, and although she loved the latter, Miss Benham felt obligated to her guardian and therefore seemed to appear more attached to the son. Edmund Cobb played Buffalo Bill, who drifted in and out of the scenes at the whim of the scripters.

Dorothy Phillips returned to the screen in *The Bar-C Mystery* following the death of her director husband, Allan Hollubar. Cast as a modiste in a smart Fifth Avenue shop, she suddenly inherited a large ranch in the West. A bearded prospector, "Nevada" (Wallace MacDonald), had willed her the property and then disappeared on a trip into the desert. On her way across the country to take possession of her new-found wealth, she met a suave gambler (Philo McCullough) and a dance-hall owner (Ethel Clayton), who were the instigators of a plot to gain the ranch. They knew that it contained much wealth in mineral resources, along with a hidden gold mine. Robbins, the gambler, attempted to pose as an agent of her benefactor in order to deceive her into giving up control of the land. The stranger who came to her rescue turned out to be Nevada, minus the dirt and beard, and all ended happily.

Nat Levine, who had done state-right features and was soon to found Mascot Pictures, produced an independent serial in connection with Sam Bischoff of California Studios. A dog which had appeared in numerous Levine features was renamed Silver Streak and cast as the central character, with Malcolm MacGregor and Louise Lorraine supporting the canine star. The serial was originally entitled *The Sky Skidder,* but Levine was able to talk Universal into distributing it and the release title became *The Silent Flyer.* Levine was to make quite a large number of independent serials after founding Mascot, which quickly became one of the best producing units in the later silent-serial period.

Davis Distributing Division had great plans for the 1926 season. Back in 1925, Ken Maynard had made a series of inexpensive western features which had been released and exploited for the full value. Drawing the prints out of circulation, Davis decided to wring every possible cent out of the name and reputation of Maynard, who had gone to First National. The features were recut, assembled into a not very coherent serial entitled *The Range Fighter,* and put back on the market. The first real serial Davis made for 1926 turned out to be the last joint effort of the Wilson-Gerber team. As we have seen, in 1925, Davis had contracted with Vital Exchanges for the release of its serial product in those areas where the latter firm's exchanges were established to handle distribution. The other areas of the country were state-righted. Vital became very greedy and began to establish outlets all over the nation in an effort to handle all distribution of the Davis product. Expansion was so rapid that suddenly the foundation of the exchange firm began to shake and hurried consultations were held with J. Charles Davis II, president of Davis Distributing Division. Upon learning of the difficulties which Vital was encountering, Davis immediately sought financial backing to buy out the exchange system—after being assured by the owners of its basic stability.

Imagine Davis' surprise when he returned to Indianapolis

after a successful trip for funds only to find that Vital had collapsed and gone into receivership during February, 1926. Stunned, he immediately took steps to protect his product but was unable to halt the backslide. Davis Distributing Division went bankrupt and into receivership in a few short weeks. Litigation dragged on for weeks, and the situation worsened until the receivers sold distribution rights to the final two Davis serials, *The Power God* and *Officer 444* to Goodwill Pictures of California. Thus the last Wilson-Gerber offering went into release almost unheralded and never did a great deal of business. Full of action, much of it took place in sewer tunnels, where "The Frog" held court behind many sliding panels. Jack Mower did a fine turn as the Irish cop who was the sidekick of 444, Ben Wilson. Near the end of one chapter, the police were battling with numerous henchmen of the master criminal and Mower, getting his hands on a young crook, pulled him over his knee and properly spanked the boy. Jack showed a fine flair for comedy, but Ben Wilson showed mainly his age. Miss Gerber was her usual demure self and demonstrated that she had not lost her ability to register terror effectively.

The year 1926 seemed to be a fine time for independents to go bankrupt. Arrow placed its last serial on the market in April. Produced for release by the Hurricane Film Company, it was entitled *Lightning Hutch*. This was a ten-episode comeback attempt by Charles Hutchison, but his efforts were hampered by the fact that Arrow fell into receivership at about the same time the serial was being released. The chapter play was obscured by the financial difficulties of its distributor and never got off the ground. Hutchison was finished, and so was Arrow.

Allene Ray's first 1926 release was another high-quality production. An original screenplay by Frank Leon Smith, *Snowed In* created high suspense by allowing the movements of many of the characters to cloud the issue for the hero and heroine. The initial episode served to create interest at the very beginning, and it was well maintained throughout all ten chapters. The action was placed in the snowbound Sierras. A series of spectacular mail robberies had occurred in the vicinity, and Miss Ray's brother, an air-mail pilot, was accused of deliberately wrecking his plane in order to steal its cargo, which contained government bonds worth millions of dollars. The pilot was held for trial and his sister and a forest ranger (Walter Miller) tried to unravel the mystery. Miller had provided evidence which served to tighten the noose around the flyer's neck, but was uncertain of the man's guilt. The scene of the criminal activities centered upon an abandoned hotel in the wilderness. The master criminal, Redfield, emerged at periodic intervals from Room 28, masked and clothed in a black commando suit. His identity was withheld from the audience very successfully as everyone in the cast took turns entering and leaving Room 28. Interiors were shot at the old Fine Arts Studio, which had been used by D. W. Griffith, while a location crew attempted to find snow for the outdoor scenes. That particular year, New York City had most of the white stuff, but McCall, Idaho, finally provided the deep snow desired. Brought in under the wire at less than $90,000, the serial provided Pathé with the huge profit it had come to expect from its chapter plays. An unexpected dividend came in the form of an unqualified endorsement from the California Federation of Women's Clubs, which had given serials a hard time over the previous few years.

Allene took a well-earned vacation while Miller was cast as second lead in *The Fighting Marine,* which starred Gene Tunney. Preparations had been made for another Ray-Miller epic, but Pathé had signed Tunney, who had only a short time before he was to begin training for his heavyweight fight with Jack Dempsey, and they had to make immediate use of his services. Smith characteristically whipped up a story and shooting began. Many precautions were taken to avoid a serious injury to the pugilist, for he could not risk hurting himself in the rough work involved in a fast-action serial. Pathé took a large risk with this production. If Tunney had lost the fight, the serial would have been a lost cause. Tunney won, though, and the film was rushed to theaters around the country to cash in on his popularity. Pathé felt that the outcome of the bout meant an additional half-million dollars to the value of the film.

131

Tunney was cast as a reporter who found himself drafted as a bodyguard for a titled Englishwoman who was required to reside in a western mining town for six months under the terms of an eccentric will. Sinister interests wished to remove her from her residence, and Tunney was on hand to see that they didn't. It certainly gave him a fine opportunity to display his particular talent; he licked twelve opponents in the first three reels and many more by the last chapter.

Miller and Miss Ray went back to work in *House Without A Key,* a Smith adaptation of the first Charlie Chan novel. It concerned the enmity between two elderly brothers in Hawaii over a crime supposedly committed by the wealthy one some twenty years before. Evidence concerning the crime was contained in a "treasure chest" which a nephew (Miller) was commissioned to destroy. Before this could be carried out, the chest fell into other hands. This led to a succession of situations in an effort to regain the evidence. It was another fine effort by the cast and Spencer Bennet, but the chest did not take the place of a strong character of mystery in sustaining interest. Allene portrayed the daughter of the honest brother's partner, and Frank Lackteen again filled the heavy's shoes.

CHAPTER EIGHT

THE CLOSING WEB

IN 1927, WALL STREET FINALLY TOOK over the motion-picture industry more or less completely; the year was also marked by an economy wave to bolster what was felt to be a sagging profit margin. The economy cuts were largely in the form of actors' salaries, and the tide of unionization finally made itself effectively felt. This should have been expected and was, in fact, long overdue. Production costs and salaries of those near the top of the ladder had been out of proportion for a number of years. Salaries of stars had soared to unbelievable heights in the early twenties; directors' wages were fabulous—even supporting players were highly overpriced. Although the profits were huge, they were not enough to finance the lavish expansion of the industry. Firms merged to better their positions against competition, and still more capital was needed to carry on operations. This was where Wall Street entered the scene. It provided millions for the expanding film companies and in return, fastened a tighter and tighter grip on the industry.

Attempts to gain control of distribution and exhibition had caused bitter fights among the film moguls, with few holds barred. In an effort to keep up with its competitors, Pathé, which had already listed stock on the New York Stock Exchange for public investment, merged with Producers Distributing Corporation. This brought Cecil B. deMille under a new banner, Pathé Exchanges, Incorporated. It was an effort to shore up a sagging business and was the first step in a long downward slide for the honored old firm. The demand for short subjects, Pathé's specialty, continued to slip, and it was hoped that the merger would strengthen its feature program. As a step in acquiring a foothold in the exhibition field, an agreement was made with the Keith-Albee circuit to give Pathé preference in bookings. Under its terms, the Keith-Albee theaters were to use Pathé products at least 40 per cent of the time.

The weakest of the Ray-Miller chapter plays came along this year, *Melting Millions*. It related the adventures of a young girl who was adopted while a baby by a notorious bandit and brought up by him. At his death, the girl learned that she was the missing heiress to a large fortune. An organized band of wealthy criminals led by E. H. Calvert tried every means within their power to keep her from claiming the inheritance and used her for carrying out various machinations. Fortunately, she had the help not only of Walter Miller but also of a mysterious stranger who alternated with Miller in saving her from dire circumstances and dark plots.

An original story by George Arthur Gray marked the welcome return of a strong mystery element in the second serial which the team put forth during the year. *Hawk of The Hills* took its name from a Montana outlaw who raided mining claims with his gang. Frank Lackteen played "Hawk" to the hilt, with Paul Panzer as his chief lackey. A miner, Clyde Selby, was taken prisoner when he refused to reveal the secret mine he was working. His brother, Henry, had been appointed as the new Indian agent at Broken Knee, and while he was en route to his new post, the Hawk's men took him captive. One of the outlaws, Sheckard, impersonated Henry at the Indian agency while the Hawk attempted to force the secret from the two men. The first stumbling block in the wily outlaw's plans came when Sheckard received news that Mary Selby (Allene Ray) was on her way west to join her father, Clyde. The gang realized that the impersonation could not be kept up under these circumstances, so orders were given to do away with Mary before she reached Broken Knee and gave the scheme away. Walter Miller portrayed Laramie, one of the outlaw gang who slipped away to warn Mary of her danger and wound up protecting her. Miss Ray was especially attractive in period dress and gave her usual fine performance. A stronger plot line had given Spencer Bennet something to work with and he turned out a very creditable piece of work. His first serial western ranked with *The Green Archer* as one of his finest.

On Guard was an action serial with a military background. It dealt with the intrigues of a group of international spies who desired certain valuable information badly enough to plant their own men in the U.S. Army. As Bob Adams (Cullen Landis) was about to commit suicide, he was accosted by the leader of the spies (Walter P. Lewis), who persuaded him to think over a proposition. Put simply, it was an offer to join the army under an assumed name and receive $25,000 for his services. Assured that he would not be called upon to do anything disloyal, he accepted. However, after thinking it over, his suspicions were rightly aroused and with the assistance of a patriotic girl (Muriel Kingston), he set forth to foil the spies. A masked horseman was introduced from time to time to help him out and add to the suspense. Arch Heath, a one-time cartoonist and newspaperman, made his directoral debut under the Pathé rooster with this so-so entry.

Who stole "The Crimson Flash"? Who was "The Ghost"? And who was "Operative K–17"? The answers were supplied in ten episodes by Cullen Landis and Eugenia Gilbert, with Heath at his second try behind the megaphone. The theft of a world-famous ruby supplied the quest, and the shadowy underworld figure known as "The Ghost," who was greatly feared by his criminal contemporaries, provided the mystery element. As if one mystery figure wasn't enough, K–17 was brought into the picture at intervals to keep the audience guessing. Landis was ostensibly cast as an American importer, but in reality was a Secret Service man. The exteriors were shot on location in Charleston, South Carolina, and provided a scenic background for the action, which interwove the Treasury Department, state police, and a group of clever smugglers operating under instructions from The Ghost. Better than his first effort, *The Crimson Flash* gave indications that perhaps Heath had something on the ball. He soon ruined this impression with his third effort, *The Masked Menace,* which had a suspicious odor about it. People said it stank.

Universal's best efforts of the year threw their weight around at the box office. Three years before, the evil element in a western community had been disposed of by a masked stranger; now a gang of crooks was once more in control of the town. They were led by a sinister and evil genius who was never seen, but always relayed his instructions to his hirelings by telephone. Once again the local newspaper editor was forced by circumstance to don his dual identity, and *The Return of The Riddle Rider* heralded the reappearance of the masked man as champion of the townsfolk. William Desmond's performance in *The Riddle Rider* in 1924 had been good enough to merit a sequel, and the latter lived up to expectations. Since the audience was expected to know the identity of the Riddle Rider, it was necessary to provide the proper mystery element. Lola Todd, as Madge, took the feminine lead this time in a serial that was full of dash, pep, and vigor. It also proved that after an unproductive stint with Pathé, Robert F. Hill still had the old stuff. His associates began to realize that Pathé just hadn't provided Hill with the scripts he needed.

Angus Blake, world-renowned criminologist, was persuaded to leave retirement by Lady Diana Blanton (Gloria Gray) in order to capture the nefarious "Spider." Blake (Hayden Stevenson) had formerly been associated with Scotland Yard and his reputation was an enviable one. It seemed that the master crook had plagued Lady Diana's father, Lord Blanton, in an attempt to steal the secret formula for transforming base metal into gold. Many eventful happenings, including a trip to Canada and the discovery of a deceitful nephew, occurred before the final episode of *Blake of Scotland Yard* faded from the screen. A mysterious woman in white was seemingly always on hand to give an assist when needed, and this role was well filled by Grace Cunard. Popular reception of this serial called for a sequel, which came about in due time.

Although *Trail of The Tiger* sounded much like a jungle picture, it really concerned the three-ring atmosphere of a circus. The first chapter introduced the mysterious organization called "The Mystic Mountebanks," which had a dual function in the plot. It was entrusted with looking after the welfare of the heroine, Frances Teague, and with the attempt to gain revenge on the vil-

136

lain (Jack Mower), who had double-crossed the organization and heaped disgrace and shame wrongfully upon the girl's father. Jack Daugherty turned in his usual good performance and Miss Teague was satisfactory as the girl, but had she been given more than a decorative function, she might have given a more positive portrayal. As he had done so many times in the past, Mower gave an excellent performance as the double-dyed villain. Two so-so offerings of the year were *The Fire Fighters,* a story built around a large city fire department, and a version of the favorite western story *Whispering Smith Rides* which dealt with the famous railroad detective.

Weiss Brothers Artclass got into the act with an independent production, *Perils of The Jungle,* which brought forth once again the old Selig zoo and its menagerie of wild animals. A routine plot provided the action, and it centered on a trip into the wilds of the jungle by Phyllis Manley (Eugenia Gilbert) and her father (Harry Belmore) in search of a fantastic wealth of treasure known only to the old man. They were accompanied by "Brute" Hanley (Albert J. Smith), who had posed as a sailor on the voyage to Africa in order to gain the old fellow's confidence. He plotted to steal the treasure for himself once it was located, but his plans were upset when they met young Rod Bedford (Frank Merrill). Manley became very ill in the deepest reaches of the jungle and gave the map to Bedford with the understanding that he would carry on with the search. Brute revealed his true nature at this point, and so it went for twenty-one reels. It was a change, however, from the western orientation of the serial screen, and Selig's zoo was always fascinating.

Elmo Lincoln came forth with his final serial performance in the Rayart release *King of The Jungle.* It was rather undistinguished in the long line of jungle epics and proved to be the final Rayart serial to be marketed.

CHAPTER NINE

A FIGHT FOR LIFE

PATHÉ PASSED UP ITS DIVIDEND on Class A stock in 1928 and failed to make a $150,000 payment into the sinking fund which had been established for its debenture bonds. Consequently, both stocks and bonds took a sharp dip on the market, losing up to one-third in value. The phenomenal advance in production costs and the ever decreasing market for short subjects combined to place Pathé in an extremely precarious position. Worst of all, the shorts made by Harold Lloyd and Hal Roach were the two most valuable commodities the firm had been able to offer, and both were gone. Lloyd had gone independent and into features. Roach had moved his distribution over to M-G-M.

The merger with Producers Distributing Corporation had not put Pathé in the more competitive position with features which it had hoped for and which Cecil B. deMille was actively seeking out. The Keith-Albee circuit merged with Film Booking Office, thus negating the agreement of the previous year. In the eyes of the bankers, this left Pathé in an untenable position and there was some doubt and much speculation about the continuation of the firm. At this point, J. J. Murdock, the president of Pathé, persuaded a long-time friend, Joseph P. Kennedy, to undertake a study of the situation and make recommendations. Kennedy, who was the head of F.B.O., agreed and was given an unofficial position as observer.

It is difficult to believe that Kennedy undertook this study in a mood of altruism, for many rumors had raged that a reorganization of the firm was imminent and that Murdock and Elmer Pearson, a vice-president, were on their way out. However, on

Kennedy's recommendation, Blair and Company agreed to provide the bankroll for the 1928–29 production schedule, and the reorganization of officers found both Murdock and Pearson in their old seats. By this time it was clear that the firm's days were numbered; it was merely a question of when the ax would fall. The complete demise of Pathé as a serial producer came with sound and the assumption of Joseph P. Kennedy as the chairman of the firm on April 30, 1929. Kennedy had disposed of his holdings in F.B.O. at a tidy profit in December, 1928, and went about his work seriously as a Pathé adviser. It has been said that he instituted economy measures which saved the firm some $30,000 weekly, but the truth of this is unverified. Knowing Kennedy's keen interest in building a property up prior to milking off a fat profit, it may very well be fact and not fiction. At any rate, he was able to put Pathé on its knees again. Finding that the firm had lost $415,389 through April, 1928, he instituted an issue of $100,000 shares of common stock, which was placed on the market at $11.50 net per share in order to gain additional working capital. His stewardship began to prove itself with a $65,338 profit through July 14, 1928, and an additional $167,798 through October 6. Pathé ended the year with a net profit of $187,436. However, Kennedy placed little faith in the value of serials, and when the 1928–29 schedule was released, that was the end.

With the exception of the Ray-Miller chapter plays, the quality of Pathé's serials had been steadily sliding downhill since 1925. Its top producing talent had left for greener fields, and only Spencer G. Bennet remained in the directoral ranks as a man above average. George B. Seitz had long departed. Robert F. Hill had brought his abilities to Pathé in late 1924, only to receive banal scripts and little co-operation. He soon left. Arch Heath turned out four serials, none of which merited a great deal of praise. He also left. The entire operation had begun to crack at the seams by early 1928, and the firm's serial products showed it.

Serialwise, Universal was not in much better shape. Its top stars were Desmond and Daugherty, but no one in the front office could decide what to do with them. Where Pathé had continued to grind out serials in the past few years, Universal had hesitated several times, cutting back and then expanding production. For the first time since *Lucille Love, Girl of Mystery* back in 1914, Universal's advance trade notices gave a hint of what was brewing. These listed the 1928–29 schedule complete with casts, but when the products went before the camera, their casts had been altered completely from the leading role down. This was the first time in fourteen years that the exhibitor found he couldn't believe the firm's advance publicity. The serials were hastily put in the can and cautiously released. No more high-priced advertising spreads heralded their release, and the lack of ballyhoo was deafening. An era was rapidly coming to a close.

The one bright spot in the dimming picture centered around Mascot Pictures, founded by Nat Levine. Its first release in January, 1927, had found favor with independent exchange men and the public. Encouraged, Levine released a total of five serials in 1927–28. Using stars who had worn out their welcome at the larger studios, Levine turned out serial epics still remembered today for their fast action, deep intrigue, offbeat plots, production values, and general interest. In short, Mascot's releases harked back to a simpler, uncomplicated past using up-to-date techniques. The firm was financed by Consolidated Film Industries, a film-lab service owned by Herbert J. Yates of the American Tobacco Company. Mascot was to last well into the thirties, when it merged with Consolidated, Monogram, and several smaller independents to form Republic Pictures Corporation.

Mascot's two releases of the year were a match in thrills, excitement, and all-round interest with anything turned out by the major studios. Richard Thorpe gave an excellent effort in *Vultures of The Sea,* which had exceptional production values that were out of the ordinary at this point in silent-serial history. The story took place in the midst of a rough crew on board ship. A murder had been committed for the sake of a fortune which had been hidden aboard. An innocent man, found guilty of the crime and sentenced to the gallows, had only thirty days to live. Convinced of his innocence, his son shipped back on board the vessel in order to find

140

the real murderer. While involved in his personal vendetta, he fell in love with the girl owner of the ship, who had been left in the charge of a cruel mate. Johnnie Walker and Shirley Mason certainly got a great deal of mileage out of their roles. Attempts were made to do them both in, but these failed, and the search continued until the money and the guilty party were each found.

Dire villany, deep intrigue, daring rescues, and fast action characterized *The Vanishing West,* Mascot's second release, which looked back to the earlier days of the serial in its treatment of an old plot line. The time-worn theme dealt with Mickey Bennett as a boy whose father (Jack Perrin) was unjustly accused of a crime and thus was a fugitive from justice. A villainous uncle sought to gain the position of guardian over the child in hopes that he could eventually gain sole possession of a mysterious fortune. An excellent all-round performance was turned in by the cast, all veterans of westerns and serials. Mascot was rapidly gaining an enviable position as a leader in low-budget serials of extremely high quality, compared to their competition.

Joe Bonomo came forth with a fast-action thriller which represented the last major effort of Francis Ford as a silent director. Produced for Syndicate Pictures, *The Chinatown Mystery* found Bonomo portraying Joe Masters, a Secret Service operative. Ruth Hiatt possessed the secret formula for producing artificial diamonds and Masters fought a determined ten-chapter struggle with the evil "Sphinx" (Francis Ford) to save both the girl and the valuable paper. The quick-paced plot gave Bonomo ample opportunity to demonstrate his strength again, as in one instance when he picked up Al Baffert (six feet, 210 pounds) and threw him halfway across the room.

Weiss Brothers Artclass Productions announced *The Mysterious Airman* and *You Can't Win* for release and then rescheduled *Police Reporter* to precede both. Walter Miller and Eugenia Gilbert starred in the last-named item, and apparently nothing ever came of *You Can't Win*. It is possible that it was made and released, but no mention was ever made in the trade papers of such.

The 1928 Pathé releases were mediocre efforts, to say the

least. The only exceptions were the items turned out by Spencer Bennet with Allene Ray, and they did not represent the best work of either. In fact, Bennet carried the major load of the serial program by directing four of the six releases. Arch Heath did it for the last time under the Pathé flag. *Mark of The Frog* utilized a routine serial plot, but it was a poorly paced, implausible, and illogical attempt that never did get its feet off the ground. Really, it was like kicking a man when he was down to put this one out at a time when the firm was in trouble. The story developed from the fact that two crooks had stolen a million dollars some twenty years before. One had to go somewhere in a hurry, so he entrusted the entire sum to his cohort. This ungentlemanly character then proceeded to gather about him a group of unsavory persons, mostly criminals and tramps, each of whom wore the brand of a frog on his arm as an identifying mark. Once organized, they terrorized New York City, with the result that the police were completely baffled. The master crook was hooded, and even his close associates didn't know who he was. Actually, this was just as well. They might have laughed themselves to death. Donald Reed, as the hero, set out to unmask "The Frog" and tried his best, but it all seemed rather ludicrous. A lack of continuity didn't help, either. After this try, Heath threw up his hands and quit serials.

Jimmie Fulton came along with ten chapters that equaled Heath's efforts. Perhaps the two were competing to see who could do the worst. At any rate, *Eagle of The Night* didn't begin to measure up anywhere near the standard which was once necessary to wear proudly the rooster trade-mark. Although the theme was up to date (it was a vehicle for airplanes and stunting), it lacked real serial appeal. In fact, it lacked an engrossing story, a supply of thrills, interesting situations, and much more. What action one found was stereotyped and provided no dash or vigor. The release version committed one of the cardinal sins of serials: situations overlapped and were repeated time and again. The kindest way to treat Fulton's work is to say that his direction was not likely to provoke enthusiasm. The plot concerned the efforts of unscrupulous border smugglers to steal the "Magic Muffler," an invention

142

of Joseph Swickard which would silence the motor of a plane in flight. The smugglers had an idea that it would be useful to them in their line of endeavor, so they captured Swickard and tried to kidnap his daughter, Shirley Palmer. Frustrated in their attempts to find the plans in her home, they set it afire after rifling the place. Frank Clarke undertook to square things up, and some fans who remember this item still wonder how he did it. A few still wonder why he even bothered.

Spencer Bennet led off the year with another Ray-Miller epic, *The Man Without A Face*. This opened with a bang and a bank holdup foiled by James Brisbane, a daring young teller (Walter Miller). His efforts resulted in the capture of the crooks and impressed the bank president to no end. It seemed that he had been looking for some time for a man of courage to undertake a dangerous and difficult mission in the interior of China. Miller was to go to a besieged city where a rebellion was under way and locate two sisters who had recently come into a great deal of wealth (Miss Ray and Jeanette Loff). The other part of his job was to bring them safely back to the United States. Unexpected opposition developed in the form of "The Man Without A Face," also called "The Master," who was determined that they should not reach their destination. Suspense was built up in the fine Bennet manner for the unmasking in Chapter 10. Jeanette Loff's cold, classic beauty struck a fine balance with the warmth which Allene Ray projected.

After co-starring Miss Ray in eight consecutive serials with Walter Miller, Pathé placed her in *The Yellow Cameo*, with Edward Hearn and Cyclone, a dog. Alluring as ever, Allene gave a good portrayal in a story of a yellow cameo which held the secret to buried treasure near a Spanish mission out west. Summoned by her brother, she started west with the mysterious item and ran into a group of crooks who just happened to be seeking the key to the treasure's location.

Drawing upon Edgar Wallace's book *The Terrible People*, Pathé found the right type of material with which to reunite Miller and Ray. The serial of the same title opened with a threat of vengeance by a criminal condemned to die and followed the threat with two villains: the "Professor," who was the leader of "The Terrible People," and one of his henchmen, who was garbed in a flowing black robe and possessed hairy claws instead of hands.

Universal's five releases found two sleepers, one surprise, and two duds in the lot. William Desmond led off the year with *The Vanishing Rider*, which, although not a sequel, was close in spirit to *The Return of The Riddle Rider*. A beautiful young brunette, Ethlyne Clair, was drafted to play the female lead, and she began a very brief but extremely promising career in serials. Born in Talladega, Alabama, in 1908, she was raised in Atlanta, Georgia. Ethlyne attended Brenan College and the National Academy of Fine and Applied Arts in Washington, D.C., where she studied art. In 1924, she went to New York City and began a career as a bit player in *Sandra*. Other small parts followed, and these led to a contract in 1926 for the role of Mrs. Newlywed in *The Newlyweds and Their Baby* series, which Stern Brothers released through Universal.

Desmond undertook a dual role as a mysterious horseman with a price on his head who was blamed for the villainous activities of the Butch Bradley gang. At the end of Episode 2, "The Vanishing Rider" was captured and unmasked by the sheriff. He turned out to be Jim Davis, foreman of the Allen Ranch. Although Mary Allen (Miss Clair) proclaimed his innocence, the sheriff started to ride away with his captive when lo and behold, the real masked man appeared on the horizon. Freeing Davis, the sheriff gave pursuit but lost his quarry. Throughout the remainder of the chapters, Bradley and his gang were continually blocked in their efforts to gain the gold bullion which the masked horseman had stolen in Episode 1. The final chapter unmasked the mystery man as the twin brother of Davis and told the audience that they were really Secret Service agents sent to capture the Bradley gang. Desmond turned in another fine performance and should live forever in serial history, for his masked roles were among the best western-adventure chapter plays ever made.

He capped his colorful portrayals of masked heroes in his last thriller, *The Mystery Rider,* which found him in the role of Winthrop Lane, the sweetheart of Grace Wentworth (Derelys Perdue). After years of experimentation, Grace's father finally achieved the secret of producing rubber from the sap of the mesquite plant. Breathlessly confiding the formula to her, he also admitted that he feared deeply for his life now that he had found success. A man with a deformed, clawlike hand had once tried to rob him, and Wentworth felt that "The Claw" would someday return. His worst fear came true as he met with death over a cliff at the hands of the villain. The crime was neatly placed at the feet of "The Mystery Rider" as The Claw (Tom London, formerly known as Leonard Clapham) went free to pursue his villany.

The surprise of 1928 came in the form of Frank Merrill as Tarzan in *Tarzan, The Mighty.* A former stunt man, it was claimed that he had won the title "The World's Most Perfect Man" in a contest, but Joe Bonomo must certainly have challenged *that* claim. With a small cast of humans and a large number of animals, this serial detailed the encounters between Tarzan and Black John (Al Ferguson), the ruler of an African village of pirates' descendants. Tarzan came upon Mary Trevor (Natalie Kingston) bathing in a pool and was enamored of her, but she was about to become the bride of Black John. Lord Greystoke (Lorimer Johnston), Tarzan's uncle, arrived to look for the family heir and Black John attempted to pass himself off as the real one. He nearly got away with it and was about to wed Mary in England when Tarzan arrived and set matters straight. Originally scheduled as a twelve-episode release, it was successful enough to be extended to fifteen chapters.

The two duds came in the form of Francis X. Bushman, Jr.'s serial debut and a remake of the 1918 Universal serial *Brass Bullet.* Entitled *Haunted Island,* the latter was loosely adapted from the same story, *Pleasure Island,* but failed to measure up to the standards set by the Juanita Hansen chiller. Helen Foster took the role of the heiress to a hoard of pirate gold. Marooned on the island where the gold was supposedly hidden, she was in constant danger from her nasty uncle (Al Ferguson) and his henchmen, who sought to kill her and gain the gold. Jack Daugherty was her only source of aid. Ho-hum!

The Scarlet Arrow was a story of the Royal Canadian Mounted Police, the Canadian fur trade, and a lost gold mine thrown in for good measure. Francis X. Bushman, Jr. was starred as Bob North of the RCMP, and a fine-looking Mountie he was. His only problem seemed to be his affinity for falling into rivers at the end of the chapters. When he was not soaking himself, he spent much of the rest of his time being extricated from debris which just happened to crash down on him in alternate chapters. You know, mine explosions, cave-ins, and avalanches can be a nuisance at times. It was the first of three nightmares for Director Ray Taylor.

CHAPTER TEN

THE END OF THE TRAIL

THE FINAL SILENT SERIAL turned out by Mascot Pictures
was *The Fatal Warning,* another excellent example of the
work Richard Thorpe had been doing as chief director for Nat
Levine. It was another low-budget serial that had all of the necessary ingredients for success. An intriguing film filled with mystery,
suspense, and action, its adventures were cleverly interlapped for
maximum effect. Although the story was not at all convincing in
places, at least it moved at a fast enough pace to allow the viewer
to overlook the few times that logic and the script did not coincide.
A fine performance by the cast capped the fade-out of Levine's
silent serials. As Dorothy Rogers, Helen Costello turned in a very
creditable job. The daughter of a banker who had mysteriously
disappeared (George Periolat), she called on a friend, Russ Thorne
(Ralph Graves) to assist her in solving the case. Boris Karloff made
another of his frequent appearances in Mascot pictures and Tom
Lingham, an old favorite who had helped Helen Holmes in and out
of many rough spots, also had a small role.

The first entry in the "silent-sound" serial appeared in August under the title *King of The Kongo.* This was no departure
from Mascot's specialty of producing serials which left the audience in a very uneasy frame of mind as each episode closed. As
a matter of fact, it was easily one of the best Mascot entries of
the twenties, and with all of the frills added to the sound version,
it really caught the viewer in the pit of his stomach. It had a theme
song, *Love Thoughts of You,* which was dedicated to Jacqueline
Logan, the heroine, and a special synchronized musical score by
Lee Zahler, plus sound effects. The sound was all done on discs

147

by the Victor system, and although it was a bit shaky by nature of the recording and playback process, it really caught the patrons off guard. Walter Miller took the role of a Secret Service man who had journeyed to a far-off jungle temple in order to solve the mysterious disappearance of another agent, who also happened to be his brother. The only clue Miller found was a golden trinket which pointed to the possibility of buried treasure near the temple. Returning to the trading post, he met Miss Logan, who was trying to locate her father. Miller was only mildly interested in her until he discovered that she possessed a trinket identical to the one he had found. Together, they returned to the temple to search further for evidence which might help them, only to find that a band of desperate criminals had occupied it as a headquarters while searching for the same treasure. The mystery was projected to a high degree with the revelation of a man who was being held prisoner in the dungeon of the temple because he refused to disclose the location of the hidden wealth. Their efforts were hampered by a ferocious gorilla which plagued their every move, but by the last episode, the matter had been satisfactorily disposed of.

Pathé released its last three serials, ending a lengthy span of chapter plays with the final Miller-Ray offering, *The Black Book*. This outlined the search for a book holding the key to a mysterious code which was needed to unravel the mystery set before Allene, as a girl detective, and Miller, as her adoring lover. The acting was capable, but the chapters took their time in arousing interest, and the item turned out to be just another ordinary affair. It received an average reception among fans and was an unfortunate item with which to close the door. Spencer Bennet had done his best with what had been given him during 1928–29, but he had other problems besides poor scripts. As a second-unit director earlier in his serial career, Bennet had never received screen credit for his efforts. During his last days at Pathé, he was highly indignant at the fact that he had to share screen credit with his second-unit director, Thomas L. Storey. His resentful attitude was perhaps justified when you consider that Storey was an unknown quantity. He also happened to be a brother of the executive who

148

had replaced Frank Leon Smith as head of serial production. This type of problem was to plague Bennet through a very long and productive career in the sound era.

Universal plunged back into the serial field in 1929 with a fury. After a season of doubt coupled with poor releases, Fred J. McConnell, the short-subjects sales manager, declared that the serial was regaining favor at the box office. Hoping to use that vehicle to lure children into the theater and thus regain lost patronage, he declared at several sales meetings: "Every child is a walking 24-sheet." The theory behind this statement was that wherever you found children, the parents were certain to be. Thus if the kids could be enticed back to theater seats, their parents would most likely be with them.

The first release of 1929 was a remake of the 1921 Universal chapter play *The Diamond Queen*. Adapted from a novel by Jacques Futrelle, the new version was entitled *The Diamond Master* and concerned the adventures of a young and attractive woman (Louise Lorraine) whose father had invented a machine which made pure diamonds from dust. Of course, a relentless group of criminals coveted the machine and only Hayden Stevenson, as a detective, was able to protect her and her inheritance from the dastardly band.

A Final Reckoning was set during the gold rush in Australia and starred the sixteen-year-old wonder boy of Universal western shorts, Newton House. Obviously aimed at the juvenile trade, it was too similar to a western story to be very original or interesting, and Louise Lorraine easily took all acting honors as the rest of the cast indulged in flagrant overacting. In conception, it might have been a good idea, but in execution, it was worse than many of the old melodramatic serials. As the story went, Ruben Whitney (House) and his sister (Lorraine) were living alone in England while their father sought his fortune in the Australian gold fields. Striking it rich, the father sent for them and enclosed a copy of a map pinpointing the location of the strike. The map was sent for a very good reason. A desperado called "Black Jack" and his gang of bushrangers wanted the mine and killed the old man while trying to extract its location from him. The body was found by a Captain Wilson, a friend of old Whitney, who vowed vengeance on the murderers and helped the children foil the evil designs of Black Jack. Ray Taylor could have done better with a decent script.

Right on the heels of this came another juvenile effort called *Pirate of Panama*. A cross between an exaggerated western and a pirate story, it starred Jay Wilsey, who had played a featured role in the previous release. Wilsey was better known as Buffalo Bill, Jr., but he had hit the downward trail and was paired with former Sennett comedienne Natalie Kingston in a plot which failed to progress sensibly and lacked continuity throughout. Naturally, the story dealt with buried treasure and a map. Ray Taylor had made many serials over the years and you couldn't expect them all to be top notch, but this pair marked some kind of a bottom in his career.

The Ace of Scotland Yard had many reasons to be commended. It regained prestige for Taylor and was a fine sequel to *Blake of Scotland Yard*. It was also the first Universal effort in the serial field to come with sound effects, dialogue, and a synchronized musical score. Crauford Kent took the role of Blake, a retired Scotland Yard man who came out of his self-imposed seclusion when the life of his lady friend was threatened. Her father was one of England's most prominent collectors of ancient Egyptian relics, and his latest acquisition, "The Love Ring," was sought by criminals. In due time, Blake took care of them. Well-paced, it was a spooky item with much creeping about in the night, sudden attacks, and the disappearance of many objects. The excellent work done by the cast proved that the serial might well have a new life ahead.

Beginning with *The Ace of Scotland Yard,* Universal established a special department headed by Charles Logue. A finished print of the sound serial and all discarded footage were turned over to this group, who developed a silent story with a faster tempo and additional scenes where such were required. The cast was then called back to shoot scenes needed for continuity in the silent version. In this manner, Universal was able to provide two versions for the unsettled market. The department was to last until the fall of 1930, when part-talking serials died a sudden death.

Universal's last serial of the season was *Tarzan, The Tiger,* which came about as a result of the success that the 1928 Tarzan serial had encountered. Directed by Henry McRae, it was cast with the same people, and was supposedly based on the story *Tarzan and the Jewels of Opar.* Al Ferguson portrayed a scientist who was friendly to Tarzan (Frank Merrill) but who tried to sell Jane (Natalie Kingston) into slavery. The film was most notable in the fact that Tarzan lost his memory as a result of a blow on the head in Chapter 3 and was unable to tell his friends from his enemies until a second blow was delivered in Chapter 13.

The year 1930 was a sparse one for serials. Mascot put out its first all-talking entry, leaving only Universal to offer competition. Pathé had quit the serial field, and many of the independents had gone bankrupt. Those that were still solvent were concentrating on feature production with the hope of weathering the sound crisis. Over the years, the serial had met with low points, but at no time had things ever looked so bleak for its future. Although Universal made and released three serials in the first seven months of 1930, they were all part-talkies and left something to be desired in the pace with which they moved. The sound experts were very insistent in their belief that an outdoor action serial with a quick tempo was beyond the realm of possibility with the available equipment.

Henry McRae, Universal's top serial director, was very sincere in his belief that such a serial could be made, and he took his idea directly to Carl Laemmle. Laemmle had lost his interest in serials and McRae had to use a great deal of tact and persuasion before he received permission to try out his plan. Working closely with the sound men and solving many of the problems himself, McRae chose an adaptation of the William F. Cody story *The Great West That Was.* Co-starring Allene Ray and Tim McCoy, *The Indians Are Coming* was brought in for a total cost of $160,000. With the studio promotional force behind it, the serial netted nearly $1,000,000 and was the first picture of its kind to open for a Broadway first run at the Roxy, turning the trick in mid-September, 1930. McRae had proved his point and had opened the doors for many great talking serials to come. By this time, silent pictures provided only 7 per cent of the over-all gross, and extinction was near. Will Hays wrote Laemmle: "The entire motion picture industry owes you a debt of gratitude for *The Indians Are Coming*. It brought 20,000,000 children back to the theatre."

Thus the serial lived on. From its beginning to its end as a silent quantity, it had proved to be a potent money-maker and an interesting item in itself. It had created many top stars who lived on in the memories of their fans long after death. Good stories as well as poor ones came to the screen, but I believe that when you consider the number of good ones as a percentage of total production, the resulting figure is higher than its counterpart for feature production in the silent era. This work merely scratches the surface of the serial's history. Much remains to be told about the stars, directors, and others who took part in putting those grand adventures on the screen, and I sincerely hope that someone will accept the challenge.

SERIALS FROM 1912 TO 1930

1912

What Happened To Mary?

DIRECTOR: Unknown

CAST: Mary Fuller, Ben Wilson, Marc MacDermott, Charles Ogle, Barry O'Moore, William Wadsworth

RELEASE DATE: 26 July 1912   RELEASING COMPANY: Edison

CHAPTER TITLES: 1 reel each

1. The Escape From Bondage
2. Alone in New York
3. Mary in Stageland
4. The Affair at Raynor's
5. A letter to the Princess
6. A Clue to Her Parentage
7. False to Their Trust
8. A Will and a Way
9. A Way to the Underworld
10. The High Tide of Misfortune
11. A Race to New York
12. Fortune Smiles

1913

The Adventures of Kathlyn

DIRECTOR: F. J. Grandon

CAST: Kathlyn Williams, Tom Santschi, Charles Clary, William Carpenter, Goldie Coldwell, Hurri Tsingh

RELEASE DATE: 29 Dec. 1913   RELEASING COMPANY: Selig

CHAPTER TITLES:

1. The Unwelcome Throne (3 reels)
2. The Two Ordeals
3. In The Temple of the Lion

CONTINUED NEXT WEEK

4. The Royal Slave
5. A Colonel in Chains
6. Three Bags of Silver
7. The Garden of Brides
8. The Cruel Crown
9. The Spellbound Multitude
10. The Warrior Maid
11. The Forged Parchment
12. The King's Will
13. The Court of Death

Who Will Marry Mary?

DIRECTOR: Unknown

CAST: Mary Fuller

RELEASE DATE: 26 July 1913 RELEASING COMPANY: Edison

CHAPTER TITLES: 1 reel each

1. A Proposal From the Duke
2. A Proposal From the Spanish Don
3. A Proposal From the Sculptor
4. A Proposal From Nobody
5. A Proposal Deferred
6. A Proposal From Mary

1914

The Active Life of Dolly of The Dailies

DIRECTOR: Walter Edwin

CAST: Mary Fuller, Yale Boss, Charles Ogle, Harry Beaumont, Gladys Hulette, William West, Edwin Clark, Richard Neil

RELEASE DATE: 31 Jan. 1914 RELEASING COMPANY: Edison

CHAPTER TITLES: 1 reel each

1. The Perfect Truth
2. The Ghost of Mother Eve
3. An Affair of Dress
4. Putting One Over
5. The Chinese Fan
6. On The Heights
7. The End of the Umbrella
8. A Tight Squeeze
9. A Terror of the Night
10. Dolly Plays Detective
11. Dolly at the Helm
12. The Last Assignment

The Beloved Adventurer

DIRECTOR: Arthur V. Johnson

CAST: Arthur V. Johnson, Lottie Briscoe, Florence Hackett, Ruth Bryan, Howard M. Mitchell, J. Robinson Hall, Jeanette Hackett, Ed McLaughlin, Josephine Longworth, D. B. Bentley

RELEASE DATE: 14 Sept. 1914   RELEASING COMPANY: Lubin

CHAPTER TITLES:

1. Lord Cecil Intervenes
2. An Untarnished Shield
3. An Affair of Honor
4. An American Heiress
5. The Girl From The West
6. The Golden Hope
7. The Holdup
8. A Partner to Providence
9. Lord Cecil Plays A Part
10. Lord Cecil Keeps His Word
11. The Serpent Comes to Eden
12. Fate's Tangled Threads
13. Through Desperate Hazards
14. A Perilous Passage
15. In Port O' Dreams

The Exploits of Elaine

DIRECTORS: Louis Gasnier, George B. Seitz

CAST: Pearl White, Creighton Hale, Arnold Daly, Sheldon Lewis, Floyd Buckley

RELEASE DATE: 29 Dec. 1914   RELEASING COMPANY: Pathé

CHAPTER TITLES:

1. The Clutching Hand
2. The Twilight Sleep
3. The Vanishing Jewels
4. The Frozen Safe
5. The Poisoned Room
6. The Vampire
7. The Double Trap
8. The Hidden Voice
9. The Death Ray
10. The Life Current
11. The Hour of Three
12. The Blood Crystals
13. The Devil Worshippers
14. The Reckoning

The Hazards of Helen

DIRECTORS: J. P. McGowan for Miss Holmes, James Davis for Miss Gibson

CAST: Helen Holmes, Helen Gibson, Robyn Adair, Ethel Clisbee, Tom Trent, G. A. Williams, Pearl Anibus, P. S. Pembroke, Roy Watson

RELEASE DATE: 13 Nov. 1914   RELEASING COMPANY: Kalem

CHAPTER TITLES: 1 reel each

1. Helen's Sacrifice
2. The Plot at the R.R. Cut
3. The Girl at the Throttle
4. The Stolen Engine
5. The Flying Freight's Captive
6. The Black Diamond Express
7. The Escape on the Limited
8. The Girl Telegrapher's Peril
9. The Leap From the Water Tower
10. The Broken Circuit
11. The Fast Mail's Danger
12. The Little Engineer
13. Escape of the Fast Freight
14. The Red Signal
15. The Engineer's Peril
16. The Open Drawbridge
17. The Death Train
18. Night Operator at Buxton
19. Railroad Raiders of '62
20. The Girl at Lone Point
21. A Life in the Balance
22. The Girl on the Trestle
23. The Girl Engineer
24. A Race For A Crossing
25. The Box Car Trap
26. The Wild Engine
27. A Fiend at the Throttle
28. The Broken Train
29. A Railroader's Bravery
30. The Human Chain
31. The Pay Train
32. Near Eternity
33. In Danger's Path
34. The Midnight Limited
35. A Wild Ride
36. A Deed of Daring
37. The Girl on the Engine
38. The Fate of #1
39. The Substitute Fireman
40. The Limited's Peril
41. A Perilous Chance
42. Train Order #45
43. The Broken Rail
44. Nerves of Steel
45. A Girl's Grit
46. A Matter of Seconds
47. The Runaway Boxcar
48. The Water Tank Plot
49. A Test of Courage (Miss Gibson's first, 16 Oct. 1915)
50. A Mile A Minute
51. Rescue of the Brakeman's Children
52. Danger Ahead
53. The Girl and the Special
54. The Girl on the Bridge
55. The Dynamite Train
56. The Tramp Telegrapher
57. Crossed Wires
58. The Wrong Train Order
59. A Boy at the Throttle
60. At the Risk of Her Life
61. When Seconds Count
62. The Haunted Station
63. The Open Track
64. Tapped Wires
65. The Broken Wire
66. Peril of the Rails
67. A Perilous Swing
68. The Switchman's Story
69. A Girl Telegrapher's Nerve

70. A Race for a Life
71. The Girl Who Dared
72. The Detective's Peril
73. The Trapping of "Peeler White"
74. The Record Run
75. The Race for a Siding
76. The Governor's Special
77. The Trail of Danger
78. The Human Telegram
79. The Bridge of Danger
80. One Chance in a Hundred
81. The Capture of Red Stanley
82. Spiked Switch
83. Treasure Train
84. A Race Through The Air
85. The Mysterious Cypher
86. The Engineer's Honor
87. To Save The Road
88. The Broken Brake
89. In Death's Pathway
90. A Plunge From The Sky
91. A Mystery of The Rails
92. Hurled Through The Drawbridge
93. With The Aid of The Wrecker
94. At Danger's Call
95. Secret of The Box Car
96. Ablaze on The Rails
97. The Hoodoo of Division B
98. Defying Death
99. The Death Swing
100. The Blocked Track
101. To Save The Special
102. A Daring Chance
103. The Last Messenger
104. The Gate of Death
105. The Lone Point Mystery
106. The Runaway Sleeper
107. The Forgotten Train Order
108. The Trial Run
109. The Lineman's Peril
110. The Midnight Express
111. The Vanishing Box Car
112. A Race With Death
113. The Morgul Mountain Mystery
114. The Fireman's Nemesis
115. The Wrecked Station
116. Railroad Claim Intrigue
117. The Death Siding
118. The Prima Donna's Special
119. The Side Tracked Sleeper

Lucille Love, Girl of Mystery

DIRECTOR: Francis Ford

CAST: Francis Ford, Grace Cunard, Harry Rattebury, Ernest Shields

RELEASE DATE: 14 April 1914   RELEASING COMPANY: Universal

CHAPTER TITLES: 15 chapters

The Man Who Disappeared

DIRECTOR: Charles J. Brabin

CONTINUED NEXT WEEK

CAST: Marc MacDermott, Miriam Nesbitt, Barry O'Moore

RELEASE DATE: 7 April 1914 RELEASING COMPANY: Edison

CHAPTER TITLES: 1 reel each

1. The Black Mask
2. The Hunted Animal
3. The Double Cross
4. The Light on The Wall
5. With His Hands
6. The Gap
7. Face to Face
8. A Matter of Minutes
9. The Living Dead
10. By The Aid of A Film

The Master Key

DIRECTOR: Robert Leonard

CAST: Robert Leonard, Ella Hall, Harry Carter, Alan Forest, Jean Hathaway, Alfred Hickman

RELEASE DATE: 16 Nov. 1914 RELEASING COMPANY: Universal

CHAPTER TITLES: 15 chapters (31 reels)

The Million Dollar Mystery

DIRECTOR: Howell Hansell

CAST: Florence LaBadie, Marguerite Snow, James Cruze, Frank Farrington, Sidney Bracy, Creighton Hale, Mitchell Lewis, Irving Cummings

RELEASE DATE: 22 June 1914 RELEASING COMPANY: Thanhouser (Re-released in 1918 in 6 reels by Randolph Film Corporation)

CHAPTER TITLES:

1. The Airship in the Night
2. The False Friend
3. A Leap in the Dark
4. The Top Floor Flat
5. At The Bottom of The Sea
6. The Coaching Party of The Countess
7. The Doom of the Auto Bandits
8. The Wiles of A Woman
9. The Leap From An Ocean Liner
10. Unknown
11. In The Path of The Fast Express

12–14. Unknown
15. The Borrowed Hydroplane
16. Drawn into the Quicksand
17. A Battle of Wits
18–21. Unknown
22. The Million Dollar Mystery
23. The Mystery Solved

The Perils of Pauline

DIRECTORS: Louis Gasnier, Donald MacKenzie

CAST: Pearl White, Crane Wilbur, Paul Panzer, Edward Jose, Francis Carlyle, Eleanor Woodruff, Clifford Bruce, Sam Ryan, Donald MacKenzie

RELEASE DATE: 31 March 1914 RELEASING COMPANY: Pathé

CHAPTER TITLES: 20 episodes

The Trey O' Hearts

DIRECTOR: Wilfred Lucas

CAST: Cleo Madison, George Larkin, Edward Sloman, Tom Walsh, Roy Hanford

RELEASE DATE: 4 August 1914 RELEASING COMPANY: Universal

CHAPTER TITLES:

1. Flower O' Flames (3 reels)
2. White Water
3. The Sea Venture
4. Dead Reckoning
5. The Sunset Bride
6. The Crack O' Doom
7. Stalemate
8. The Mock Rose
9. As The Crow Flies
10. Steel Ribbons
11. The Painted Hills
12. The Mirage
13. Jaws of Death
14. The First Law
15. The Last Trump

Zudora (The Twenty Million Dollar Mystery)

DIRECTOR: Howell Hansell

CAST: James Cruze, Marguerite Snow, Harry Benham, Sidney Bracy, Mary Elizabeth Forbes, Frank Farrington

RELEASE DATE: 23 Nov. 1914   RELEASING COMPANY: Thanhouser

CHAPTER TITLES:

1. The Mystic Message of the Spotted Collar
2. The Mystery of the Sleeping House
3. The Mystery of the Dutch Cheese Maker
4. The Mystery of the Frozen Laugh
5. The Secret of the Haunted Hills
6. The Mystery of the Perpetual Glare
7. The Mystery of the Lost Ships
8. The Foiled Elopement
9. Kidnapped or the Mystery of the Missing Heiress
10. Zudora in the $20,000,000 Mystery or The Gentlemen Crooks and the Lady
11. A Message From the Heart
12. A Bag of Diamonds
13. The Raid on the Madhouse or The Secret of Dr. Munn's Sanitarium
14. The Missing Million
15. The Ruby Coronet
16. The Battle on the Bridge
17. The Island of Mystery
18. The Cipher Code
19. The Prisoner in the Pilot House
20. The Richest Woman in the World

1915

Ⓢ *The Black Box*

DIRECTOR: Otis Turner

CAST: Herbert Rawlinson, Anna Little, William Worthington, Mark Fenton, Laura Oakley, Frank MacQuarrie, Frank Lloyd, Helen Wright, Beatrice Van

RELEASE DATE: 14 March 1915   RELEASING COMPANY: Universal

CHAPTER TITLES:

1. An Apartment House Mystery
2. The Hidden Hands
3. The Pocket Wireless
4. An Old Grudge
5. On the Rack
6. The Unseen Terror
7. The House of Mystery
8. The Inherited Sin
9. Lost in London
10. The Ship of Horror

11. A Desert Vengeance
12. Neath Iron Wheels
13. Tongues of Flame
14. A Bolt From the Blue
15. The Black Box

The Broken Coin

DIRECTOR: Francis Ford

CAST: Francis Ford, Grace Cunard, Harry Mann, Eddie Polo, John Ford, Mina Cunard, Harry Schumm, Ernest Shields

RELEASE DATE: 21 June 1915 RELEASING COMPANY: Universal

CHAPTER TITLES:

1. The Broken Coin
2. The Satan of the Sands
3. When the Throne Rocked
4. The Face at the Window
5. The Underground Foe
6. A Startling Discovery
7. Between Two Fires
8. The Prison in the Palace
9. Room 22
10. Cornered
11. The Clash of Arms
12. A Cry in the Dark
13. War
14. On The Battlefield
15. The Deluge
16. Kitty in Danger
17. The Castaways
18. The Underground City
19. The Sacred Fire
20. Between Two Fires
21. A Timely Rescue
22. An American Queen

The Diamond From The Sky

DIRECTORS: William Desmond Taylor, Jacques Jaccard

CAST: Lottie Pickford, Irving Cummings, William Russell, Charlotte Burton, Eugenie Ford, George Periolat, Orral Humphrey, W. J. Tedmarsh, Lillian Buckingham

RELEASE DATE: 3 May 1915 RELEASING COMPANY: North American Film Corporation (American)

CHAPTER TITLES:

1. The Heritage of Hate
2. An Eye For An Eye
3. The Silent Witness
4. The Prodigal's Progress
5. For the Sake of A False Friend
6. Shadows at Sunrise

7. The Fox and the Pig	18. Charm Against Harm
8. A Mind in the Past	19. Fire, Fury and Confusion
9. A Runaway Match	20. The Soul Stranglers
10. Old Foes With New Faces	21. The Lion's Bride
11. The Web of Destiny or Plaything of the Papoose	22. The Rose in the Dust
	23. The Double Cross
12. To the Highest Bidder	24. The Mad Millionaire
13. The Man in the Mask	25. A House of Cards
14. For Love and Money	26. The Garden of the Gods
15. Desperate Chances	27. Mine Own People
16. The Path of Peril	28. The Falling Aeroplane
17. King of Diamonds and The Queen of Hearts	29. A Deal With Destiny
	30. The American Earl

🌀 *The Fates and Flora Fourflush (The Ten Billion Dollar Vitagraph Mystery Serial)*

DIRECTOR: Wally Van

CAST: Clara Kimball Young, Charles Brown, L. Rogers Lytton, Temple Saxe, George Stevens

RELEASE DATE: 4 Jan. 1915   RELEASING COMPANY: Vitagraph

CHAPTER TITLES:

1. Treachery in the Clouds	3. A Race For Life
2. The Temple of Bhosh	

🌀 *The Girl and The Game*

DIRECTOR: J. P. McGowan

CAST: Helen Holmes, J. P. McGowan, Leo Maloney, George McDaniel

RELEASE DATE: 27 Dec. 1915   RELEASING COMPANY: Signal Film Corporation (Mutual)

CHAPTER TITLES:

1. Helen's Race With Death	3. A Life in Peril
2. The Winning Jump	4. Helen's Perilous Escape

162

5. The Fight at the Signal Station
6. Helen's Wild Ride
7. Spike's Awakening
8. A Race For the Right of Way
9. A Close Call
10. A Dash Through Flames
11. The Salting of Superstition Mine
12. Buried Alive
13. A Fight For A Fortune
14. Helen's Race Against Time
15. Driving the Last Spike

The Goddess

DIRECTOR: Ralph Ince

CAST: Anita Stewart, Earle Williams, Paul Scardon, William Dangman, Ned Finley

RELEASE DATE: 10 May 1915 RELEASING COMPANY: Vitagraph

CHAPTER TITLES: 15 episodes

Graft

DIRECTOR: Richard Stanton

CAST: Hobart Henley, Harry D. Carey, Nanine Wright, Richard Stanton, Hayward Mack, Jane Novak, Glen White, L. M. Wells, W. Horne, Mary Ruby, Edward Brown

RELEASE DATE: 11 Dec. 1915 RELEASING COMPANY: Universal

CHAPTER TITLES:

1. Liquor and the Law
2. The Tenement House Evil
3. The Traction Grab
4. The Power of the People (Carey took over the role of attorney in this chapter)
5. Grinding Life Down
6. The Railroad Monopoly
7. America Saved From War
8. Old King Coal
9. The Insurance Swindlers
10. The Harbor Transportation Trust
11. The Illegal Bucket Shops
12. The Milk Battle
13. Powder Trust and the War
14. The Iron Ring
15. The Patent Medicine Danger
16. The Pirates of Finance
17. The Queen of the Prophets
18. The Hidden City of Crime
19. The Photo Badger Game
20. The Final Conquest

Neal of The Navy

DIRECTOR: W. M. Harvey

CAST: Lillian Lorraine, William Courtleigh, Jr., Ed Brady, Henry Stanley, William Conklin

RELEASE DATE: 2 Sept. 1915 RELEASING COMPANY: Pathé

CHAPTER TITLES:

1. The Survivors
2. The Yellow Packet
3. The Failure
4. The Tattered Parchment
5. A Message From the Past
6. The Cavern of Death
7. The Gun Runners
8. The Yellow Peril
9. The Sun Worshippers
10. The Rolling Terror
11. The Dreadful Pit
12. The Worm Turns
13. White Gods
14. The Final Goal

The New Exploits of Elaine

DIRECTOR: George B. Seitz

CAST: Pearl White, Creighton Hale, Arnold Daly, Edwin Arden

RELEASE DATE: 5 April 1915 RELEASING COMPANY: Pathé

CHAPTER TITLES:

1. The Serpent Sign
2. The Cryptic Ring
3. The Watching Eye
4. The Vengeance of Wu Fang
5. The Saving Circles
6. Spontaneous Combustion
7. The Ear in the Wall
8. The Opium Smugglers
9. The Tell-Tale Heart
10. Shadows of War

The Red Circle

DIRECTOR: Sherwood MacDonald

CAST: Ruth Roland, Frank Mayo, Philo McCullough, Gordon Sackville

RELEASE DATE: 16 Dec. 1915 RELEASING COMPANY: Pathé

CHAPTER TITLES:

1. Nevermore
2. Pity the Poor
3. Twenty Years Ago
4. In Strange Attire
5. Weapons of War
6. False Colors
7. Third Degree or Two Captives

8. Peace at Any Price
9. Dodging the Law
10. Excess Baggage
11. Seeds of Suspicion
12. Like A Rat in A Trap
13. Branded As A Thief
14. Judgment Day

℗ The Road of Strife

DIRECTOR: John Ince

CAST: Crane Wilbur, Mary Charleson, Jack Standing, Rosetta Brice, Charles Brandt, Howard M. Mitchell

RELEASE DATE: 5 April 1915   RELEASING COMPANY: Lubin

CHAPTER TITLES:

1. The House of Secrets
2. Face of Fear
3. The Silver Cup
4. The Ring of Death
5. No Other Way
6. Strength of Love
7. Into the Night
8. In the Wolf's Den

9. The Iron Hand of Law
10. The Unsparing Sword
11. The Valley of the Shadow
12. The Sacrifice
13. The Man Who Did Not Die
14. A Story of the Past
15. The Coming of the Kingdom

℗ The Romance of Elaine

DIRECTOR: George B. Seitz

CAST: Pearl White, Creighton Hale, Arnold Daly, Lionel Barrymore

RELEASE DATE: 14 June 1915   RELEASING COMPANY: Pathé

CHAPTER TITLES:

1. The Lost Torpedo
2. The Gray Friar

3. The Vanishing Man
4. The Submarine Harbor

5. The Conspirators
6. The Wireless Detective
7. The Death Cloud
8. The Searchlight Gun
9. The Life Chain
10. The Flash
11. The Disappearing Helmet
12. The Triumph of Elaine

Runaway June

DIRECTOR: Oscar Engle

CAST: Norma Phillips, Margaret Loveridge, J. W. Johnston, Charles Mason, Rica Allen

RELEASE DATE: 13 Jan. 1915 RELEASING COMPANY: Reliance

CHAPTER TITLES:

1. The Runaway Bride
2. The Man With The Black Vandyke
3. Discharged
4. The New Governess
5. Trapped In A Gambling House or A Woman in Trouble
6. The Siege of the House of O'Keefe
7. The Tormentors
8. Her Enemies
9. Kidnapped
10. Trapped On A Liner
11. In the Clutch of the River Thieves
12. The Spirit of the Marsh
13. Trapped
14. In the Grip of Poverty
15. At Last, My Love

Under The Crescent

DIRECTOR: Burton King

CAST: Ola Humphrey, Edward Sloman, William Dowlan, Carmen Phillips, Helen Wright, Edna Mason

RELEASE DATE: 1 June 1915 RELEASING COMPANY: Universal

CHAPTER TITLES:

1. The Purple Iris
2. The Cage of the Golden Bars
3. In the Shadow of the Pyramids
4. For the Honor of A Woman
5. In the Name of the King
6. The Crown of Death

⑤ *The Ventures of Marguerite*

DIRECTORS: Hamilton Smith, John E. Mackin, Robert Ellis

CAST: Marguerite Courtot, Richard Purdon, E. T. Roseman, Paula Sherman

RELEASE DATE: 29 Oct. 1915   RELEASING COMPANY: Kalem

CHAPTER TITLES: 1 reel each

1. When Appearances Deceive
2. The Rogue Syndicate
3. The Kidnapped Heiress
4. The Veiled Priestess
5. A Society Schemer
6. The Key to A Fortune
7. The Ancient Coin
8. The Secret Message
9. The Oriental's Plot
10. The Spy's Ruse
11. The Crossed Clues
12. The Tricksters
13. The Sealskin Coat
14. The Lurking Peril
15. The Fate of America
16. The Trail's End

1916

⑤ *The Adventures of Peg O' The Ring*

DIRECTORS: Francis Ford, Jacques Jaccard

CAST: Francis Ford, Grace Cunard, Ruth Stonehouse, Peter Gerald, Charles Munn, G. Raymond Nye, Eddie Polo, Mark Fenton, Jean Hathaway

RELEASE DATE: 1 May 1916   RELEASING COMPANY: Universal

CHAPTER TITLES:

1. The Leopard's Mark (3 reels)
2. A Strange Inheritance
3. In The Lion's Den
4. The Circus Mongrels
5. The House of Mystery
6. The Cry For Help or Cry of the Ring
7. The Wreck
8. Outwitted
9. The Leap
10. In The Hands of the Enemy
11. The Stampede
12. On The High Seas
13. The Clown Act
14. The Will
15. Retribution

⑤ *Beatrice Fairfax*

DIRECTORS: Theodore and Leo Wharton

CAST: Harry Fox, Grace Darling, Robin Townley, Olive Thomas (guest appearances by Elaine Hammerstein, Nigel Barre, Mae Hopkins, Mary Cranston, Betty Howe)

RELEASE DATE: 7 Aug. 1916   RELEASING COMPANY: International Film Service

CHAPTER TITLES:

1. The Missing Watchman
2. Adventures of the Jealous Wife
3. Billie's Romance
4. The Stone God
5. Mimosa San
6. The Forbidden Room
7. A Name For the Baby
8. At the Ainsley Ball
9. Outside the Law
10. Play Ball
11. The Wages of Sin
12. Curiosity
13. The Ringer
14. The Hidden Menace
15. Wrist Watches

⑤ *The Crimson Stain Mystery*

DIRECTOR: T. Hayes Hunter

CAST: Maurice Costello, Ethel Grandin, Eugene Strong, Thomas J. McGrane

RELEASE DATE: 21 Aug. 1916   RELEASING COMPANY: Consolidated Film Company (Metro)

CHAPTER TITLES:

1. The Brand of Satan
2. In The Demon's Spell
3. The Broken Spell
4. The Mysterious Disappearance
5. The Figure in Black
6. The Phantom Image
7. The Devil's Symphony
8. In the Shadow of Death
9. The Haunting Specter
10. The Infernal Fiend
11. The Tortured Soul
12. The Restless Spirit
13. Despoiling Brutes
14. The Bloodhound
15. The Human Tiger
16. The Unmasking

🎬 *Gloria's Romance*

DIRECTOR: Walter Edwin

CAST: Billie Burke, David Powell, Frank McGlynn, Henry Kolker, William Roselle, William T. Carleton, Jule Power, Henry Weaver, Helen Hart

RELEASE DATE: 22 May 1916   RELEASING COMPANY: Kleine

CHAPTER TITLES:

1. Lost in the Everglades
2. Caught by the Seminoles
3. A Perilous Love
4. The Social Vortex
5. The Gathering Storm
6. Hidden Fires
7. The Harvest of Sin
8. The Mesh of Mystery
9. The Shadow of Scandal
10. Tangled Threads
11. The Fugitive Witness
12. Her Fighting Spirit
13. The Midnight Riot
14. The Floating Trap
15. The Murderer at Bay
16. A Modern Pirate
17. The Tell-Tale Envelope
18. The Bitter Truth
19. Her Vow Fulfilled
20. Love's Reward

🎬 *The Grip of Evil*

DIRECTORS: W. A. Douglas, Harry Harvey

CAST: Jackie Saunders, Roland Bottomley

RELEASE DATE: 17 July 1916   RELEASING COMPANY: Pathé

CHAPTER TITLES:

1. Fate
2. The Underworld
3. The Upper Ten
4. The Looters
5. The Way of A Woman
6. The Hypocrites
7. The Butterflies
8. In Bohemia
9. The Dollar Kings
10. Down to the Sea
11. Mammon and Moloch
12. Into the Pits
13. Circumstantial Evidence
14. Humanity Triumphant

🎬 *The Iron Claw*

DIRECTOR: Edward Jose

CAST: Pearl White, Creighton Hale, Sheldon Lewis, Harry Fraser, J. E. Dunn

RELEASE DATE: 27 Feb. 1916   RELEASING COMPANY: Pathé

CHAPTER TITLES:

1. The Vengeance of Legar
2. The House of Unhappiness
3. The Cognac Mask
4. The Name and The Game
5. The Incorrigible Captive
6. The Spotted Warning
7. The Hooded Helper
8. The Stroke of 12
9. Arrows of Hate
10. The Living Dead
11. The Saving of Dan O'Mara
12. The Haunted Canvas
13. The Hidden Face
14. The Plunge For Life
15. The Double Resurrection
16. The Unmasking of Davy
17. The Vanishing Fakir
18. The Green-Eyed God
19. The Cave of Despair
20. The Triumph of The Laughing Mask

✐ *Lass of The Lumberlands*

DIRECTORS: J. P. McGowan, Paul C. Hurst

CAST: Helen Holmes, Thomas Lingham, L. D. Maloney, Ned Chapman, Paul C. Hurst, Katherine Goodrich, F. L. Hemphill

RELEASE DATE: 23 Oct. 1916   RELEASING COMPANY: Signal Film Corporation (Mutual)

CHAPTER TITLES:

1. The Lumber Pirate
2. The Wreck in the Fog
3. First Blood
4. A Deed of Daring
5. The Burned Record
6. The Spiked Switch
7. The Runaway Car
8. The Fight in Camp I
9. The Double Fight
10. The Gold Rush
11. The Ace High Loses
12. The Main Line Wreck
13. Unknown
14. The Indian's Hand
15. Retribution

✐ *Liberty, A Daughter of The U.S.A.*

DIRECTORS: Jacques Jaccard, Henry McRae

CAST: Marie Walcamp, Jack Holt, Neal Hart, G. Raymond Nye, L. M. Wells, Eddie Polo, Hazel Buckham, Roy Stewart, Maude Emory, Bertram Grassby

RELEASE DATE: 14 Aug. 1916 RELEASING COMPANY: Universal

CHAPTER TITLES:

1. The Fangs of the Wolf (3 reels)
2. Riding With Death
3. American Blood
4. Dead or Alive
5. Love and War
6. The Desert of Lost Souls
7. Liberty's Sacrifice
8. Clipped Wings
9. A Daughter of Mars
10. The Buzzard's Prey
11. The Devil's Triumph
12. For the Flag
13. Strife and Sorrow
14. A Modern Joan of Arc
15. Flag of Truce
16. Court-Martialled
17. A Trail of Blood
18. The Wolf's Nemesis
19. An Avenging Angel
20. A Daughter of the U.S.A.

The Mysteries of Myra

DIRECTORS: Theodore and Leo Wharton

CAST: Jean Sothern, Howard Estabrook, Allen Murnane, M. W. Rale, Bessie Wharton

RELEASE DATE: 24 April 1916 RELEASING COMPANY: International Film Service (Pathé)

CHAPTER TITLES:

1. Unknown (3 reels)
2. Unknown
3. The Mystic Mirrors
4–8. Unknown
9. The Invisible Destroyer
10. Levitation
11. The Fire-Elemental
12. The Elixir of Youth
13. Witchcraft
14. Suspended Animation
15. The Thought Monster

Pearl of The Army

DIRECTOR: Edward Jose

CAST: Pearl White, Ralph Kellard, Marie Wayne, Floyd Buckley, Theodore Friebus, W. T. Carleton

RELEASE DATE: 3 Dec. 1916 RELEASING COMPANY: Pathé

CHAPTER TITLES:

1. The Traitor
2. Found Guilty
3. The Silent Menace
4. War Clouds
5. Somewhere in Grenada
6. Major Brent's Perfidy
7. For the Stars and Stripes
8. International Diplomacy
9. The Monroe Doctrine
10. The Silent Army
11. A Million Volunteers
12. The Foreign Alliance
13. Modern Buccaneers
14. The Flag Despoiler
15. The Colonel's Orderly

Perils of Our Girl Reporters

DIRECTOR: George W. Terwilliger

CAST: Helen Green, Earl Metcalfe, Zena Keefe, William Turner

RELEASE DATE: 28 Dec. 1916 RELEASING COMPANY: Niagara Film Company (Mutual)

CHAPTER TITLES:

1. The Jade Necklace
2. The Black Door
3. Ace High
4. The White Trail
5. Many A Slip
6. The Long Lane
7. Smite of Conscience
8. Birds of Prey
9. Misjudged
10. Taking Chances
11. The Meeting
12. Outwitted
13. The Schemers
14. The Counterfeiters
15. Kidnapped

The Purple Mask

DIRECTOR: Francis Ford

CAST: Francis Ford, Grace Cunard, Jean Hathaway, Peter Gerald, Jerry Ash, Mario Bianchi, John Featherstone, John Duffy

RELEASE DATE: 31 Dec. 1916 RELEASING COMPANY: Universal

CHAPTER TITLES:

1. The Vanished Jewels (3 reels)
2. Suspected
3. The Capture
4. Facing Death
5. The Demon of the Sky
6. The Silent Feud
7. The Race for Freedom
8. Secret Adventure
9. A Strange Discovery
10. House of Mystery
11. Garden of Surprise
12. The Vault of Mystery
13. The Leap
14. The Sky Monsters
15. Floating Signal
16. A Prisoner of Love

The Scarlet Runner

DIRECTORS: Wally Van, William P. S. Earle

CAST: Earle Williams, Jean Stuart, Arthur Robinson, Billie Billings, Thomas R. Mills, Alex Kyle, Zena Keefe, Walter McGrail, Josephine Earle, Harold Forshay, Betty Howe, Nellie Anderson, Ray Walburn

RELEASE DATE: 2 Oct. 1916 RELEASING COMPANY: Vitagraph

CHAPTER TITLES:

1. The Car and His Majesty
2. The Nuremberg Watch
3. The Masked Ball
4. The Hidden Prince
5. The Jacobean House
6. The Red Whiskered Man
7. The Mysterious Motor Car
8. The Glove and the Ring
9. The Gold Cigarette Case
10. The Lost Girl
11. The Missing Chapter
12. The Car and the Girl

The Secret of The Submarine

DIRECTOR: George Sargent

CAST: Juanita Hansen, Tom Chatterton, William Tedmarsh, Lamar Johnstone, Hylda Hollis, George Clancy, Harry Edmundson, George Webb, Hugh Bennett

RELEASE DATE: 22 May 1916 RELEASING COMPANY: American (Mutual special feature)

CHAPTER TITLES: 15 chapters

✪ *The Sequel to The Diamond From The Sky*

DIRECTOR: Edward Sloman

CAST: William Russell, Charlotte Burton, Rhea Mitchell, William Tedmarsh, Orral Humphrey

RELEASE DATE: 27 Nov. 1916   RELEASING COMPANY: American (Mutual)

CHAPTER TITLES:

1. Fate and Death	3. Sealed Lips
2. Under Oath	4. The Climax

✪ *The Shielding Shadow*

DIRECTORS: Louis Gasnier, Donald MacKenzie

CAST: Grace Darmond, Leon Bary, Ralph Kellard, Madeline Traverse

RELEASE DATE: 1 Oct. 1916   RELEASING COMPANY: Pathé

CHAPTER TITLES:

1. The Treasure Trove	9. The Incorrigible Captive
2. Into the Depths	10. The Vanishing Mantle
3. The Mystic Defender	11. The Great Sacrifice
4. The Earthquake	12. The Stolen Shadow
5. Through Bolted Doors	13. The Hidden Menace
6. The Disappearing Shadow	14. Absolute Black
7. The Awakening	15. The Final Chapter
8. The Haunting Hand	

✪ *The Strange Case of Mary Page*

DIRECTOR: J. Charles Haydon

CAST: H. B. Walthall, Edna Mayo, Ernest Cossart, Sydney Ainsworth, Harry Dunkinson, Tom Cummerford

RELEASE DATE: 24 Jan. 1916   RELEASING COMPANY: Essanay

CHAPTER TITLES:

1. The Tragedy
2. The Trial
3. The Web
4. The Mark
5. The Alienist
6. The Depths
7. A Confession
8. The Perjury
9. The Accusing Eye
10. The Clew
11. The Raid
12. The Slums
13. Dawning Hope
14. Recrimination
15. The Verdict

The Yellow Menace

DIRECTOR: William Steiner

CAST: Edwin Stevens, Florence Malone, Margaret Gale, Gerald Griffen, Marie Treador, Armand Cortes, J. A. Hall

RELEASE DATE: 4 Sept. 1916 (SR)

RELEASING COMPANY: Serial Film Company (Unity Sales)

CHAPTER TITLES:

1. Hidden Power
2. The Mutilated Hand
3. The Poisonous Tarantula
4. Plot of A Demon
5. The Haunted House
6. The Torture Chamber
7. Drops of Blood
8. The Time-Clock Bomb
9. The Crystal Globe
10. A Message From the Sky
11. The Half-Breed's Hatred
12. Aeroplane Accident
13. The Spy and the Submarine
14. Interrupted Nuptials
15. The Pay of Death
16. The Final Strand

1917

The Fatal Ring

DIRECTOR: George B. Seitz

CAST: Pearl White, Earle Fox, Warner Oland, Floyd Buckley, Caesare Gravina, Ruby Hoffman, Henry G. Sell, Mattie Ferguson

RELEASE DATE: 8 July 1917   RELEASING COMPANY: Pathé

CHAPTER TITLES:

1. The Violet Diamond
2. The Crushing Wall
3. Borrowed Identity
4. The Warning on the Ring
5. Danger Underground
6. Rays of Death
7. The Signal Lantern
8. The Switch in the Safe
9. The Dice of Death
10. The Perilous Plunge
11. The Short Circuit
12. A Desperate Chance
13. A Dash for Arabia
14. The Painted Safe
15. The Dagger Duel
16. The Double Disguise
17. The Death Weight
18. The Subterfuge
19. The Cryptic Maze
20. The End of the Trail

The Fighting Trail

DIRECTOR: William Duncan

CAST: William Duncan, Carol Holloway, George Holt, Joe Ryan, Walter Rodgers, Fred Burns

RELEASE DATE: 10 Sept. 1917   RELEASING COMPANY: Vitagraph

CHAPTER TITLES:

1. The Priceless Ingredient (3 reels)
2. The Story of Ybarra
3. Will Yaqui Joe Tell?
4. The Other Half
5. The Torrent Rush
6. The Ledge of Despair
7. The Lion's Prey
8. Strands of Doom
9. The Bridge of Death
10. The Sheriff
11. Parched Trails
12. The Desert of Torture
13. The Water Trap
14. The Trestle of Horrors
15. Out of the Flame

The Gray Ghost

DIRECTOR: Stuart Paton

CAST: Harry Carter, Priscilla Dean, Emory Johnson, Eddie Polo, Howard Crampton, Sidney Dean, Lou Short, Gypsy Hart, Gertrude Astor, T. D. Crittenden, J. Morris Foster, Richard la Reno, John Cook

RELEASE DATE: 1 July 1917   RELEASING COMPANY: Universal

CHAPTER TITLES:

1. The Bank Mystery (3 reels)
2. The Mysterious Message
3. The Warning
4. The Fight
5. Plunder
6. The House of Mystery
7. Caught in the Web
8. The Double Floor
9. The Pearl Necklace
10. Shadows
11. The Flaming Meteor
12. The Poisoned Ring
13. The Tightening Snare
14. At Bay
15. The Duel
16. From Out of the Past

꧁ The Great Secret

DIRECTOR: William Christy Cabanne

CAST: Francis X. Bushman, Beverly Bayne, Belle Bruce, Fred R. Stanton, Tom Blake, Sue Balfour, Charles Ripley, Ed Connelly, Helen Dunbar, Art Ortego, Charles Fang, Tammany Young, Dorothy Haydel, W. J. Butler

RELEASE DATE: 8 Jan. 1917   RELEASING COMPANY: Serial Producing Company (Metro)

CHAPTER TITLES:

1. The Whirlpool of Destiny or The Secret Seven (3 reels)
2. The Casket of Tainted Treasure
3. The Hidden Hand
4. From Sunshine to Shadow
5. The Trap
6. The Dragon's Den
7. The Yellow Claw
8. A Clue From the Klondike
9. Cupid's Puzzle
10. The Woman and the Game
11. A Shot in the Dark
12. Caught in the Web
13. The Struggle
14. The Escape
15. Test of Death
16. The Crafty Hand
17. The Missing Finger
18. The Great Secret

꧁ The Hidden Hand

DIRECTOR: Unknown

CAST: Doris Kenyon, Sheldon Lewis, Arline Pretty, Mahlon Hamilton

RELEASE DATE: 25 Nov. 1917 RELEASING COMPANY: Pathé

CHAPTER TITLES:

1. The Gauntlet of Death
2. Counterfeit Faces
3. The Island of Dread
4. The False Locket
5. The Air-Lock
6. The Flower of Death
7. The Fire Trap
8. Slide for Life
9. Jets of Flame
10. Cogs of Death
11. Trapped by Treachery
12. Eyes in the Wall
13. Jaws of the Tiger
14. The Unmasking
15. The Girl of the Prophecy

Jimmy Dale Alias The Grey Seal

DIRECTOR: Harry Webster

CAST: E. K. Lincoln, Doris Mitchell, Edna Hunter, Paul Panzer

RELEASE DATE: 23 March 1917 RELEASING COMPANY: Monmouth Film Company (Mutual)

CHAPTER TITLES:

1. The Grey Seal
2. The Stolen Rubies
3. The Counterfeit Five
4. The Metzer Murder Mystery
5. A Fight for Honor
6. Below the Deadline
7. The Devil's Work
8. The Underdog
9. The Alibi
10. Two Crooks and A Knave
11. A Rogue's Defeat
12. The Man Higher Up
13. Good for Evil
14. A Sheep Among Wolves
15. The Tapped Wires
16. The Victory

The Lost Express

DIRECTOR: J. P. McGowan

CAST: Helen Holmes, Thomas Lingham, L. D. Maloney, John McKinnon, Ed Hearn, William Brunton

RELEASE DATE: 17 Sept. 1917 RELEASING COMPANY: Signal Film Corporation (Mutual)

CHAPTER TITLES:

1. The Lost Express
2. The Destroyed Document
3. The Wreck at the Crossing
4. The Oil Well Conspiracy
5. In Deep Waters
6. High Voltage
7. The Race with the Limited
8. The Mountain King
9. The Looters
10. The Secret of the Mine
11. A Fight for A Million
12. Law Is Law or Daring Death
13. Disowned or The Escape
14. Trapped or Unmasked
15. The Found Express or Return of the Lost Express

The Mystery of The Double Cross

DIRECTOR: William Parke

CAST: Mollie King, Leon Bary, Ralph Stuart, Gladden James, Theodore Friebus, Harry Fraser

RELEASE DATE: 18 March 1917 RELEASING COMPANY: Pathé

CHAPTER TITLES:

1. The Lady in Number 7
2. The Masked Strangers
3. An Hour To Live
4. Kidnapped
5. The Life Current
6. The Dead Come Back
7. Into Thin Air
8. The Stranger Disposes
9. When Jailbirds Fly
10. The Hole-in-the-Wall
11. Love's Sacrifice
12. The Riddle of the Cross
13. The Face of the Stranger
14. The Hidden Brand
15. The Double Cross

The Mystery Ship

DIRECTOR: Harry Harvey, Henry McRae

CAST: Ben Wilson, Neva Gerber, Kingsley Benedict, Duke Worne

RELEASE DATE: 1 Dec. 1917 RELEASING COMPANY: Universal

CHAPTER TITLES:

1. The Crescent Scar
2. The Grip of Hate

3. Adrift
4. The Secret of the Tomb
5. The Fire God
6. Treachery
7. One Minute to Live
8. Hidden Hands
9. The Black Masks
10. The Rescue
11. The Line of Death
12. The Rain of Fire
13. The Underground House
14. The Masked Riders
15. The House of Trickery
16. The Forced Marriage
17. The Deadly Torpedo
18. The Fight in Mid-Air

The Neglected Wife

DIRECTOR: William Bertram

CAST: Ruth Roland, Roland Bottomley, Corrine Grant, Neil Hardin, Philo McCullough

RELEASE DATE: 13 May 1917 RELEASING COMPANY: Pathé

CHAPTER TITLES:

1. The Woman Alone
2. The Weakening
3. In the Crucible
4. Beyond Recall
5. Under Suspicion
6. On the Precipice
7. The Message on the Mirror
8. A Relentless Fate
9. Deepening Degradation
10. A Veiled Intrigue
11. A Reckless Indiscretion
12. Embittered Love
13. Revolting Pride
14. Desperation
15. A Sacrifice Supreme

Patria

DIRECTORS: The Whartons (Ithaca scenes), Jacques Jaccard (Hollywood scenes)

CAST: Irene Castle, Warner Oland, Milton Sills, Floyd Buckley, Marie Walcamp, George Maharoni, Allen Murnane, Dorothy Green

RELEASE DATE: 14 Jan. 1917 RELEASING COMPANY: International Film Service (Pathé)

CHAPTER TITLES:

1. Last of the Fighting Channings (3 reels)
2. The Treasure
3. Winged Millions
4. Double Crossed
5. The Island God Forgot
6. Alias Nemesis
7. Red Dawn
8. Red Night
9. Cat's Paw and Scapegoat
10. War in the Dooryard
11. Sunset Falls
12. Peace on the Border or Peace
    Which Passeth All Under-
    standing
13. Wings of Death
14. Border Peril
15. For the Flag

The Railroad Raiders

DIRECTOR: J. P. McGowan

CAST: Helen Holmes, Thomas Lingham, L. D. Maloney, Paul C.
Hurst, William Brunton, F. L. Hemphill, William Behrens,
J. P. McGowan, William Buhler, Marvin Martin

RELEASE DATE: 9 April 1917   RELEASING COMPANY: Signal Film
Corporation (Mutual)

CHAPTER TITLES:

1. Circumstantial Evidence
2. A Double Steal
3. Inside Treachery
4. A Race for A Fortune
5. A Woman's Wit
6. The Overland Disaster
7. Mistaken Identity
8. A Knotted Cord
9. A Leap for Life
10. A Watery Grave
11. A Desperate Deed
12. A Fight for A Franchise
13. The Road Wrecker
14. The Trap
15. Mystery of the Counterfeit
    Tickets

The Red Ace

DIRECTOR: Jacques Jaccard

CAST: Marie Walcamp, Larry Peyton, Yvette Mitchell, Bobby
Mack, L. M. Wells, Charles Brindley, Miriam Shelby, Noble
Johnson, Harry Archer

RELEASE DATE: 22 Oct. 1917   RELEASING COMPANY: Universal

CHAPTER TITLES:

1. Silent Terror
2. Lure of the Unattainable
3. A Leap for Liberty
4. The Undercurrent
5. In Mid-Air
6. Fighting Blood
7. The Lion's Claws
8. Lair of the Beast
9. A Voice From the Dead or Voice From the Past
10. Hearts of Steel
11. The Burning Span
12. Overboard
13. New Enemies
14. The Fugitives
15. Hell's Riders
16. Virginia's Triumph

The Secret Kingdom

DIRECTORS: Theodore Marston, Charles J. Brabin

CAST: Charles Richman, Dorothy Kelly, Arline Pretty, Joseph Kilgour, Ned Finley, Charles Wellesley, William Dunn

RELEASE DATE: 1 Jan. 1917 RELEASING COMPANY: Vitagraph

CHAPTER TITLES:

1. Land of the Intrigue (3 reels)
2. Royalty at Red Wing (3 reels)
3. Sealed Packet
4. Honorable Mr. Oxenham
5. Carriage Call #101
6. Human Flotsam
7. Ghost Ship
8. Rum Cay
9. Swamp Adder
10. A Goat Without Horns
11. The White Witch
12. The Shark's Nest
13. The Tragic Masque
14. The Portrait of A King
15. The Tocsin

The Seven Pearls

DIRECTOR: Donald MacKenzie

CAST: Mollie King, Creighton Hale, Floyd Buckley, Leon Bary, Henry G. Sell, John J. Dunn

RELEASE DATE: 16 Sept. 1917 RELEASING COMPANY: Pathé

CHAPTER TITLES:

1. The Sultan's Necklace (3 reels)
2. The Bowstring
3. The Air Peril
4. Amid The Clouds

5. Between Fire and Water
6. The Abandoned Mine
7. The False Pearl
8. The Man Trap
9. The Message on the Wire or The Warning on the Wire
10. The Hold-up
11. Gems of Jeopardy
12. Buried Alive
13. Over the Falls
14. The Tower of Death
15. The Seventh Pearl

Vengeance and The Woman

DIRECTOR: William Duncan

CAST: William Duncan, Carol Holloway, George Holt, Tex Allen, Vincente Howard, Fred Burns, S. E. Jennings, Walter Rodgers

RELEASE DATE: 24 Dec. 1917   RELEASING COMPANY: Vitagraph

CHAPTER TITLES:

1. The Oath
2. Loaded Dice
3. The Unscaled Peak
4. The Signalling Cipher
5. The Plunge of Destruction
6. Lure of Hate
7. Wolf Trap
8. Mountain of Devastation
9. Buried Alive
10. The Leap for Life
11. The Cavern of Terror
12. The Desperate Chance
13. Sands of Doom
14. The Hand of Fate
15. The Reckoning

The Voice on The Wire

DIRECTOR: Stuart Paton

CAST: Neva Gerber, Ben Wilson, Francis McDonald, Ernest Shields, Joseph W. Girard, Frank Tokonaga, Howard Crampton

RELEASE DATE: 18 March 1917   RELEASING COMPANY: Universal

CHAPTER TITLES:

1. The Oriental Death Punch
2. The Mysterious Man in Black
3. The Spider's Web
4. The Next Victim
5. The Spectral Hand
6. The Death Warrant

7. The Marked Room
8. High Finance
9. A Stern Chase
10. The Guarded Heart
11. The Thought Machine
12. The Sign of the Thumb or The Fifth Victim
13. 'Twixt Death and Dawn
14. The Light of Dawn
15. The Living Death

Ⓢ *Who Is Number One?*

DIRECTOR: William Bertram

CAST: Kathleen Clifford, Cullen Landis

RELEASE DATE: 29 Oct. 1917   RELEASING COMPANY: Paramount

CHAPTER TITLES:

1. The Flaming Cross
2. The Flying Fortress
3. The Sea Crawler
4. A Marine Miracle
5. Halls of Hazard
6. The Flight of the Fury
7. Hearts in Torment
8. Walls of Gas
9. Struck Down
10. Wires of Wrath
11. The Rail Raiders
12. The Show Down
13. Cornered
14. No Surrender
15. The Round Up

1918

Ⓢ *The Brass Bullet*

DIRECTOR: Ben Wilson

CAST: Juanita Hansen, Jack Mulhall, Charles Hill Mailes, Joseph W. Girard, Harry Dunkinson, Helen Wright, Ashton Dearholt

RELEASE DATE: 10 August 1918   RELEASING COMPANY: Universal

CHAPTER TITLES:

1. A Flying Start
2. The Muffled Man
3. The Mysterious Murder or Locked in the Tower
4. Smoked Out
5. The Mock Bride
6. A Dangerous Honeymoon
7. Pleasure Island or The Depth Bomb
8. The Magnetic Rug

9. The Room of Flame
10. A New Peril
11. Evil Waters
12. Caught by Wireless
13. $500.00 Reward
14. On Trial For His Life
15. In the Shadow
16. The Noose
17. The Avenger
18. The Amazing Confession

Bull's Eye

DIRECTOR: James W. Horne

CAST: Eddie Polo, Vivian Reed, Hal Cooley, Roy Hanford, Frank Lanning, William Welsh, Noble Johnson

RELEASE DATE: 9 Feb. 1918 RELEASING COMPANY: Universal

CHAPTER TITLES:

1. First Blood
2. The Fearless One
3. Desperate Odds
4. Still In the Ring
5. The Swing of Death
6. On the Brink
7. Riding Wild
8. Dynamite
9. The Flaming Crisis
10. Coyotes of the Desert
11. Fired
12. Burning Sands
13. Sold at Auction
14. The Firing Squad
15. The Stained Face
16. Running Wild
17. In Irons
18. The Runaway

A Daughter of Uncle Sam

DIRECTOR: James Morton

CAST: William Sorelle, Jane Vance, Henry Carleton, Lewis Dayton

RELEASE DATE: 19 Jan. 1918 RELEASING COMPANY: Jaxon (General Film Corporation)

CHAPTER TITLES: 12 chapters (1 reel each)

The Eagle's Eye

DIRECTORS: George A Lessey, Wellington Playter

CAST: King Baggot, Marguerite Snow, William N. Bailey, Florence

Short, Bertram Marburgh, Paul Everton, John P. Wade, Fred Jones

RELEASE DATE: 27 March 1918 RELEASING COMPANY: Wharton–
(SR)   American

CHAPTER TITLES:

1. Hidden Death
2. The Naval Ball Conspiracy
3. The Plot Against the Fleet
4. Von Rintelen, the Destroyer
5. The Strike Breeders
6. The Plot Against Organized Labor
7. Brown Port Folio
8. The Kaiser's Death Messenger
9. The Munitions Campaign
10. The Invasion of Canada
11. The Burning of Hopewell
12. The Canal Conspirators
13. The Reign of Terror
14. The Infantile Paralysis Epidemic
15. The Campaign Against Cotton
16. The Raid of the U–53
17. Germany's U–Base in America
18. The Great Hindu Conspiracy
19. The Menace of the I.W.W.
20. The Great Decision

⟲ A Fight For Millions

DIRECTOR: William Duncan

CAST: William Duncan, Edith Johnson, Joe Ryan, Walter Rodgers

RELEASE DATE: 15 July 1918 RELEASING COMPANY: Vitagraph

CHAPTER TITLES:

1. The Snare
2. Flames of Peril
3. The Secret Stockade
4. Precipice of Horror
5. Path of Thrills
6. Spell of Evil
7. Gorge of Destruction
8. In the Clutches
9. The Estate
10. The Secret Tunnel
11. The Noose of Death
12. The Tide of Disaster
13. The Engine of Terror
14. The Decoy
15. The Sealed Envelope

⟲ Hands Up

DIRECTOR: James W. Horne

186

CAST: Ruth Roland, George Chesebro, George Larkin, Easter Walters

RELEASE DATE: 18 August 1918 RELEASING COMPANY: Pathé

CHAPTER TITLES:

1. Bride of the Sun (3 reels)
2. The Missing Prince
3. The Phantom and the Girl
4. The Phantom Trail
5. The Runaway Bride
6. Flames of Vengeance
7. Tossed into the Torrent
8. The Fatal Jewels
9. A Leap Through Space
10. The Sun Message
11. Stranger From the Sea
12. The Silver Book
13. The Last Warning
14. The Oracle's Decree
15. The Celestial Messenger

✦ The House of Hate

DIRECTOR: George B. Seitz

CAST: Pearl White, Antonio Moreno, Floyd Buckley, Peggy Shanor, Paul Dillon, John Gilmour

RELEASE DATE: 10 March 1918 RELEASING COMPANY: Pathé

CHAPTER TITLES:

1. The Hooded Terror (3 reels)
2. The Tiger's Eye
3. A Woman's Perfidy
4. The Man From Java
5. Spies Within
6. A Living Target
7. Germ Menace
8. The Untold Secret
9. Poisoned Darts
10. Double Crossed
11. Haunts of Evil
12. Flashes in the Dark
13. Enemy Aliens
14. Underworld Allies
15. The False Signal
16. The Vial of Death
17. The Death Switch
18. At the Pistol's Point
19. The Hooded Terror Unmasked
20. Following Old Glory

✦ The Iron Test

DIRECTORS: R. N. Bradbury, Paul C. Hurst

CAST: Antonio Moreno, Carol Holloway

RELEASE DATE: 21 Oct. 1918   RELEASING COMPANY: Vitagraph

CHAPTER TITLES:

1. Ring of Fire
2. Van of Disaster
3. Blade of Hate
4. The Noose
5. Tide of Death
6. Fiery Fate
7. The Whirling Trap
8. The Man Eater
9. The Pit of Lost Hope
10. In the Coils
11. The Red Mask's Prey
12. The Span of Terror
13. Hanging Peril
14. Desperate Odds
15. Riding With Death

The Lion's Claw

DIRECTORS: Jacques Jaccard, Harry Harvey

CAST: Marie Walcamp, Thomas Lingham, Gertrude Astor, Alfred Allen, Edwin August, Leonard Clapham, Harry Von Meter, Frank Lanning, Roy Hanford

RELEASE DATE: 6 April 1918   RELEASING COMPANY: Universal

CHAPTER TITLES:

1. A Woman's Honor
2. Beasts of the Jungle
3. Net of Terror
4. A Woman's Scream
5. The Secret Document
6. The Dungeon of Terror
7. Quicksand
8. Into the Harem
9. The Human Pendulum
10. Escape Thru the Flames
11. Caught in the Toils
12. The Spies' Cave
13. In Disguise
14. Hell Let Loose
15. Bridge of the Beast
16. The Jungle Pool
17. The Well of Horror or The Danger Pit
18. The Doom of Rej Hari or Triumph

Lure of The Circus

DIRECTOR: J. P. McGowan

CAST: Eddie Polo, Josie Sedgwick, Eileen Sedgwick

RELEASE DATE: 18 Nov. 1918   RELEASING COMPANY: Universal

CHAPTER TITLES:

1. The Big Tent
2. The Giant's Leap
3. Beaten Back
4. The Message on the Cuff
5. The Lip Reader
6. The Aerial Disaster
7. The Charge of the Elephant
8. The Human Ladder
9. The Flying Loop
10. A Shot For Life
11. The Dagger
12. A Strange Escape
13. A Plunge For Life
14. Flames
15. The Stolen Record
16. The Knockout
17. A Race With Time
18. The Last Trick

The Silent Mystery

DIRECTOR: Francis Ford

CAST: Francis Ford, Rosemary Theby, Mae Gaston, Elsie Van Name

RELEASE DATE: 1918 (SR)   RELEASING COMPANY: Burston
(Silent Mystery Corporation)

CHAPTER TITLES:

1–3. Unknown
4. Dens of Iniquity
5–15. Unknown

Wolves of Kultur

DIRECTOR: Joseph A. Golden

CAST: Leah Baird, Charles Hutchison, Sheldon Lewis

RELEASE DATE: 13 Oct. 1918   RELEASING COMPANY: Pathé

CHAPTER TITLES:

1. The Torture Trap (3 reels)
2. The Iron Chair
3. Trapping the Traitors
4. The Ride to Death
5. Through the Flames
6. Trails of Treachery
7. The Leap of Despair
8. In the Hands of the Hun
9. Precipice of Death
10. When Woman Wars
11. Betwixt Heaven and Earth
12. Tower of Tears
13. The Huns' Hell Trap
14. Code of Hate
15. Reward of Patriotism

189

🔗 A Woman In The Web

DIRECTORS: Paul C. Hurst, David Smith

CAST: Hedda Nova, J. Frank Glendon

RELEASE DATE: 8 April 1918   RELEASING COMPANY: Vitagraph

CHAPTER TITLES:

1. Caught in The Web
2. The Open Switch
3. The Speeding Doom
4. The Clutch of Terror
5. The Hand of Mystery
6. Full Speed Ahead
7. The Crater of Death
8. The Plunge of Horror
9. The Fire Trap
10. Out of The Dungeon
11. In The Desert's Grip
12. Hurled to Destruction
13. The Hidden Menace
14. The Crash of Fate
15. Out of The Web

1919

🔗 The Adventures of Ruth

DIRECTOR: George Marshall

CAST: Ruth Roland, Herbert Heyes, Thomas Lingham, Charles Bennett, Helen Case, William Human, Helen Deliane

RELEASE DATE: 28 Dec. 1919   RELEASING COMPANY: Pathé

CHAPTER TITLES:

1. The Wrong Countess
2. The Celestial Maiden
3. The Bewitching Spy
4. The Stolen Picture
5. The Bank Robbery
6. The Border Fury
7. The Substitute Messenger
8. The Harem Model
9. The Cellar Gangsters
10. The Forged Check
11. The Trap
12. The Vault of Terror
13. Within Hollow Walls
14. The Fighting Chance
15. The Key to Victory

🔗 The Black Secret

DIRECTOR: George B. Seitz

CAST: Pearl White, George B. Seitz, Walter McGrail, Wallace McCutcheon

RELEASE DATE: 9 Nov. 1919   RELEASING COMPANY: Pathé

CHAPTER TITLES:

1. The Great Secret (3 reels)
2. Marked For Death
3. The Gas Chamber
4. Below the Waterline
5. The Acid Bath
6. The Unknown
7. The Betrayal
8. A Crippled Hand
9. Woes of Deceit
10. Inn of Dread
11. The Death Studio
12. The Chance Trail
13. Wings of Mystery
14. The Hidden Way
15. The Secret Host

Bound and Gagged

DIRECTOR: George B. Seitz

CAST: Marguerite Courtot, George B. Seitz, Frank Redman, Nellie Burt, Joe Cuny, Harry Semele, Harry Stone, Tom Goodwin, John Reinhard

RELEASE DATE: 26 Oct. 1919   RELEASING COMPANY: Pathé

CHAPTER TITLES:

1. The Wager
2. Overboard
3. Help, Help
4. An Unwilling Princess
5. Held For Ransom
6. Out Again, In Again
7. The Fatal Error
8. Arrested
9. A Harmless Princess
10. Hopley Takes the Liberty

The Carter Case (The Craig Kennedy Serial)

DIRECTOR: Donald MacKenzie

CAST: Herbert Rawlinson, Marguerite Marsh, Ethel Grey Terry, Kempton Green, William Pike, Coit Albertson, Joseph Marba, Don Hall, Louie R. Wolheim, Gene Baker, Leslie Stowe, Frank Wunderlee

RELEASE DATE: 17 March 1919   RELEASING COMPANY: Oliver Films (SR)

CHAPTER TITLES:

1. The Phosgene Bullet (3 reels)
2. The Vacuum Room
3. The Air Terror
4. The Dungeon
5. Unknown
6. The Wireless Detective
7. The Nervagraph
8. The Silent Shot
9. The Camera Trap
10. The Moonshiners
11. The White Damp
12. The X-Ray Detective
13. The Ruse
14–15. Unknown

Ⓢ Elmo, The Mighty

DIRECTOR: Henry McRae

CAST: Elmo Lincoln, Grace Cunard, Fred Starr, Virginia Craft, Ivor McFadden, James Cole

RELEASE DATE: 16 June 1919   RELEASING COMPANY: Universal

CHAPTER TITLES:

1. The Mystery of Mad Mountain
2. Buried Alive
3. Flames of Hate
4. A Fiendish Revenge
5. The Phantom Rescue
6. The Puma's Paws
7. The Masked Pursuer
8. The Flaming Pit
9. The House of A Thousand Tortures
10. Victims of the Sea
11. The Burning Den
12. Lashed to the Rocks
13. Into the Chasm
14. The Human Bridge
15. Crashing to Earth
16. Parachute Perils
17. The Plunge
18. Unmasked

Ⓢ The Fatal Fortune

DIRECTOR: Donald MacKenzie

CAST: Helen Holmes, Lieutenant Jack Levering, Leslie King, Bill Black, Frank Wunderlee, Floyd Buckley, Sidney Dalbrook, Nellie Lindrith

RELEASE DATE: 15 Dec. 1919   RELEASING COMPANY: SLK Serial
(SR)   Corporation

CHAPTER TITLES:

1. The Trader's Secret
2. Men of Tigerish Mold
3. Tortured by Flames
4. A Climb For Life
5. The Forced Marriage
6. Desperate Chances
7. A Plunge to Death
8. A Struggle in Midair
9. The Deadly Peril
10. Sure Death
11. A Leap for Life
12. A Fiendish Plot
13. Set Adrift
14. The Hidden Treasure
15. Unmasked

The Great Gamble

DIRECTOR: Joseph A. Golden

CAST: Anne Luther, Charles Hutchison, Richard Neil, Billy Moran, William Cavanaugh, Warner Cook

RELEASE DATE: 3 August 1919   RELEASING COMPANY: Pathé

CHAPTER TITLES:

1. The Great Gamble
2. The Clock of Doom
3. Into the Chasm
4. In the Law's Grip
5. Draught of Death
6. Out of the Clouds
7. The Crawling Menace
8. The Ring of Fire
9. Through Iron Doors
10. Written in Blood
11. The Stolen Identity
12. The Wolf Pack
13. Barriers of Flame
14. Under Arrest
15. Out of the Shadows

The Great Radium Mystery

DIRECTORS: Robert Broadwell, Robert F. Hill

CAST: Cleo Madison, Robert Reeves, Eileen Sedgwick, Robert Kortman, Ed Brady

RELEASE DATE: 13 Oct. 1919   RELEASING COMPANY: Universal

CHAPTER TITLES:

1. The Mystic Stone
2. The Death Trap
3. The Fatal Ride
4. The Swing For Life
5. The Torture Chamber
6. The Tunnel of Doom
7. A Flash in the Dark
8. In the Clutches of the Mad Man
9. The Roaring Volcano
10. Creeping Flames
11. Perils of Doom
12. Shackled
13. The Scalding Pit
14. Hemmed In
15. The Flaming Arrow
16. Over the Cataract
17. The Wheels of Death
18. Liquid Flames

⑤ Lightning Bryce

DIRECTOR: Paul C. Hurst

CAST: Jack Hoxie, Ann Little, Steve Clemente, Ben Corbett, Walter Patterson, George Champion, Slim Lucas, George Hunter, Paul C. Hurst

RELEASE DATE: 15 Oct. 1919 (SR)   RELEASING COMPANY: National Film Corporation (Arrow)

CHAPTER TITLES:

1. The Scarlet Moon
2. Wolf Nights
3. Perilous Trails
4. The Noose
5. The Dragon's Den
6. Robes of Destruction
7. Bared Fangs
8. The Yawning Abyss
9. The Voice of Conscience
10. Poison Waters
11. Walls of Flame
12. A Voice From The Dead
13. Battling Barriers
14. Smothering Tides
15. The End of The Trail

⑤ The Lightning Raider

DIRECTOR: George B. Seitz

CAST: Pearl White, Warner Oland, Henry G. Sell

RELEASE DATE: 5 Jan. 1919   RELEASING COMPANY: Pathé

CHAPTER TITLES:

1. The Ebony Block
2. The Counterplot
3. Underworld Terrors
4. Through The Doors of Steel
5. The Brass Key
6. The Mystic Box
7. Meshes of Evil
8. Cave of Dread
9. Falsely Accused
10. The Baited Trap
11. Bars of Death
12. Hurled into Space
13. The White Roses
14. Cleared of Guilt
15. Wu Fang Atones

The Lion Man

DIRECTORS: Albert Russell, Jack Wells

CAST: Kathleen O'Connor, Jack Perrin, Mack Wright, J. Barney Sherry, Gertrude Astor, Henry Barrows, Leonard Clapham, Robert Walker

RELEASE DATE: 29 Dec. 1919   RELEASING COMPANY: Universal

1. Flames of Hate
2. Rope of Death
3. Kidnappers
4. A Devilish Device
5. In the Lion's Den
6. House of Horrors
7. Doomed
8. Dungeon of Despair
9. Sold into Slavery
10. Perilous Plunge
11. At the Mercy of Monsters
12. Jaws of Destruction
13. When Hell Broke Loose
14. Desperate Deeds
15. Furnace of Fury
16. Relentless Renegades
17. In Cruel Clutches
18. In the Nick of Time

The Lurking Peril

DIRECTOR: George Morgan

CAST: Anne Luther, George Larkin, Ruth Dwyer, William Betchel, Peggy Shanor

RELEASE DATE: 15 Dec. 1919   RELEASING COMPANY: Wistaria
(SR)   (Arrow)

CHAPTER TITLES:

1. The $25,000 Contract
2. At The Edge of The Cliff

195

3. The Aviator's Victim
4. A Bolt From Heaven
5. The Man Trap in The Woods
6. A Duel of Wits
7. A Satanic Plot
8. Helpless in A Madhouse
9. The Hiding Place in The Slums
10. The Den in Chinatown
11. At A Maniac's Mercy
12. Six Inches of Steel
13. Trapped By Telegraph
14. The Dynamite Ship
15. The Last Plot of Bates

Man of Might

DIRECTOR: William Duncan

CAST: William Duncan, Edith Johnson, Joe Ryan

RELEASE DATE: Jan. 1919 RELEASING COMPANY: Vitagraph

CHAPTER TITLES:

1. The Riven Flag
2. The Leap Through Space
3. The Creeping Death
4. The Gripping Hand
5. The Human Shield
6. The Height of Torment
7. Into The Trap
8. The One Chance
9. The Crashing Horror
10. Double Crossed
11. The Ship of Dread
12. The Volcano's Prey
13. The Flood of Despair
14. The Living Catapult
15. The Rescue

The Masked Rider

DIRECTOR: Aubrey M. Kennedy

CAST: Harry Myers, Ruth Stonehouse, Paul Panzer

RELEASE DATE: May 1919 RELEASING COMPANY: Arrow (SR)

CHAPTER TITLE: 15 chapters

The Master Mystery

DIRECTOR: Burton King

CAST: Harry Houdini, Marguerite Marsh, Ruth Stonehouse, William Pike, Charles Graham, Edna Britton, Floyd Buckley

RELEASE DATE: 1 March–
1 May 1919 (SR)

RELEASING COMPANY: Octagon
Films, Incorporated

CHAPTER TITLES:

1. Unknown (3 reels)
2-14. Unknown

15. Unmasking of The Automaton

The Midnight Man

DIRECTOR: James W. Horne

CAST: James J. Corbett, Orral Humphrey, Sam Polo, Kathleen O'Connor, Joseph W. Girard, Frank Jonasson, Noble Johnson, William Sauter, Georgia Woodthorpe, Joseph Singleton

RELEASE DATE: 1 Sept. 1919   RELEASING COMPANY: Universal

CHAPTER TITLES:

1. Cast Adrift
2. Deadly Enemies
3. Ten Thousand Dollars Reward
4. At Bay
5. Unmasked
6. Elevator Mystery
7. The Electric Foe
8. Shadow of Fear
9. The Society Hold-Up
10. Blazing Torch
11. The Death Ride
12. The Tunnel of Terror
13. A Fight to the Finish
14. Jaws of Death
15. Wheel of Terror
16. Hurled From the Heights
17. The Cave of Destruction
18. A Wild Finish

The Mystery of 13

DIRECTOR: Francis Ford

CAST: Francis Ford, Rosemary Theby, Pete Girard, Mark Fenton, Phil Ford, Jack Saville, Doris Dare, Jack Lawton, V. Orilo, Ruth Maureice, Nigel De Brouiller

RELEASE DATE: August 1919
(SR)

RELEASING COMPANY: Burston
Films

CHAPTER TITLES:

1. Bitter Bondage

2. Lights Out

3. The Submarine Gardens
4. The Lone Rider
5. Blown to Atoms
6. Single Handed
7. Fire and Water
8. Pirate Loot
9. The Phantom House
10. The Raid
11. Bare Handed
12. The Death Ride
13. Brother Against Brother
14. The Man Hunt
15. The 13th Card

The Perils of Thunder Mountain

DIRECTORS: R. N. Bradbury, W. J. Bauman

CAST: Antonio Moreno, Carol Holloway, Kate Price

RELEASE DATE: 26 May 1919 RELEASING COMPANY: Vitagraph

CHAPTER TITLES:

1. Spear of Malice
2. The Bridge Trap
3. Teeth of Steel
4. Cave of Terror
5. Cliff of Treachery
6. Tree of Torture
7. Lightning Lure
8. Iron Clutch
9. Prisoner of the Deep
10. The Flaming Sacrifice
11. In the Ocean's Grip
12. Rushing Horror
13. River of Dread
14. Hut of Disaster
15. Fate's Verdict

The Red Glove

DIRECTOR: J. P. McGowan

CAST: Marie Walcamp, Pat O'Malley, Truman Van Dyke, Evelyn Selbie, Alfred Allen, Andrew Waldron, Thomas Lingham, Leon de la Mothe

RELEASE DATE: 17 March 1919 RELEASING COMPANY: Universal

CHAPTER TITLES:

1. Pool of Lost Souls
2. Claws of the Vulture
3. The Vulture's Vengeance
4. Passing of Gentleman Geoff
5. At the Mercy of a Monster
6. Flames of Death
7. A Desperate Chance
8. Facing Death

9. A Leap For Life
10. Out of Death's Shadow
11. In the Depths of the Sea
12. In Death's Grip
13. Trapped
14. The Lost Millions
15. The Mystery Message
16. In Deadly Peril
17. The Rope of Death
18. Run to Earth

Smashing Barriers

DIRECTOR: William Duncan

CAST: William Duncan, Edith Johnson, Walter Rodgers, George Stanley, Fred Darnton, Slim Cole, William McCall

RELEASE DATE: Sept. 1919

RELEASING COMPANY: Vitagraph (Recut and re-released as 6-reel feature in September 1923)

CHAPTER TITLES:

1. Test of Courage
2. Plunge of Death
3. Tree-Hut of Torture
4. Deed of A Devil
5. Living Grave
6. Downward to Doom
7. The Fatal Flight
8. The Murder Car
9. The Dynamite Tree
10. Overpowered
11. The Den of Deviltry
12. Explosive Bullets
13. Dead Fall
14. Trapped Like Rats
15. The Final Barrier

The Terror of The Range

DIRECTOR: Stuart Paton

CAST: Betty Compson, George Larkin, H. P. Carpenter, Fred M. Malatesta, Ora Carew

RELEASE DATE: 2 Feb. 1919

RELEASING COMPANY: Pathé

CHAPTER TITLES:

1. Prowlers of the Night
2. The Hidden Chart
3. The Chasm of Fear
4. The Midnight Raid
5. A Threat From the Past
6. Tangled Tales
7. Run to Earth

The Tiger's Trail

DIRECTOR: Robert Ellis, Paul C. Hurst

CAST: Ruth Roland, George Larkin, Fred Kohler, Easter Walters, Harry G. Moody, George Field, Mark Strong

RELEASE DATE: 20 April 1919 RELEASING COMPANY: Pathé

CHAPTER TITLES:

1. The Tiger Worshipers
2. Glowing Eyes
3. The Human Chain
4. Danger Signals
5. The Tiger Trap
6. The Secret Assassin
7. Flaming Waters
8. Danger Ahead
9. Raging Torrent
10. Bringing in the Law
11. In the Breakers
12. The Two Amazons
13. The False Idol
14. The Mountain Hermit
15. The Tiger Face

Trail of The Octopus

DIRECTOR: Duke Worne

CAST: Ben Wilson, Neva Gerber, William Dyer, Howard Crampton, William Carroll, Marie Pavis

RELEASE DATE: Oct. 1919 (SR) RELEASING COMPANY: Hallmark Pictures Corporation

CHAPTER TITLES:

1. The Devil's Trade-Mark (3 reels)
2. Purple Dagger
3. Face to Face
4. The Hand of Wang
5. The Eye of Satan
6. Behind the Mask
7. The Dance of Death
8. Satan's Soulmate
9. The Chained Soul
10. The Ape Man
11. The Red Death
12. The Poisoned Talon
13. The Phantom Mandarin
14. The House of Shadows
15. The Yellow Octopus

1920

The Branded Four

DIRECTOR: Duke Worne

CAST: Ben Wilson, Neva Gerber, Joseph Girard, William Dyer, Ashton Dearholt, Pansy Porter, William Carroll

RELEASE DATE: 1 August 1920 RELEASING COMPANY: Select

CHAPTER TITLES:

1. A Strange Legacy
2. The Devil's Trap
3. Flames of Revenge
4. The Blade of Death
5. Fate's Pawn
6. The Hidden Cave
7. Shanghaied
8. Mutiny
9. The House of Doom
10. Ray of Destruction
11. Buried Alive
12. Lost to the World
13. Valley of Death
14. From the Sky
15. Sands of Torment

Bride 13

DIRECTOR: Richard Stanton

CAST: Marguerite Clayton, John O'Brien, Greta Hartman, William Lawrence, Mary Christensen, Arthur Earle

RELEASE DATE: Sept. 1920 RELEASING COMPANY: Fox Film Corporation

CHAPTER TITLES:

1. Snatched From the Altar
2. The Pirate's Fangs
3. The Craft of Despair
4. The Vulture's Prey
5. The Torture Chamber
6. The Tarantula's Trail
7. Tongues of Flame
8. Entombed
9. Hurled From the Clouds
10. The Cavern of Terror
11. Greyhounds of the Sea
12. The Creeping Peril
13. Reefs of Treachery
14. The Fiendish Tribesmen
15. Thundering Vengeance

⑤ *Daredevil Jack*

DIRECTOR: W. S. Van Dyke

CAST: Jack Dempsey, Josie Sedgwick, Lon Chaney, Spike Robinson, Ruth Langston, Hershall Mayall, Fred Starr, Frank Lanning, Albert Cody, Al Kaufman

RELEASE DATE: 15 Feb. 1920   RELEASING COMPANY: Pathé

CHAPTER TITLES:

1. The Mysterious Bracelets (3 reels)
2. The Ball of Death
3. Wheels of Fate
4. Shanghaied
5. Race for Glory
6. A Skirmish of Wits
7. A Blow in the Dark
8. Blinding Hate
9. Phantoms of Treachery
10. Paths of Destruction
11. Flames of Wrath
12. The Unseen Menace
13. Baiting the Trap
14. A Terrible Vengeance
15. The Triple Chase

⑤ *The Dragon's Net*

DIRECTOR: Henry McRae

CAST: Marie Walcamp, Harlan Tucker, Otto Lederer, Wadsworth Harris

RELEASE DATE: 23 August 1920   RELEASING COMPANY: Universal

CHAPTER TITLES:

1. The Mysterious Murder
2. Thrown Overboard
3. A Watery Grave
4. Into the Chase
5. A Jump For Life
6. Captured in China
7. The Unseen Foe
8. Trailed to Peking
9. On the Great Wall of China
10. The Train of Death
11. The Shanghai Peril
12. The Unmasking

⑤ *Elmo, The Fearless*

DIRECTOR: J. P. McGowan

CAST: Elmo Lincoln, Louise Lorraine, William Chapman, Ray Watson, Frank Ellis, V. L. Barnes, Gordon McGregor

RELEASE DATE: 9 Feb. 1920 RELEASING COMPANY: Universal

CHAPTER TITLES:

1. Wreck of the Santiam
2. The Racing Death
3. The Life Line
4. The Flames of Death
5. The Smugglers Cave
6. The Battle Under the Sea
7. The House of Mystery
8. The Fatal Crossing
9. The Assassin's Knife
10. The Fatal Bullet
11. The Temple of the Dragon
12. Crashing Through
13. The Hand on the Latch
14. The Avalanche
15. The Burning Fuse
16. The House of Intrigue
17. The Trap
18. The Fateful Letter

The Evil Eye

DIRECTORS: J. Gordon Cooper, Wally Van

CAST: Benny Leonard, Stuart Holmes, Ruth Dwyer, Maria Shotwell, Madam Marstini, Bernard Randall

RELEASE DATE: April 1920 (SR) RELEASING COMPANY: Hallmark (Asher's Enterprise)

CHAPTER TITLES:

1. Below the Deadline
2. In the House of the Blind Men
3. The Golden Locket
4. Vengeance of the Dead
5. Trapped by Treachery
6. On the Wings of Death
7. The Double Cross

8–10. Unknown

11. A Monstrous Menace

12–15. Unknown

Fantomas

DIRECTOR: Edward Sedgwick

CAST: Edna Murphy, Ed Roseman, Eva Balfour, Johnny Walker, Lionel Adams, John Willard

RELEASE DATE: 19 Dec. 1920 RELEASING COMPANY: Fox Film Corporation

CHAPTER TITLES:

1. On the Stroke of 9
2. The Million Dollar Reward
3. The Triple Peril
4. Blades of Terror
5. Heights of Horror
6. Altar of Sacrifice
7. Flames of Sacrifice
8. At Death's Door
9. The Haunted Hotel
10. The Fatal Card
11. The Phantom Sword
12. The Danger Signal
13. On the Count of 3
14. The Blazing Train
15. The Sacred Necklace
16. The Phantom Shadow
17. The Price of Fang Wu
18. Double-Crossed
19. The Hawk's Prey
20. The Hell Ship

The Fatal Sign

DIRECTOR: Stuart Paton

CAST: Claire Anderson, Harry Carter, Joseph W. Girard, Boyd Irwin, Leo Maloney

RELEASE DATE: 1 Feb. 1920 RELEASING COMPANY: Arrow (SR)

CHAPTER TITLES:

1. The Sign of the Rat
2. The Lair of the Rat
3. The Devil's Web
4. Out of the Night

5–14. Unknown

The Flaming Disc

DIRECTOR: Robert F. Hill

CAST: Elmo Lincoln, Louise Lorraine, Lee Kohlmar, Ray Watson, George Williams, Monty Montague, Jenks Harris

RELEASE DATE: 21 Nov. 1920 RELEASING COMPANY: Universal

CHAPTER TITLES:

1. Rails of Death
2. Span of Life
3. Perilous Leap
4. Fires of Hate
5. Vanishing Floor
6. Pool of Mystery
7. Circle of Fire
8. Through Walls of Steel

9. The Floating Mine
10. Spiked Death
11. The Dynamite Trail
12. The Tunnel of Flames
13. Caged In
14. The Purple Rays
15. Poisoned Waters
16. Running Wild
17. Rails of Destruction
18. End of the Trail

The Hawk's Trail

DIRECTOR: W. S. Van Dyke

CAST: King Baggot, Rhea Mitchell, Grace Darmond, Harry Lorraine, Fred Windermere, Stanton Heck, George Siegmann

RELEASING DATE: 13 Jan. 1920 RELEASING COMPANY: Burston Films

CHAPTER TITLES:

1. False Faces
2. The Superman
3. Yellow Shadows
4. Stained Hands
5. House of Fear
6. Room Above
7. The Bargain
8. The Phantom Melody
9. The Lure
10. The Swoop
11. One Fatal Step
12. Tides That Tell
13. Face to Face
14. The Substitute
15. The Showdown

Hidden Dangers

DIRECTOR: William Bertram

CAST: Joe Ryan, Jean Page

RELEASE DATE: July 1920 RELEASING COMPANY: Vitagraph

CHAPTER TITLES:

1. The Evil Spell
2. The Murder Mood
3. Plucked From Peril
4. The Fatal Choice
5. Hands of Horror
6. Springing the Trap
7. Hindoo Hate
8. Hemmed In

9. An Inch From Doom
10. A Fanatic's Revenge
11. The Tank's Secret
12. Human Bait
13. A Woman's Grit
14. The Fatal Escape
15. The Lifting Fog

The Invisible Hand

DIRECTOR: William J. Bowman

CAST: Antonio Moreno, Pauline Curley, Brinsley Shaw, Jay Morley, Sam Polo, George Mellcrest

RELEASE DATE: Jan. 1920

RELEASING COMPANY: Vitagraph

CHAPTER TITLES:

1. Setting the Snare (3 reels)
2. T. N. T.
3. Winged Death
4. Gassed
5. Dodging Disaster
6. The Closing Jaw
7. The Submarine Cave
8. Outwitted
9. A Heathen Sacrifice
10. Fender of Flesh
11. Flirting With Death
12. Dungeon of Despair
13. Plunging Peril
14. A Modern Mazeppa
15. Closing the Net

The Invisible Ray

DIRECTOR: Harry Pollard

CAST: Jack Sherrill, Ruth Clifford, Sidney Bracy, Ed Davis, Corrine Uzzell, W. H. Tooker

RELEASE DATE: 1 July 1920 (SR)

RELEASING COMPANY: Frohman Amusement Corporation (Joan Film Sales)

CHAPTER TITLES: 15 chapters

King of The Circus

DIRECTOR: J. P. McGowan

CAST: Eddie Polo, Corrine Porter, Harry Madison, Kittoria Beveridge, Charles Fortune

RELEASE DATE: 22 Nov. 1920 RELEASING COMPANY: Universal

CHAPTER TITLES:

1. Blood Money
2. The Mushroom Bullet
3. Stolen Evidence
4. Facing Death
5. The Black Wallet
6. The Lion's Claws
7. Over the City
8. Treachery
9. Dynamite
10. The Mystic's Power
11. Man and Beast
12. Deep Water
13. A Fight For Life
14. Out of the Clouds
15. The Woman in Black
16. The Cradle of Death
17. The Final Reckoning
18. The Lost Heritage

The Lost City

DIRECTOR: E. A. Martin

CAST: Juanita Hansen, George Chesebro, Frank Clark, Hector Dion

RELEASE DATE: Feb. 1920 (SR) RELEASING COMPANY: Warner Brothers

CHAPTER TITLES:

1. The Lost Princess (3 reels)
2. The City of Hanging Gourds
3. The Flaming Tower
4. Jungle Death
5. The Puma's Victim
6. The Man Eater's Prey
7. The Bride of Death
8. A Tragedy in the Sky
9. In the Palace of Black Walls
10. The Tug of War
11. In the Lion's Jaw
12. The Jungle Fire
13. In the Cave of Eternal Fire
14. The Eagle's Nest
15. The Lost City

The Moon Riders

DIRECTORS: Reeves Eason, Albert Russell

CONTINUED NEXT WEEK

CAST: Art Acord, Mildred Moore, George Field, Beatrice Dominguez, Charles Newton, Tote DuCrow

RELEASE DATE: 26 April 1920 RELEASING COMPANY: Universal

CHAPTER TITLES:

1. Over the Precipice
2. Masked Marauders
3. Red Rage of Jealousy
4. Vultures of the Hills
5. Death Trap
6. Caves of Mystery
7. The Menacing Monster
8. At the Rope's End
9. The Triple Menace
10. The Moon Rider's Bride
11. Death's Door
12. Pit of Fire
13. House of Doom
14. Unmasked
15. His Hour of Torture
16. The Flaming Peril
17. Rushing Waters
18. Clearing Skies

The Mystery Mind

DIRECTORS: William Davis, Fred Sittenham

CAST: J. Robert Pauline, Peggy Shanor, Paul Panzer, Ed Rogers, Violet MacMillian, De Sacia Saville

RELEASE DATE: 6 Sept. 1920 (SR) RELEASING COMPANY: Supreme Pictures (Pioneer Film Corporation)

CHAPTER TITLES:

Prologue: The Road to Yesterday
1. The Hypnotic Clue
2. The Fires of Fury
3. The War of Wills
4. The Fumes of Fear
5. Thought Waves
6. A Halo of Help
7. The Nether World
8. The Mystery Mind
9. Dual Personality
10. Hounds of Hate
11. The Sleepwalker
12. The Temple of the Occult
13. The Binding Ray
14. The Water Cure
15. The Gold of the Gods

The $1,000,000 Reward

DIRECTOR: George A. Lessey

CAST: Lillian Walker, Coit Albertson, George A. Lessey, William Pike, Joseph Marba, Leora Spellman, Bernard Randall, Charles Middleton

RELEASE DATE: Jan. 1920 (SR) RELEASING COMPANY: Grossman Pictures

CHAPTER TITLES:

1. Unknown (3 reels) 2–15. Unknown

🌀 *The Phantom Foe*

DIRECTOR: Bertram Millhauser

CAST: Juanita Hansen, William N. Bailey, Warner Oland, Harry Semels, Wallace McCutcheon, Nina Cassavant, Tom Goodwin, Joe Cuny

RELEASE DATE: 17 Oct. 1920 RELEASING COMPANY: Pathé

CHAPTER TITLES:

1. Doom
2. Disappearance of Janet Dale
3. Trail of the Wolf
4. The Open Window
5. The Tower Room
6. The Crystal Ball
7. Gun Fire
8. The Man Trap
9. The Mystic Summons
10. The Foe Unmasked
11. Through Prison Walls
12. Behind the Veil
13. Attack at the Inn
14. Confession
15. Retribution

🌀 *Pirate Gold*

DIRECTOR: George B. Seitz

CAST: Marguerite Courtot, George B. Seitz, Frank Redman, William Burt, Joe Cuny, Harry Stone, Harry Semels

RELEASE DATE: 15 August 1920 RELEASING COMPANY: Pathé

CHAPTER TITLES:

1. In Which Hoey Buys A Map 2. Dynamite

3. The Dead Man's Story
4. Treasure at Last
5. Drugged
6. Kidnapped
7. Under Suspicion
8. Knifed
9. The Double Cross
10. Defeat and Victory

Ruth of The Rockies

DIRECTOR: George Marshall

CAST: Ruth Roland, Herbert Heyes, Thomas Lingham, Fred Burns, Norma Bichole, William Gilliss, Jack Rollens

RELEASE DATE: 29 August 1920 RELEASING COMPANY: Pathé

CHAPTER TITLES:

1. The Mysterious Trunk
2. The Inner Circle
3. The Tower of Danger
4. Between Two Fires
5. Double Crossed
6. The Eagle's Nest
7. Troubled Waters
8. Danger Trails
9. The Perilous Path
10. Outlawed
11. The Fatal Diamond
12. The Secret Order
13. The Surprise Attack
14. The Secret of Regina Island
15. The Hidden Treasure

The Screaming Shadow

DIRECTOR: Duke Worne

CAST: Ben Wilson, Neva Gerber, William Dyer, Howard Crampton, William Carroll, Fred Gamble, Joseph W. Girard, Francis Terry, Pansy Porter, Claire Mille, Joseph Manning

RELEASE DATE: 22 Feb. 1920 (SR) RELEASING COMPANY: Hallmark Picture Corporation

CHAPTER TITLES:

1. A Cry in the Dark
2. The Virgin of Death
3. The Fang of the Beast
4. The Black Seven
5. The Vapor of Death
6. The Hidden Menace or The Crawling Horror
7. Into the Depths

8. The White Terror
9. The Sleeping Death
10. The Prey of Mong
11. Liquid Fire
12. Cold Steel
13. The Fourth Symbol
14. Entombed Alive
15. Unmasked

The Silent Avenger

DIRECTOR: William Duncan

CAST: William Duncan, Edith Johnson, Jack Richardson, Virginia Nightingale, Ernest Shields, Willis L. Robards, William S. Smith

RELEASE DATE: April 1920 RELEASING COMPANY: Vitagraph

CHAPTER TITLES:

1. The Escape (3 reels)
2. Fighting Back
3. Within The Noose
4. Tearing Through
5. Blotted Out
6. The Hidden Blow
7. Dynamite Doom
8. The Crusher
9. Into the Jaws
10. Blades of Horror
11. Shot into Space
12. Facing Eternity
13. A Human Pendulum
14. The Lakes of Fire
15. The Final Trump

Son of Tarzan

DIRECTORS: Harry Revier, Arthur J. Flaven

CAST: P. Dempsey Tabler, Karla Schram, Manilla Martan, Gordon Griffith, Lucille Rubey, Kamuela C. Searle, De Sacia Saville, Kathleen May, Frank Morrell, Ray Thompson, Eugene Burr, Frank Earle, Mae Giraci

RELEASE DATE: Dec. 1920 (SR) RELEASING COMPANY: National Film Corporation

CHAPTER TITLES:

1. Call of the Jungle (3 reels)
2. Out of the Lion's Jaws
3. The Girl of the Jungle
4. The Sheik's Revenge
5. The Pirate's Prey
6. The Killer's Mate

7. The Quest of the Killer
8. Coming of Tarzan
9. The Kiss of the Beast
10. Tarzan Takes the Trail
11. Ashes of Love

12. Meriem's Ride in the Night
13. Double Crossed
14. Blazing Hearts
15. An Amazing Denouement

᥆ The Third Eye

DIRECTOR: James W. Horne

CAST: Eileen Percy, Warner Oland, Jack Mower, Olga Grey, Mark Strong

RELEASE DATE: 23 May 1920   RELEASING COMPANY: Pathé

CHAPTER TITLES:

1. The Poisoned Dagger
2. The Pendulum of Death
3. In Destruction's Path
4. Daggers of Death
5. The Black Hand Bag
6. The Death Spark
7. The Crook's Ranch or The Double Trap

8. Trails of Danger or Dangerous Trails
9. The Race For Life
10. The House of Terrors
11. The Long Arm of Vengeance
12. Man Against Man
13. Blind Trails of Justice
14. At Bay
15. Triumph of Justice

᥆ Thunderbolt Jack

DIRECTORS: Francis Ford, Murdock MacQuarrie

CAST: Jack Hoxie, Marin Sais, Chris Frank, Steve Clemente, Alton Hoxie, Edith Stayart

RELEASE DATES 1 Nov. 1920   RELEASING COMPANY: Berwilla
(SR)   Film Corporation (Arrow)

CHAPTER TITLES:

1. The Thunderbolt Strikes
2. Eight to One

3–10. Unknown

212

The Tiger Band

DIRECTOR: Gilbert P. Hamilton

CAST: Helen Holmes, Jack Mower, Dwight Crittenden, Omar Whitehead, Billy Brunton

RELEASE DATE: 1920 (SR)

RELEASING COMPANY: Holmes Producing Corporation (Warner Brothers)

CHAPTER TITLES:

1. Chang the Mighty
2. The Brand of Hate
3. The Stolen Engine
4. In the Power of Chang
5. The Great Leap
6. The Mysterious Friend
7. At Close Quarters
8. A Race With Death
9. A Perilous Escape
10. Trapped
11. The Informer
12. The Death Hazard
13. The Flaming Peril
14. The Masked Man's Treachery
15. The Masked Man's Claws

Trailed by Three

DIRECTOR: Perry Vekroff

CAST: Frances Mann, Stuart Holmes, John Webb Dillon, Wilfred Lytell, William Welsh, Ruby Hoffman, John Wheeler

RELEASE DATE: 4 April 1920

RELEASING COMPANY: Pathé

CHAPTER TITLES:

1. The Mystery Pearls (3 reels)
2. Trapped in Chinatown
3. Tyrant of the South Seas
4. The Prison Ship
5. Buried Alive
6. Wanted For Burglary
7. In the Pasha's House
8. The Fifteenth Wife
9. The Pasha's Revenge
10. The Slave Market
11. The Torture Trap
12. The Burning Fuse
13. The Door of Death
14. The Hidden Crime
15. The Reckoning

⑤ *The Vanishing Dagger*

DIRECTORS: Ed Kull, Eddie Polo

CAST: Eddie Polo, Thelma Percy, Leach Cross, Laura Oakley, G. Norman Hammond, Arthur Jerris, Ray Ripley, Thomas Lingham, Ruth Royce, Peggy O'Dare

RELEASE DATE: 7 June 1920   RELEASING COMPANY: Universal

CHAPTER TITLES:

1. The Scarlet Confession
2. The Night of Terror
3. In Death's Clutches
4. On the Trail of the Dagger
5. The End of the Rustlers
6. A Terrible Calamity
7. Plunged To His Doom
8. In Unmerciful Hands
9. Ferocious Foes
10. When London Sleeps
11. A Race to Scotland
12. An Evil Plot
13. Spears of Death
14. Walls of Doom
15. The Great Pendulum
16. Beneath the Sea
17. Beasts of the Jungle
18. Silver Linings

⑤ *Vanishing Trails*

DIRECTOR: Leon de la Mothe

CAST: Franklyn Farnum, Mary Anderson, L. M. Wells, Duke R. Lee, Harry Lonsdale, Vester Pegg, W. A. Orlamond, Pedro León, Prince (dog)

RELEASE DATE: Sept. 1920   RELEASING COMPANY: Canyon
(SR)   Picture Corporation

CHAPTER TITLES:

1. The Midnight Mystery
2. Silent Joe's Death Warrant
3. The Dreadful Scourge
4. Vengeance
5. Death Pursues
6. The Brand of Hate
7. Death Shadows
8. The Dare-Devil
9. A Livid Fate
10. The Mansion of Mystery
11. Rails of Destruction
12. The Final Hour
13. The Death Trap
14. For Murder
15. Unmasked

The Veiled Mystery

DIRECTORS: Antonio Moreno, Webster Cullison, William J. Bowman

CAST: Antonio Moreno, Pauline Curley, H. A. Barrows, Nenette de Courey, W. L. Rogers, George Reed

RELEASE DATE: Sept. 1920 RELEASING COMPANY: Vitagraph

CHAPTER TITLES:

1. The Menace
2. The Quicksand
3. The Sea Demon
4. Trapped in Mid-Air
5. The Well of Despair
6. The Fiery Furnace
7. Human Targets
8. The Span of Death
9. A Slide For Life
10. A Demon's Device
11. The Smoke of Doom
12. A Climax of Hate
13. The Sinister Stroke
14. The Veil's Secret
15. The Accounting

Velvet Fingers

DIRECTOR: George B. Seitz

CAST: George B. Seitz, Marguerite Courtot, Tommy Carr, Harry Semels, Lucille Lennox, Frank Redman, Joe Cuny

RELEASE DATE: 5 Dec. 1920 RELEASING COMPANY: Pathé

CHAPTER TITLES:

1. To Catch A Thief
2. The Face Behind The Curtain
3. The Hand From Behind The Door
4. The Man in The Blue Spectacles
5. The Deserted Pavilion
6. Unmasked
7. The House of 1000 Veils
8. Aiming Straight
9. The Broken Necklace
10. Shots in The Dark
11. The Other Woman
12. Into Ambush
13. The Hidden Room
14. The Trap
15. Out of The Web

🎬 The Whirlwind

DIRECTOR: Joseph A. Golden

CAST: Charles Hutchison, Edith Thornton, Richard Neil, Ben Walker

RELEASE DATE: 17 Jan. 1920 (SR)

RELEASING COMPANY: Allgood Picture Corporation (Republic)

CHAPTER TITLES:

1. The Trap
2. The Waters of Death
3. Blown Skyward
4. The Drop to Death
5. Over The Precipice
6. On The Brink
7. In Mid-Air
8. A Fight For Life
9. Amid The Flames
10. The Human Bridge
11. Thrown Overboard
12. A Fight At Sea
13. In The Lion's Cage
14. A Life At Stake
15. The Missing Bride

🎬 A Woman In Grey

DIRECTOR: James Vincent

CAST: Arline Pretty, Henry G. Sell, Fred Jones, Margaret Fielding, James A. Heenan, Ann Brodie, Violet de Bicari, Adelaine Fitzgallen

RELEASE DATE: 22 Jan. 1920 (SR)

RELEASING COMPANY: Serico Producing Corporation

CHAPTER TITLES:

1. The House of Mystery
2. The Dagger of Death
3. The Trap of Steel
4. The Strangle Knot
5. The Chasm of Fear
6. Unknown
7. At The Mercy of Flames
8. The Drop To Death
9. Burning Strands
10. House of Horrors
11–15. Unknown

1921

The Adventures of Tarzan

DIRECTOR: Robert F. Hill

CAST: Elmo Lincoln, Louise Lorraine, Percy Pembroke, Frank Whitson, James Inslee, Lillian Worth, George Momberg, Frank Merrill, Joe Martin (orangutan), Charles Gay, Maceo Bruce Sheffield

RELEASE DATE: 1 Dec. 1921 (SR)

RELEASING COMPANY: Weiss Brothers–Numa Picture Corporation (Recut and re-released in 10 episodes, with sound effects, in 1928 by Weiss Brothers Artclass)

CHAPTER TITLES:

1. Jungle Romance (3 reels)
2. City of Gold
3. Sun Death
4. Stalking Death
5. Flames of Hate
6. The Ivory Tomb
7. The Jungle Trap
8. The Tornado
9. Fangs of The Lion
10. The Simoon
11. The Hidden Foe
12. Dynamite Trail
13. The Jungle's Prey
14. Flaming Arrows
15. The Last Adventure

The Avenging Arrow

DIRECTORS: William J. Bowman, W. S. Van Dyke

CAST: Ruth Roland, Ed Hearn, Frank Lackteen, Virginia Ainsworth, Vera Sisson, Otto Lederer

RELEASE DATE: 13 March 1921

RELEASING COMPANY: Pathé

CHAPTER TITLES:

1. Vow of Mystery
2. The Enemy Strikes
3. The Hand of Treachery
4. A Life in Jeopardy

5. The Message Stone
6. The Midnight Attack
7. The Double Game
8. The Strange Pact
9. The Auction Block
10. Outwitted
11. Dangerous Waters
12. House of Treachery
13. On Perilous Grounds
14. Shifting Sands
15. The Toll of the Desert

The Blue Fox

DIRECTOR: Duke Worne

CAST: Ann Little, J. Morris Foster, Joseph W. Girard, Charles Mason, William LaRock, Hope Loring, Lon Seefield

RELEASE DATE: May 1921   RELEASING COMPANY: Arrow (SR)

CHAPTER TITLES:

1. Message of Hate
2. Menace From The Sky
3. Mysterious Prisoner
4. A Perilous Ride
5. A Woman's Wit
6. A Night of Terror
7. Washed Ashore
8. A Perilous Leap
9. Lost Identity
10. In Close Pursuit
11. The Wilds of Alaska
12. The Camp of the Charkas
13. The Secret Skull
14. The Desert Island
15. Home and Happiness

Breaking Through

DIRECTOR: Robert Ensminger

CAST: Carmel Myers, Wallace MacDonald, Vincente Howard

RELEASE DATE: 25 Sept. 1921   RELEASING COMPANY: Vitagraph

CHAPTER TITLES: 15 chapters

The Diamond Queen

DIRECTOR: Ed Kull

CAST: Eileen Sedgwick, George Chesebro, Al Smith, Frank Clarke, Lou Short, Josephine Scott

218

RELEASE DATE: 15 March 1921 RELEASING COMPANY: Universal

CHAPTER TITLES:

1. Vow of Vengeance
2. Plunge of Doom
3. Perils of The Jungle
4. Fires of Hate
5. Tide of Destiny
6. The Colossal Game
7. An Amazing Ultimatum
8. In Merciless Clutches
9. A Race With Rogues
10. The Betrayal
11. In Torture's Grip
12. The Kidnapping
13. Weird Walls
14. The Plunge
15. The Decoy
16. The Dip of Death
17. The Hand of Fate
18. The Hour of Reckoning

✪ Do or Die

DIRECTOR: J. P. McGowan

CAST: Eddie Polo, J. P. McGowan, Inez McDonald, Magda Lane, Jay Marchant, Jean Perkins

RELEASE DATE: 30 May 1921 RELEASING COMPANY: Universal

CHAPTER TITLES:

1. The Buccaneer's Bride
2. The Hornet's Nest
3. The Secret of the Sea
4. The Hidden Danger
5. The Bandit's Victim
6. The Escape
7. In Hiding
8. The Trap
9. Under Sentence
10. The Secret Cavern
11. Satan's Twin
12. The Lost Ring
13. The Cipher Key
14. The Midnight Attack
15. The Race For Life
16. The Crystal Lake
17. A Fight To the Finish
18. Hidden Treasure

✪ Double Adventure

DIRECTOR: W. S. Van Dyke

CAST: Charles Hutchison, Josie Sedgwick, Ruth Langston, Carl Stockdale, S. E. Jennings, Louis D'Or

RELEASE DATE: 23 Jan. 1921 RELEASING COMPANY: Pathé

CHAPTER TITLES:

1. On the Trail of Fate (3 reels)
2. The Harbor Bandits
3. Hearts of Stone
4. The Gun Runner
5. The Rebel's Nest
6. Troubled Trail
7. War in the Oil Fields
8. Grill of Fate
9. Black Whirlpool
10. A Devil's Bargain
11. The Danger Ledge
12. Hazardous Heights
13. By Air and Sea
14. House in the Canyon
15. Wages of Crime

Fighting Fate

DIRECTOR: William Duncan

CAST: William Duncan, Edith Johnson, Larry Richardson, Ford West, Frank Weed, William McCall

RELEASE DATE: Jan. 1921   RELEASING COMPANY: Vitagraph

CHAPTER TITLES:

1. A Borrowed Life
2. Playing The Game
3. A Modern Daniel
4. A Desperate Dilemma
5. Double Crossed
6. The Crown Jewel Clue
7. A Demon's Bluff
8. The Treasure Hunt
9. The Air Avenger
10. The Stolen Bride
11. A Choice of Death
12. Indian Vengeance
13. Mystery Mountain
14. When Thieves Fall Out
15. Cleaning the Bolt

The Great Reward

DIRECTOR: Francis Ford

CAST: Francis Ford, Ella Hall

RELEASE DATE: May 1921 (SR)   RELEASING COMPANY: Burston Films (National Exchanges)

CHAPTER TITLES:

1. His Living Image
2. The Life Current
3. In Bondage
4. The Duel

5. The Madman
6. Caves of Doom
7. Burning Sands
8. The Thunderbolt
9. Cross Fires
10. Forgotten Halls
11. On The Brink
12. At Bay
13. The Silent Hour
14. High Treason
15. The Reward

The Hope Diamond Mystery

DIRECTOR: Stuart Paton

CAST: Grace Darmond, George Chesebro, Harry Carter, William Marion, Boris Karloff, Carmen Phillips, William Puckley, May Yohe

RELEASE DATE: March 1921 (SR)

RELEASING COMPANY: Kosmik Films

CHAPTER TITLES:

1. The Hope Diamond Mystery
2. The Vanishing Hand
3. The Forged Note
4. The Jewel of Sita
5. A Virgin's Love
6. The House of Terror
7. Flames of Despair
8. Yellow Whisperings
9. The Evil Eye
10. In The Spider's Web
11. The Cup of Fear
12. The Ring of Death
13. The Lash of Hate
14. Primitive Passions
15. An Island of Destiny

Hurricane Hutch

DIRECTOR: George B. Seitz

CAST: Charles Hutchison, Lucy Fox, Warner Oland, Diana Deer, Ann Hastings, Harry Semels, Frank Redman

RELEASE DATE: 25 Sept. 1921

RELEASING COMPANY: Pathé

CHAPTER TITLES:

1. The Secret Cipher
2. The Cycle Bullet
3. The Millionth Chance
4. Smashing Through
5. One Against Many
6. At The Risk of His Neck

7. On A Dangerous Coast
8. Double Crossed
9. Overboard
10. The Show Down
11. Hare and Hounds

12. Red Courage
13. Neck and Neck
14. The Secret of the Flame
15. The Last Duel

⑤ Miracles of The Jungle

DIRECTORS: E. A. Martin, James Conway

CAST: Ben Hagerty, Wilbur Higby, Irene Wallace, Genevieve Burte, Al Ferguson, Frederic Peters, John George

RELEASE DATE: 16 July 1921 (SR)

RELEASING COMPANY: Warner Brothers

CHAPTER TITLES:

1. The City of Lions (3 reels)
2. The Passage of Death
3. The Jungle Attack
4. The Leopard's Revenge
5. The Storm in the Desert
6. To The Rescue
7. The Leopard's Lair
8. Doomed to Death

9. In The Hands of The Apes
10. Midst Raging Tigers
11. Twelve Against One
12. Cheating Death
13. The Heart of An Elephant
14. The Lion's Leap
15. All's Well That Ends Well

⑤ The Mysterious Pearl

DIRECTOR: Ben Wilson

CAST: Ben Wilson, Neva Gerber

RELEASE DATE: Dec. 1921 (SR)

RELEASING COMPANY: Photoplay Serials Company

CHAPTER TITLES:

1. The Pearl Web
2. The Brass Spectre
3. The Hand in the Fog
4. Four Black Pennies
5. Through the Door

6. The Bride of Hate
7. The Getaway
8. Broken Fetters
9. Leering Faces
10. The Graven Image

11. The Phantom Husband
12. The Door Between
13. The Living Death
14. The Sting of The Lash
15. The Pearl

The Purple Riders

DIRECTOR: William Bertram

CAST: Joe Ryan, Elinor Field, Joseph Rixon, William Shields, Vincente Howard, Maude Emory

RELEASE DATE: Feb. 1921 RELEASING COMPANY: Vitagraph

CHAPTER TITLES:

1. Love or Duty
2. The Pool's Prey
3. The Decoy
4. The Fiery Trail
5. The Fatal Pursuit
6. Double Destruction
7. Red Feather's Secret
8. The Camouflage Trap
9. The Betrayal
10. The Fire Curtain
11. The Stolen Millions
12. The Infernal Machine
13. A Devil Fish Foe
14. The Frame-Up
15. Buried Alive

The Secret Four

DIRECTORS: Albert Russell, Perry Vekroff

CAST: Eddie Polo, Kathleen Myers, Doris Dean, Hal Wilson

RELEASE DATE: 19 Dec. 1921 RELEASING COMPANY: Universal

CHAPTER TITLES:

1. Behind The Mask
2. The House of Intrigue
3. Across The Chasm
4. The Dive of Despair
5. Black Waters
6. The Highway of Fate
7. The Creeping Doom
8. The Flaming Forest
9. The Fight in The Dark
10. The Burning Pit
11. The Stampede of Death
12. Floods of Fury
13. The Man Trap
14. The Hour of 12
15. Black Gold

The Sky Ranger

DIRECTOR: George B. Seitz

CAST: June Caprice, George B. Seitz, Harry Semels, Peggy Shanor, Frank Redman, Joe Cuny

RELEASE DATE: 1 May 1921 RELEASING COMPANY: Pathé

CHAPTER TITLES:

1. Out of the Clouds
2. The Sinister Signal
3. In Hostile Hands
4. Desert Law
5. Mid-Air
6. The Crystal Prism
7. Danger's Doorway
8. Dropped From the Clouds
9. The House on the Roof
10. Trapped
11. The Seething Pool
12. The Whirling Menace
13. At the Last Minute
14. Liquid Fire
15. The Last Raid

Terror Trail

DIRECTOR: Ed Kull

CAST: Eileen Sedgwick, George Larkin, Albert J. Smith, Barney Furey

RELEASE DATE: July 1921 RELEASING COMPANY: Universal

CHAPTER TITLES:

1. The Mystery Girl
2. False Clues
3. The Mine of Menace
4. The Door of Doom
5. The Bridge of Disaster
6. The Ship of Surprise
7. The Palace of Fear
8. The Peril of the Palace
9. The Desert of Despair
10. Sands of Fate
11. The Menace of the Sea
12. The Isle of Eternity
13. The Forest of Fear
14. The Lure of the Jungle
15. The Jaws of Death
16. The Storm of Despair
17. The Arm of the Law
18. The Final Reckoning

The White Horseman

DIRECTOR: Albert Russell

CAST: Art Acord, Eva Forrestor, Beatrice Dominguez

RELEASE DATE: 30 March 1921   RELEASING COMPANY: Universal

CHAPTER TITLES:

1. Cave of Despair (3 reels)
2. The Spider's Web
3. The Mummy Man
4. The Death Trap
5. Trails of Treachery
6. Furnace of Fear
7. Brink of Eternity
8. Pit of Evil
9. The Opal Bracelet
10. In The Enemy's Hands
11. A Race With Death
12. The Bridge of Fear
13. The Hill of Horror
14. A Jest of Fate
15. A Conquest of Courage
16. Fires of Fury
17. The Wings of Destiny
18. The Avenging Conscience

Winners of The West

DIRECTOR: Ed Laemmle

CAST: Art Acord, Burton C. Law, Percy Pembroke, Jim Corey, Burt Wilson, Myrtle Lind

RELEASE DATE: 26 Sept. 1921   RELEASING COMPANY: Universal

CHAPTER TITLES:

1. Power of Gold
2. Blazing Arrow
3. Perils of the Plains
4. The Flame of Hate
5. The Fight For A Fortune
6. Buried Alive
7. Fires of Fury
8. Pit of Doom
9. Chasm of Peril
10. Sands of Fear
11. Poisoned Pool
12. Duel in the Night
13. Web of Fate
14. Trail of Mystery
15. Unmasked
16. Hidden Gold
17. Cave of Terror
18. The End of the Trail

The Yellow Arm

DIRECTOR: Bertram Millhauser

CAST: Juanita Hansen, Marguerite Courtot, Warner Oland, William N. Bailey, Tom Keith, Stephan Carr

CONTINUED NEXT WEEK

RELEASE DATE: 19 June 1921 RELEASING COMPANY: Pathé

CHAPTER TITLES:

1. House of Alarms
2. Vengeance of the East
3. A Strange Disappearance
4. At Bay
5. Danger Ahead
6. A Nest of Knaves
7. Into The Dead of Night
8. Smuggled Aboard
9. Kingdom of Deceit
10. The Water Peril
11. Pawns of Power
12. Price of A Throne
13. Behind The Curtain
14. The False Goddess
15. The Miracle

1922

[S] *The Adventures of Robinson Crusoe*

DIRECTOR: Robert F. Hill

CAST: Harry Myers, Noble Johnson, Gertrude Olmstead, Percy Pembroke, Aaron Edwards, Joseph Swickard, Gertrude Claire, Emmet King

RELEASE DATE: 29 March 1922 RELEASING COMPANY: Universal

CHAPTER TITLES:

1. The Sea Raiders
2. Shipwrecked
3. The Cannibals' Captives
4. Hidden Gold
5. Ship of Despair
6. Friday's Faith
7. Swamp of Terror
8. Marooned
9. The Jaguar Trap
10. A Prisoner of The Sun
11. No Greater Love
12. Island of Happiness
13. Sword of Courage
14. The Buccaneers
15. Jolly Roger
16. The Idol's Bride
17. When the Heart Calls
18. Back To The Primitive

[S] *Captain Kidd*

DIRECTOR: J. P. McGowan

CAST: Eddie Polo, Katherine Myers, Leslie J. Casey, Sam Polo, Malveen Polo

RELEASE DATE: June 1922
(SR)

RELEASING COMPANY: Star Serial
Corporation

CHAPTER TITLES:

1. Shanghaied (3 reels)
2. The Pirate's Slave
3. Hidden Treasure
4. The Lost Fortune
5. The Missing Plans
6. Trapped
7–9. Unknown

10. Double Crossed
11. Unknown
12. A Fight For Fortune
13. Unknown
14. A Fight In Mid-Air
15. Victory And Happiness

A Dangerous Adventure

DIRECTORS: Sam and Jack Warner

CAST: Grace Darmond, Philo McCullough, Jack Richardson, Robert Agnew, Derelys Perdue, Mabel Stark, Captain J. R. Riccarde

RELEASE DATE: 25 Feb. 1922
(SR)

RELEASING COMPANY: Warner
Brothers (Re-released as 7-reel
feature in fall of 1922)

CHAPTER TITLES:

1. The Jungle Storm or The
   Stolen Medal (3 reels)
2. The Sacrifice
3. The Lion Pit
4. Brandon's Revenge
5. At The Leopard's Mercy
6. The Traitor
7. The Volcano

8. The Escape
9. The Leopard's Cave
10. The Jungle Water Hole
11. The Hippopotamus Swamp
12. The Lion's Prey
13. In The Tiger's Lair
14. The Treasure Cave
15. The Rescue

Go Get 'Em Hutch

DIRECTOR: George B. Seitz

CAST: Charles Hutchison, Marguerite Clayton, Richard R. Neil, Frank Hagney, Pearl Shepard, Joe Cuny, Cecile Bonnel

CONTINUED NEXT WEEK

RELEASE DATE: 9 April 1922 RELEASING COMPANY: Pathé

CHAPTER TITLES:

1. Chained To The Anchor (3 reels)
2. The Falling Wall
3. The Runaway Car
4. The Crushing Menace
5. Shot Into Space
6. Under the Avalanche
7. On Danger's Highway
8. The Broken Life Line
9. Under The Cauldron
10. The Edge of The Roof
11. The Air-Line Route
12. Between The Rails
13. Under The Ice
14. In The Doorway of Death
15. Ten Minutes to Live

[S] *In The Days of Buffalo Bill*

DIRECTOR: Ed Laemmle

CAST: Art Acord, Dorothy Woods, Duke R. Lee

RELEASE DATE: 11 Sept. 1922 RELEASING COMPANY: Universal

CHAPTER TITLES:

1. Bonds of Steel
2. In The Enemies' Hands
3. The Spy
4. The Sword of Grant and Lee
5. The Man of The Ages
6. Prisoners of the Sioux
7. Shackles of Fate
8. The Last Shot
9. From Tailor to President
10. Empire Builders
11. Perils of the Plains
12. The Hand of Justice
13. Trails of Peril
14. The Scarlet Doom
15. Men of Steel
16. The Brink of Eternity
17. A Race to The Finish
18. Driving the Golden Spike

[S] *The Jungle Goddess*

DIRECTOR: James Conway

CAST: Elinor Field, Truman Van Dyke, Vonda Phelps, Marie Pavis, Olin Francis, William Platt, H. G. Wells, George Reed

RELEASE DATE: 15 May 1922 (SR) RELEASING COMPANY: Export-Import Film Company (Re-released in fall of 1929)

CHAPTER TITLES:

1. Sacrificed to The Lions (3 reels)
2. The City of Blind Waters
3. Saved By The Great Ape
4. The Hell Ship
5. Wild Beasts in Command
6. Sky High With A Leopard
7. The Rajah's Revenge
8. The Alligator's Victim
9. At Grips With Death
10. The Leopard Woman
11. Soul of Buddha
12. Jaws of Death
13. Cave of Beasts
14. Jungle Terrors
15. The Mad Lion

Nan of The North

DIRECTOR: Duke Worne

CAST: Ann Little, Leonard Clapham, Joseph W. Girard, Hal Wilson, Howard Crampton, J. Morris Foster, Edith Stayart

RELEASE DATE: March 1922 RELEASING COMPANY: Arrow (SR)

CHAPTER TITLES:

1. Missil From Mars
2. Fountain of Fury
3. Brink of Despair
4. In Cruel Clutches
5. On Terror's Trail
6. The Cards of Chance
7. Into The Depths
8. Burning Sands
9. Power of Titano
10. A Bolt From The Sky
11. The Ride For A Life
12. Adrift
13. Facing Death At Sea
14. The Volcano
15. Consequences

Perils of The Yukon

DIRECTORS: Perry Vekroff, Jay Marchant, J. P. McGowan

CAST: William Desmond, Laura La Plante, Ruth Royce, Clarke Comstock, Joseph W. Girard, Fred R. Stanton, Joe McDermott, George A. Williams, Mack Wright, Princess Neela, Chief Harris

RELEASE DATE: 24 July 1922 RELEASING COMPANY: Universal

CHAPTER TITLES:

1. Fangs of Jealousy
2. Doomed
3. Tricked by Fate
4. Master and Man
5. Terrors of the North
6. Menace of Death
7. Trapped by Fire
8. Hurled Into Space
9. The Gold Rush
10. Valley of Death
11. A Race For Life
12. The Path of Doom
13. Martial Law
14. Trail of Vengeance
15. The Final Reckoning

The Radio King

DIRECTOR: Robert F. Hill

CAST: Roy Stewart, Louise Lorraine, Al Smith, Sidney Bracey, Clark Comstock, Ernest Butterworth, Jr.

RELEASE DATE: 30 Oct. 1922 RELEASING COMPANY: Universal

CHAPTER TITLES:

1. A Cry For Help
2. The Secret of The Air
3. A Battle of Wits
4. Warned by Radio
5. Ship of Doom
6. S. O. S.
7. Saved by Wireless
8. The Master Wave
9. The Trail of Vengeance
10. Saved by Science

Speed

DIRECTOR: George B. Seitz

CAST: Charles Hutchison, Lucy Fox, John Webb Dillon, Harry Semels, Cecile Bonnel, Winifred Verina, Joe Cuny, Tom Goodwin, Charles Raveda

RELEASE DATE: 22 Oct. 1922 RELEASING COMPANY: Pathé

CHAPTER TITLES:

1. The Getaway
2. Nerve
3. Pious Pedro
4. The Quagmire
5. Fighting Mad
6. Panic
7. Jaws of Danger
8. Caught

9. Hit or Miss	13. Risky Business
10. Buried Alive	14. The Peril Rider
11. Into The Crusher	15. Found Guilty
12. Trimmed	

⑮ The Timber Queen

DIRECTOR: Fred Jackman

CAST: Ruth Roland, Bruce Gordon, Val Paul, Leo Willis, Frank Lackteen, Bull Montana, Al Ferguson, Otto Freez, Chris Linton

RELEASE DATE: 16 July 1922   RELEASING COMPANY: Pathé

CHAPTER TITLES:

1. The Log Jam (3 reels)	9. Horned Fury
2. The Flaming Forest	10. Human Vultures
3. Guilty As Charged	11. The Runaway Engine
4. Go Get Your Man	12. The Abyss
5. The Yukon Trail	13. The Stolen Wedding
6. The Hidden Pearl	14. One Day To Go
7. Mutiny	15. The Silver Lining
8. The Smuggler's Cave	

⑮ White Eagle

DIRECTORS: W. S. Van Dyke, Fred Jackman

CAST: Ruth Roland, Earl Metcalfe, Otto Lederer, Harry Girard, Frank Lackteen, Virginia Ainsworth, Bud Osborne

RELEASE DATE: 1 Jan. 1922   RELEASING COMPANY: Pathé

CHAPTER TITLES:

1. The Sign of The Trident	7. The Mysterious Voyage
2. The Red Men's Menace	8. The Island of Terror
3. A Strange Message	9. The Flaming Arrow
4. The Lost Trail	10. The Cave of Peril
5. The Clash of the Clans	11. Danger Rails
6. The Trap	12. Win or Lose

13. Clash of the Clans
14. The Pivoted Rock

15. The Golden Pool

(S) With Stanley In Africa

DIRECTORS: William Craft, Ed Kull

CAST: George Walsh, Louise Lorraine, Charles Mason, William Welsh, Gordon Sackville

RELEASE DATE: 23 Jan. 1922   RELEASING COMPANY: Universal

CHAPTER TITLES:

1. Jaws of the Jungle
2. The Grip of the Slavers
3. Paths of Peril
4. Find Livingstone
5. The Flaming Spear
6. Lost in the Jungle
7. Trail of the Serpent
8. Pool of Death
9. Menace of the Jungle

10. The Ordeal
11. The Lion's Prey
12. The Forest of Flame
13. Buried Alive
14. The Lair of Death
15. The Good Samaritan
16. The Slave's Secret
17. The White Tribe
18. Out of The Dark

1923

(S) Around The World in 18 Days

DIRECTORS: Reeves Eason, Robert F. Hill

CAST: William Desmond, Laura La Plante, Spottiswoode Aiken, William P. DeVaul, Wade Boteler, William Welsh

RELEASE DATE: 1 Jan. 1923   RELEASING COMPANY: Universal

CHAPTER TITLES:

1. The Wager
2. Wanted By The Police
3. Apaches of Paris
4. The Man Who Broke The Bank at Monte Carlo
5. Sands of Doom
6. The Living Sacrifice

7. The Dragon's Claws
8. A Nation's Peril
9. Trapped in The Clouds
10. The Brink of Eternity
11. The Path of Peril
12. The Last Race

232

Beasts of Paradise

DIRECTOR: William Craft

CAST: William Desmond, Eileen Sedgwick, William N. Gould, Ruth Royce, Margaret Morris, Jim Welsh, Clarke Comstock, Joe Bonomo, Slim Cole

RELEASE DATE: 1 Oct. 1923 RELEASING COMPANY: Universal

CHAPTER TITLES:

1. The Mystery Ships
2. The Unseen Peril
3. The Typhoon
4. The Sea Raider
5. The Tidewater Trap
6. The Alligator Attacks
7. The Deluge
8. The Mutiny
9. Ship Aflame
10. The Mad Elephant Charge
11. Smothered in the Sand
12. Millions in Gold
13. Into The Bloodhound's Jaws
14. Into The Whirlpool
15. The Trail's End

The Eagle's Talons

DIRECTOR: Duke Worne

CAST: Fred Thomson, Ann Little, Al Wilson, Joe Bonomo

RELEASE DATE: 30 April 1923 RELEASING COMPANY: Universal

CHAPTER TITLES:

1. House of Mystery
2. Edge of Eternity
3. Hulk of Horror
4. Daring Hearts
5. A Deal in Diplomacy
6. The Flood of Fury
7. The Road to Doom
8. Against Odds
9. A Fighting Chance
10. Into the Chasm
11. The Betrayal
12. The Sacrifice
13. Dodging the Conspirators
14. The Inferno
15. The Eagle Foiled

The Fighting Skipper

DIRECTOR: Francis Ford

CAST: Peggy O'Day, Jack Perrin, Bill White

RELEASE DATE: 1 March 1923   RELEASING COMPANY: Arrow (SR)

CHAPTER TITLES:

1. Pirates of Pedro
2. Harbor of Hate
3. Pirates' Playground
4. In the Fog
5. Isle of Intrigue
6. Trapped
7. Silent Valley
8. House of Mystery

9. Snowbound
10. The Mystery Car
11. Across the Border
12. Secret of Buoy #3
13. Human Plunder
14. Lost Island
15. Love and Law

Ghost City

DIRECTOR: Jay Marchant

CAST: Pete Morrison, Margaret Morris, Al Wilson

RELEASE DATE: 3 Dec. 1923   RELEASING COMPANY: Universal

CHAPTER TITLES:

1. The Thundering Herd
2. The Bulldogger
3. The Maelstrom
4. The Water Trap
5. Foiling the Rustler
6. Death's Spectre
7. Stolen Gold
8. Midnight Intruder

9. Talons of the Night
10. The Frame-up
11. Ambushed
12. The Betrayal
13. Man to Man
14. Flames of Vengeance
15. Face to Face

Haunted Valley

DIRECTOR: George Marshall

CAST: Ruth Roland, Jack Daugherty, Larry Steers, Eulalie Jenson, Francis Ford, William Ryno, Edouard Trebeal

RELEASE DATE: 6 May 1923   RELEASING COMPANY: Pathé

CHAPTER TITLES:

1. Bound to the Enemy
   (3 reels)
2. Adventure in the Valley
3. Imperiled at Sea
4. Into the Earthquake Abyss
5. Fight at Lost River Dam
6. Brink of Eternity
7. Midnight Raid
8. Radio Trap
9. Ordeal of Fire
10. The 100th Day
11. Called to Account
12. Double Peril
13. To Hazardous Heights
14. In Desperate Flight
15. Disputed Treasure

Her Dangerous Path

DIRECTOR: Roy Clements

CAST: Edna Murphy

RELEASE DATE: 12 Aug. 1923   RELEASING COMPANY: Pathé

CHAPTER TITLES:

1. What the Sands Told (3 reels)
2. Fetters of Gold
3. At The Brink
4. Should She Become A
   Politician's Wife?
5. Should She Marry An Artist?
6. Should She Marry A Rancher?
7. Should She Become A Society
   Reporter?
8. Should She Marry A Scientist?
9. Should She Become Assistant
   To A Detective?
10. Unknown

In The Days of Daniel Boone

DIRECTOR: William Craft

CAST: Jack Mower, Eileen Sedgwick, Duke R. Lee, Charles Brinley, Albert J. Smith, Ruth Royce

RELEASE DATE: 25 June 1923   RELEASING COMPANY: Universal

CHAPTER TITLES:

1. His Country's Need
   (3 reels)
2. At Sword's Point
3. Liberty or Death
4. Foiling the Regulators
5. Perilous Paths
6. Trapped
7. In The Hands of The Enemy

CONTINUED NEXT WEEK

8. Over the Cliff
9. The Flaming Forest
10. Running the Gauntlet
11. The Wilderness Trail
12. The Fort In The Forest
13. The Boiling Springs
14. Chief Blackfish Attacks
15. Boone's Triumph

The Oregon Trail

DIRECTOR: Ed Laemmle

CAST: Art Acord, Louise Lorraine, Duke R. Lee, Jim Corey, Burton C. Law, Sidney DeGray

RELEASE DATE: 12 March 1923 RELEASING COMPANY: Universal

CHAPTER TITLES:

1. Westward Ho! (3 reels)
2. White Treachery
3. Across The Continent
4. Message of Death
5. Wagon of Doom
6. Secret Foes
7. A Man of God
8. Seeds of Civilization
9. Justice
10. The New Era
11. A Game of Nations
12. To Save An Empire
13. Trail of Death
14. On To Washington
15. Santa Fé
16. Fate of A Nation
17. For High Stakes
18. Victory

The Phantom Fortune

DIRECTOR: Robert F. Hill

CAST: William Desmond, Esther Ralston

RELEASE DATE: 19 March 1923 RELEASING COMPANY: Universal

CHAPTER TITLES:

1. It Can Be Done!
2. Never Say Die
3. Work & Win
4. Opportunity
5. Against Big Odds
6. Dangerous Waters
7. The Plunge of Doom
8. Diamond Cut Diamond
9. The Last Hope
10. A Million At Stake
11. The Speed King
12. Success

Plunder

DIRECTOR: George B. Seitz

CAST: Pearl White, Harry Semels, Warren Krech

RELEASE DATE: 28 Jan. 1923 RELEASING COMPANY: Pathé

CHAPTER TITLES:

1. The Bandaged Man
2. Held By The Enemy
3. The Hidden Thing
4. Ruin
5. To Beat A Knave
6. Heights of Hazard
7. Mocked From The Grave
8. The Human Target
9. Game Clear Through
10. Against Time
11. Spunk
12. Under The Floor
13. Swamp of Lost Souls
14. The Madman
15. A King's Ransom

Ruth of The Range

DIRECTOR: Ernest C. Warde

CAST: Ruth Roland, Bruce Gordon, Lorimer Johnston, Ernest C. Warde, Pat Harmon, Andre Peyre, Harry De Vere, V. Omar Whitehead

RELEASE DATE: 14 Oct. 1923 RELEASING COMPANY: Pathé

CHAPTER TITLES:

1. The Last Shot (3 reels)
2. The Seething Pit
3. The Danger Trail
4. The Terror Trail
5. The Temple Dungeon
6. The Pitfall
7. The Fatal Count
8. The Dynamite Plot
9. The Lava Crusher
10. Circumstantial Evidence
11. The Desert of Death
12. The Vital Test
13. The Molten Menace
14. The First Freight
15. Promises Fulfilled

The Santa Fé Trail

DIRECTORS: Ashton Dearholt, Robert Dillon

CAST: Neva Gerber, Jack Perrin

RELEASE DATE: 15 July 1923 RELEASING COMPANY: Arrow (SR)

CHAPTER TITLES:

1. Mystery of The Trail
2. Kit Carson's Daring Ruse
3. Wagon of Doom
4. The Half-Breed's Treachery
5. The Gauntlet of Death
6. Ride for Life
7. Chasm of Fate
8. Pueblo of Death
9. The Red Menace
10. A Duel of Wits
11. Buried Alive
12. Cavern of Doom
13. Scorching Sands
14. Mission Bells
15. End of The Trail

The Social Buccaneer

DIRECTOR: Robert F. Hill

CAST: Jack Mulhall, Margaret Livingston, Robert Anderson, Sidney Bracy, Percy Pembroke, Fontaine LaRue, Tote Ducrow, Wade Boteler, Lucille Ricksen

RELEASE DATE: 8 Jan. 1923 RELEASING COMPANY: Universal

CHAPTER TITLES:

1. Missing Millions
2. Secret Ally
3. Tell-Tale Coin
4. Spider's Web
5. Black Shadows
6. Into the Depths
7. A Kingdom at Stake
8. Treason
9. The Coronation
10. Justice Triumphant

The Steel Trail

DIRECTOR: William Duncan

CAST: William Duncan, Edith Johnson, Harry Carter, John Cossar, Harry Woods, Mabel Randall

RELEASE DATE: 27 Aug. 1923 RELEASING COMPANY: Universal

CHAPTER TITLES:

1. Intrigue
2. Dynamite
3. Wildfire
4. Blown From The Cliff
5. Headed On
6. Crushed
7. The Gold Rush
8. Judith's Peril
9. The Dam Bursts
10. The Trap
11. The Fight On The Cliff
12. The Tottering Bridge
13. Between Two Fires
14. Burning Fumes
15. Ten Seconds To Go

1924

Ⓢ *Battling Brewster*

DIRECTOR: Dell Henderson

CAST: Franklyn Farnum, Helen Holmes, George Wendell, Robert Walker, Roland Rand, Lafe McKee, Leon Holmes, Barbed Wire Ryan, Jerome Lacassee

RELEASE DATE: 1 Dec. 1924   RELEASING COMPANY: Rayart
(SR)

CHAPTER TITLES:

1. Crashing To Eternity (3 reels)   2–15. Unknown

Ⓢ *Days of '49*

DIRECTORS: Jacques Jaccard, Ben Wilson

CAST: Neva Gerber, Edmund Cobb, Ruth Royce, Wilbur Mc-Gaugh, Yakima Canute, Charles Brinley, Clark Coffey

RELEASE DATE: 15 March 1924   RELEASING COMPANY: Arrow
(SR)   (Recut to 6-reel feature and re-
                              released in 1925 as
                              California in '49)

CHAPTER TITLES:

1. Soldiers of Fortune   2. Red Men And White

3. A Night of Terror
4. The Empire Builders
5. A Web of Lies
6. Demetroff's Vow
7. Facing Death
8. Under The Bear Flag
9. A Ride of Peril
10. Yellow Metal and Blue Blood
11. Gold Madness
12. Crimson Nights
13. Vigilantes Justice
14. For Life and Love
15. Trail's End

The Fast Express

DIRECTOR: William Duncan

CAST: William Duncan, Edith Johnson, Albert J. Smith, Harry Woods, John Cossar, Harry Carter

RELEASE DATE: 10 March 1924 RELEASING COMPANY: Universal

CHAPTER TITLES:

1. Facing The Crisis
2. Vanishing Diamonds
3. Woman of Mystery
4. Haunted House
5. Perils of The City
6. Cipher Message
7. Bandit Raiders
8. Imposter's Scheme
9. Falsely Accused
10. Path of Danger
11. The Abduction
12. The Trial Run
13. The False Summons
14. Black Treasure
15. Retribution

The Fortieth Door

DIRECTOR: George B. Seitz

CAST: Allene Ray, Bruce Gordon, Anna May Wong, Frank Lackteen, David Dunbar, Frances Mann, Lillian Gale, Bernard Siegel

RELEASE DATE: 25 May 1924 RELEASING COMPANY: Pathé (Released as 6-reel, 6,000-foot feature)

CHAPTER TITLES:

1. The Secret Portal
2. Two Lockets

3. The Wedding
4. Buried Alive
5. Desert Trails
6. The Tomb of A King
7. Claws of The Vulture
8. Held For Hostage
9. The Rack
10. The Temple of The Forty Doors

Galloping Hoofs

DIRECTOR: George B. Seitz

CAST: Allene Ray, Johnnie Walker, J. Barney Sherry, Ernest Hilliard, Armand Cortez, William Nally, George Nardelli, Albert Roccardi

RELEASE DATE: 21 Dec. 1924 RELEASING COMPANY: Pathé (Released as feature)

CHAPTER TITLES:

1. The Sealed Box
2. The Mountain Raid
3. Neck and Neck
4. The Duplicate Box
5. The Fateful Jump
6. Raging Waters
7. Out of The Depths
8. Ambushed
9. Tricked
10. Flying Colors

Into The Net

DIRECTOR: George B. Seitz

CAST: Edna Murphy, Jack Mulhall, Constance Bennett, Harry Semels, Bradley Barker, Frank Lackteen, Frances Landau, Tom Goodwin, Paul Porter

RELEASE DATE: 3 Aug. 1924 RELEASING COMPANY: Pathé

CHAPTER TITLES:

1. The Shadow of The Web
2. The Clue
3. Kidnapped
4. Hidden Talons
5. The Raid
6. The House of The Missing
7. Ambushed
8. The Escape
9. To The Rescue
10. In The Toils

☙ The Iron Man

DIRECTOR: Jay Marchant

CAST: Lucien Albertini, Joe Bonomo, Margaret Morris, Jack Daugherty, Lola Todd, Jean DeBriac

RELEASE DATE: 18 June 1924 RELEASING COMPANY: Universal

CHAPTER TITLES:

1. Into The Sewers of Paris
2. The Imposter
3. The Dynamite Truck
4. Wings Aflame
5. The False Trail
6. The Stolen Passport
7. False Faces
8. Shadowed
9. The Missing Heirloom
10. Sinister Shadows
11. The Betrayal
12. Flames of Fate
13. The Crisis
14. Hidden Dangers
15. The Confession

☙ Leatherstocking

DIRECTOR: George B. Seitz

CAST: Edna Murphy, Harold Miller, David Dunbar, Frank Lackteen, Whitehorse

RELEASE DATE: 23 March 1924 RELEASING COMPANY: Pathé

CHAPTER TITLES:

1. The Warpath
2. The Secret Trail
3. The Hawk's Eyes
4. The Paleface Law
5. Ransom
6. The Betrayal
7. Rivenoak's Revenge
8. Out of The Storm
9. The Panther
10. Mingo Torture

☙ The Riddle Rider

DIRECTOR: William Craft

CAST: William Desmond, Eileen Sedgwick, Helen Holmes, Claude Payton, William N. Gould, Ben Corbett, Hughie Mack

RELEASE DATE: 23 Nov. 1924 RELEASING COMPANY: Universal

CHAPTER TITLES:

1. The Canyon Torrent
2. Crashing Doom
3. In The Path of Death
4. Plunged Into The Depths
5. Race For A Fortune
6. Sinister Shadows
7. The Swindle
8. The Frame-up
9. False Faces
10. At The Brink of Death
11. Thundering Steeds
12. Trapped
13. The Valley of Fate
14. The Deadline
15. The Final Reckoning

℗ *Riders of The Plains*

DIRECTOR: Jacques Jaccard

CAST: Jack Perrin, Marilyn Mills, Ruth Royce, Charles Brinley, Kingsley Benedict

RELEASE DATE: 1 Oct. 1924   RELEASING COMPANY: Arrow
   (SR)

CHAPTER TITLES:

1. Red Shadows (3 reels)
2. Dangerous Hazards
3. A Living Death
4. Flames of Fury
5. Morgan's Raid
6. Out of The Past
7. A Fighting Gamble
8. A Prisoner of War
9. Pawns of Destiny
10. Riding For Life
11. In Death's Shadow
12. Flaming Vengeance
13. Thundering Hoofs
14. Red Talons
15. The Reckoning

℗ *Ten Scars Make A Man*

DIRECTOR: William Parke

CAST: Allene Ray, Jack Mower, Rose Burdick, Lillian Gale, Larry Steers, Leon Kent, Harry Woods

RELEASE DATE: 12 Oct. 1924   RELEASING COMPANY: Pathé

CHAPTER TITLES:

1. Two Girls and A Man
2. Cowboy Chivalry

3. Westward Bound
4. The Cattle Raid
5. Through The Hills
6. Midnight Marauders
7. Unmasked
8. Liquid Gold
9. The Valley of the Legend
10. The End of the Quest

Ⓢ *Way Of A Man*

DIRECTOR: George B. Seitz

CAST: Allene Ray, Harold Miller, Florence Lee, Bud Osborne, Whitehorse, Lillian Gale, Kathryn Appleton, Chet Ryan, Lillian Adrian

RELEASE DATE: 20 Jan. 1924

RELEASING COMPANY: Pathé (Released as 7-reel, 6,904-foot feature on same date)

CHAPTER TITLES:

1. Into The Unknown
2. Redskin and White
3. In The Toils of The Torrent
4. Lost in The Wilds
5. White Medicine
6. The Firing Squad
7. Gold! Gold!
8. The Fugitive
9. California
10. Trail's End

Ⓢ *Wolves of The North*

DIRECTOR: William Duncan

CAST: William Duncan, Edith Johnson, Esther Ralston, Joseph W. Girard, Frank Rice, Joe Bonomo, Clarke Comstock, Edward Cecil, Harry Woods

RELEASE DATE: 21 Sept. 1924

RELEASING COMPANY: Universal

CHAPTER TITLES:

1. The Fur Pirates
2. The Wolf Pack
3. The Avalanche
4. Passions of War
5. The Blizzard
6. Flames of Peril
7. The Man Hunt
8. The Trail of Gold
9. A Trick of Fate
10. The Stolen Map

1925

Ace of Spades

DIRECTOR: Henry McRae

CAST: William Desmond, Mary McAllister, Jack Pratt, Albert J. Smith

RELEASE DATE: 19 Oct. 1925 RELEASING COMPANY: Universal

CHAPTER TITLES:

1. The Fatal Card
2. No Greater Love
3. Whirling Waters
4. Fires of Sacrifice
5. Thundering Hoofs
6. Flung From The Sky
7. Trail of Terror
8. Lariat of Death
9. Fingers of Fate
10. Road to Ruin
11. Chasm of Peril
12. The Avalanche
13. The Fury of Fate
14. The Chasm of Courage
15. A Deal of Destiny

Fighting Ranger

DIRECTOR: Jay Marchant

CAST: Jack Daugherty, Eileen Sedgwick, Al Wilson, William Welsh, Bud Osborne, Charles Avery, Frank Lanning, Sam Polo, Slim Cole, Gladys Roy

RELEASE DATE: 11 May 1925 RELEASING COMPANY: Universal

CHAPTER TITLES:

1. The Intruder
2. The Frame-up
3. The Secret Trail
4. Falsely Accused
5. The Betrayal
6. The Lost Fortune
7. Cattle Wolves
8. Under Fire
9. Man to Man
10. The Fatal Message
11. Hidden Fangs
12. False Friends
13. Stolen Secrets
14. Steeds of the Sky
15. Yaqui Gold
16. Left For Dead

17–18. Unknown

The Flame Fighter

DIRECTOR: Robert Dillon

CAST: Herbert Rawlinson, Brenda Lane, Jerome Legasse, Edward Fetherston, Purnell Pratt, Leigh Willard, Richard Gordon

RELEASE DATE: 10 Sept. 1925 (SR) RELEASING COMPANY: Rayart (Beacon Films)

CHAPTER TITLES:

1–2. Unknown
3. The Silent Alarm
4–10. Unknown

The Great Circus Mystery

DIRECTOR: Jay Marchant

CAST: Joe Bonomo, Louise Lorraine

RELEASE DATE: 9 March 1925 RELEASING COMPANY: Universal

CHAPTER TITLES:

1. Pact of Peril
2. A Cry For Help
3. A Race With Death
4. The Plunge of Peril
5. The Ladder of Life
6. A Leap For Liberty
7. Harvest of Hate
8. Fires of Fate
9. Cycle of Fear
10. The Leopard Strikes
11. The Sacred Ruby
12. Dive of Destiny
13. The Leap For Liberty
14. Buried Treasure
15. The Leopard Strikes

The Green Archer

DIRECTOR: Spencer G. Bennet

CAST: Allene Ray, Walter Miller, Burr McIntosh, Stephen Gratten, Frank Lackteen, Walter P. Lewis, Jack Tanner, Ray Allan, William Randall, Dorothy King, Wally Oettel

RELEASE DATE: 6 Dec. 1925 RELEASING COMPANY: Pathé

CHAPTER TITLES:

1. The Ghost of Bellamy Castle
2. The Midnight Warning
3. In The Enemy's Stronghold
4. On The Storm King Road
5. The Affair at The River
6. The Mystery Ship
7. Bellamy Baits A Trap
8. The Cottage in the Woods
9. The Battle Starts
10. The Smoke Clears Away

Idaho

DIRECTOR: Robert F. Hill

CAST: Vivian Rich, Mahlon Hamilton, Frank Lackteen, W. T. Quinn, Roy E. Bassett, Fred De Silva, Omar Whitehead, N. McDowell, William Dale, Lillian Gale, Gus Saville, George Burton, Charles Brinley, Robert Irwin

RELEASE DATE: 1 March 1925   RELEASING COMPANY: Pathé

CHAPTER TITLES:

1. Road Agents
2. Hands Up
3. The Stampede
4. Forbidden Testimony
5. Lawless Laws
6. Aroused
7. The Trap
8. The White Streak
9. Unmasked
10. Vigilantes

The Mystery Box

DIRECTOR: Alvin J. Neitz

CAST: Ben Wilson, Neva Gerber, Lafe McKee, Robert Walker, Charles Brinley, Alfred Hollingsworth, Jack Henderson

RELEASE DATE: 1 June 1925 (SR)   RELEASING COMPANY: Vital Exchanges, Incorporated (Davis Distributing Division)

CHAPTER TITLES:

1. The Fatal Box (3 reels)
2. A Tragic Legacy
3. Daring Danger
4. A Leap For Life
5. Defying Fate
6. Trapped by Outlaws
7. Pendulum of Death
8. The Miracle Rider
9. Vengeance of the Mystery Box
10. Vindicated

Perils of The Wild

DIRECTOR: Francis Ford

CAST: Joe Bonomo, Margaret Quimby, Jack Mower

RELEASE DATE: 1 Aug. 1925 RELEASING COMPANY: Universal

CHAPTER TITLES:

1. The Hurricane
2. The Lion's Fangs
3. The Flaming Jungle
4. The Treasure Cave
5. Saved by the Sun
6. The Jungle Trail
7. Pirate Peril
8. Winds of Fate
9. Rock of Revenge
10. The Rescue
11. The Stolen Wedding
12. Marooned
13. Prisoners of the Sea
14. The Leopard's Lair
15. In the Nick of Time

Play Ball

DIRECTOR: Spencer G. Bennet

CAST: Allene Ray, Walter Miller, J. Barney Sherry, Harry Semels, Mary Milnor, Wally Oettel

RELEASE DATE: 19 July 1925 RELEASING COMPANY: Pathé

CHAPTER TITLES:

1. To The Rescue
2. The Flaming Float
3. Betrayed
4. The Decoy Wire
5. Face to Face
6. The Showdown
7. A Mission of Hate
8. Double Peril
9. Into Segundo's Hands
10. A Home Plate Wedding

The Power God

DIRECTOR: Ben Wilson

CAST: Ben Wilson, Neva Gerber, Mary Brooklyn, Mary Crane, John Battaglia

RELEASING DATE: 1 May 1925   RELEASING COMPANY: Vital
  (SR)   Exchanges, Incorporated
                                             (Davis Distributing Division)

CHAPTER TITLES:

1. The Ring of Fate (3 reels)
2. Trapped
3. The Living Dead
4. Black Shadows
5. The Death Chamber
6. House of Peril
7. Hands of The Dark
8. 59th Second
9. Perilous Waters
10. The Bridge of Doom
11. Treachery
12. The Storm's Lash
13. The Purloined Papers
14. The Flaming Menace
15. The Wages of Sin

Secret Service Saunders

DIRECTOR: Duke Worne

CAST: Richard Holt, Ann Little

RELEASE DATE: 1 May 1925   RELEASING COMPANY: Rayart
  (SR)

CHAPTER TITLES: 15 episodes

Sunken Silver

DIRECTOR: George B. Seitz

CAST: Allene Ray, Walter Miller, Frank Lackteen, Ivan Linow,
  Charlie Fang

RELEASE DATE: 10 May 1925   RELEASING COMPANY: Pathé

CHAPTER TITLES:

1. Watched
2. On Secret Service
3. The Hidden Way
4. Fangs
5. Sea Tigers
6. In Double Peril
7. Face to Face
8. The Shadow on the Stairs
9. The Secret Panel
10. The End of the Trail

⑤ *Wild West*

DIRECTOR: Robert F. Hill

CAST: Jack Mulhall, Helen Ferguson, Eddie Phillips, George Burton, Milla Davenport, Virginia Warwick, Gus Saville

RELEASE DATE: 27 Sept. 1925   RELEASING COMPANY: Pathé

CHAPTER TITLES:

1. The Land Rush (3 reels)
2. On the Show
3. The Outlaw Elephant
4. Ride 'Em Cowboy!
5. The Rustler's Stampede

6. The Diamond Girl
7. The Champion Cowboy
8. Under the Buffalo
9. Stolen Evidence
10. The Law Decides

1926

⑤ *The Bar-C Mystery*

DIRECTOR: Robert F. Hill

CAST: Dorothy Phillips, Wallace MacDonald, Ethel Clayton, Philo McCullough, Violet Schram, Johnny Fox, Victor Potel, Billie Bletcher, Fred de Silva

RELEASE DATE: 25 April 1926   RELEASING COMPANY: Pathé
(Released as 5-reel, 4,756-foot feature on 14 March 1926)

CHAPTER TITLES:

1. A Heritage of Danger
2. Perilous Paths
3. The Midnight Raid
4. Wheels of Doom
5. Thundering Hoofs

6. Against Desperate Odds
7. Back From The Missing
8. Fight For A Fortune
9. The Wolf's Cunning
10. A Six-Gun Wedding

⑤ *Casey of The Coast Guard*

DIRECTOR: Will Nigh

CAST: Helen Ferguson, George O'Hara, John Jarvis, J. Barney Sherry, Coit Albertson

RELEASE DATE: 14 Feb. 1926   RELEASING COMPANY: Pathé

CHAPTER TITLES:

1. The Smugglers' Ruse
2. Shots in The Dark
3. Watchful Waiting
4. Under Suspicion
5. The Gas Chamber
6. Shot From The Depths
7. Contraband Channels
8. Smuggled Aliens
9. Meshes of The Law
10. Caught in The Net

The Fighting Marine

DIRECTOR: Spencer G. Bennet

CAST: Gene Tunney, Walter Miller, Marjorie Gay, Virginia Vance, Frank Hagney, Sherman Ross, Mike Donlin, Wally Oettel, Jack Anthony, Anna May Walthall

RELEASE DATE: 12 Sept. 1926   RELEASING COMPANY: Pathé
(Released as 7-reel, 6,997-foot feature on 24 Sept. 1926)

CHAPTER TITLES:

1. The Successful Candidate
2. The Second Attack
3. In The Enemy's Trap
4. The Desperate Foe
5. Entombed
6. The Falling Tower
7. Waylaid
8. Challenged
9. The Signal Shot
10. Fired and Hired

Fighting With Buffalo Bill

DIRECTOR: Ray Taylor

CAST: Wallace MacDonald, Elsa Benham, Grace Cunard, Howard Truesdell, Robert E. Homans, Edmund Cobb, Cuyler Supplee

RELEASE DATE: 30 Aug. 1926   RELEASING COMPANY: Universal

CHAPTER TITLES:

1. Westward
2. The Red Menace

3. The Blazing Arrow
4. The Death Trap
5. The Renegade
6. The Race For Life
7. Buried Alive
8. Desperate Chances
9. The Shadow of Evil
10. At The End of The Trail

House Without A Key

DIRECTOR: Spencer G. Bennet

CAST: Allene Ray, Walter Miller, Frank Lackteen, Charles West, John Webb Dillon, Natalie Warfield, William N. Bailey

RELEASE DATE: 21 Nov. 1926 RELEASING COMPANY: Pathé

CHAPTER TITLES:

1. The Spite Fence (3 reels)
2. The Mystery Box
3. The Missing Numeral
4. Suspicion
5. The Death Buoy
6. Sinister Shadows
7. The Mystery Man
8. The Spotted Menace
9. The Wrist Watch
10. The Culprit

Lightning Hutch

DIRECTOR: Charles Hutchison

CAST: Charles Hutchison, Edith Thornton, Virginia Pearson, Sheldon Lewis, Eddie Phillips, Ben Walker, Violet Schram

RELEASE DATE: 19 April 1926 (SR) RELEASING COMPANY: Arrow (Hurricane Film Company)

CHAPTER TITLES:

1. The Conspiracy
2. Life or Liberty
3. The Deadly Discovery
4. In The Trap
5. The Impossible Escape
6. The Thousandth Chance
7. The Mysterious Island
8. The Walls of Doom
9. The Unexpected Happens
10. A Woman's Wit

Mystery Pilot

DIRECTOR: Harry Moody

CAST: Rex Lease, Kathryn McGuire

RELEASE DATE: May 1926 (SR) RELEASING COMPANY: Rayart

CHAPTER TITLES: 10 episodes

Officer 444

DIRECTOR: Ben Wilson

CAST: Ben Wilson, Neva Gerber, Jack Mower, Phil Ford

RELEASE DATE: 15 May 1926 (SR) RELEASING COMPANY: Goodwill Pictures of California (Davis Distributing Division)

CHAPTER TITLES:

1. Flying Squadron
2. Human Rats
3. Trapped
4. Gassed
5. Missing
6. The Radio Ray
7. Death's Shadow
8. Jaws of Doom
9. Underground Trap
10. Justice

Phantom Police

DIRECTOR: Robert Dillon

CAST: Herbert Rawlinson, Gloria Joy

RELEASE DATE: March 1926 (SR) RELEASING COMPANY: Rayart

CHAPTER TITLES: 10 episodes

The Radio Detective

DIRECTORS: William Crinley, William Craft

CAST: Jack Daugherty, Margaret Quimby, Jack Mower, Florence Allen, John T. Prince, Sammy Gervon, Wallace Baldwin, Howard Enstedt & the Boy Scouts

RELEASE DATE: 26 April 1926 RELEASING COMPANY: Universal

CHAPTER TITLES:

1. The Kick-Off
2. The Radio Riddle
3. The Radio Wizard
4. Boy Scout Loyalty
5. The Radio Secret
6. Fighting For Love
7. The Tenderfoot Scout
8. The Truth Teller
9. The Fire Fiend
10. Radio Romance

The Scarlet Streak

DIRECTOR: Henry McRae

CAST: Jack Daugherty, Lola Todd, Virginia Ainsworth, Albert J. Smith, Al Prisco

RELEASE DATE: Jan. 1926   RELEASING COMPANY: Universal

CHAPTER TITLES:

1. The Face In The Crowd
2. Masks & Men
3. The Rope of Hazard
4. The Death Ray
5. The Lost Story
6. The Plunge of Peril
7. The Race of Terror
8. The Cable of Courage
9. The Dive of Death
10. Universal Peace

Scotty of The Scouts

DIRECTOR: Duke Worne

CAST: Ben Alexander, "Happy" Paddy O'Flynn

RELEASE DATE: Sept. 1926   RELEASING COMPANY: Rayart (SR)

CHAPTER TITLES: 10 episodes

The Silent Flyer

DIRECTOR: William Craft

CAST: Silver Streak (dog), Malcolm MacGregor, Louise Lorraine, Thur Fairfax, Hughie Mack, Anders Rudolph, Edith Yorke

RELEASE DATE: 8 Nov. 1926   RELEASING COMPANY: Universal

CHAPTER TITLES:

1. The Jaws of Death
2. Dynamited
3. Waters of Death
4. The Treacherous Trail
5. Plunge of Peril

6. Fight of Honor
7. Under Arrest
8. Flames of Terror
9. Hurled Through Space
10. Love and Glory

Snowed In

DIRECTOR: Spencer G. Bennet

CAST: Allene Ray, Walter Miller, Frank Austin, Tom London, John Webb Dillon, Natalie Warfield, Wally Oettel, Harrison Martell

RELEASE DATE: 4 July 1926   RELEASING COMPANY: Pathé

CHAPTER TITLES:

1. Storm Warnings
2. The Storm Starts
3. The Coming of Redfield
4. Redfield Strikes
5. Buried

6. The Enemy's Stronghold
7. The Trap
8. Thieves' Honor
9. Daybreak
10. The End of Redfield

Strings of Steel

DIRECTOR: Henry McRae

CAST: William Desmond, Eileen Sedgwick, Albert J. Smith, George Ovey, Ted Duncan, Alphonse Martel

RELEASE DATE: 28 June 1926   RELEASING COMPANY: Universal

CHAPTER TITLES:

1. The Voice on the Wire
2. The First Central
3. Fighting For Love
4. The Power of Might
5. Kings of the Wire

6. Voice of the Continent
7. Telephone Poles
8. War of the Wire
9. When Lightning Strikes
10. Love and Victory

Trooper 77

DIRECTOR: Duke Worne

CAST: Herbert Rawlinson, Hazel Deane

RELEASE DATE: Nov. 1926 RELEASING COMPANY: Rayart (SR)

CHAPTER TITLES: 10 episodes

Vanishing Millions

DIRECTOR: Alvin J. Neitz

CAST: William Fairbanks, Vivian Rich, Alec B. Francis, Sheldon Lewis, Bull Montana, Edward Cecil

RELEASE DATE: 21 Jan. 1926 RELEASING COMPANY: Sierra (SR)

CHAPTER TITLES: 15 episodes

The Winking Idol

DIRECTOR: Francis Ford

CAST: William Desmond, Eileen Sedgwick, Grace Cunard, Herbert Sutch, Jack Richardson, Helen Broneau, Les Sailor, Art Ortego

RELEASE DATE: March 1926 RELEASING COMPANY: Universal

CHAPTER TITLES:

1. The Eye of Evil
2. Buzzards' Roost
3. Crashing Timbers
4. Racing For Love
5. The Vanishing Bride
6. The Torrent of Terror
7. Flames of Fear
8. The Fight At the Falls
9. In Danger of Dynamite
10. The Lost Lode

1927

Blake of Scotland Yard

DIRECTOR: Robert F. Hill

CAST: Hayden Stevenson, Gloria Gray, Monty Montague, Grace Cunard, Albert Hart

RELEASE DATE: 15 Aug. 1927 RELEASING COMPANY: Universal

CHAPTER TITLES:

1. The Castle of Fear
2. The Spider's Web
3. The Vanishing Heiress
4. The Room Without A Door
5. Shots In The Dark
6. Ambushed
7. The Secret of The Coin
8. Into The Web
9. The Baited Trap
10. The Lady In White
11. The Closing Web
12. The Final Reckoning

The Crimson Flash

DIRECTOR: Arch B. Heath

CAST: Cullen Landis, Eugenia Gilbert, Tom Holding, J. Barney Sherry, Walter P. Lewis, Ivan Linow, Mary Gardner, Tony Hughes, Gus De Weil, Ed Roseman

RELEASE DATE: 19 June 1927 RELEASING COMPANY: Pathé

CHAPTER TITLES:

1. A Shot In The Night
2. The Ghost Takes A Hand
3. When Thieves Fall Out
4. Decoyed
5. Held in Bondage
6. Checkmate
7. The Shadow of The Menace
8. Into The Trap
9. The Flaming Menace
10. The End of The Trail

Fighting For Fame

DIRECTOR: Duke Worne

CAST: Ben Alexander

CONTINUED NEXT WEEK

RELEASE DATE: Jan. 1927 (SR) RELEASING COMPANY: Rayart

CHAPTER TITLES: 10 episodes

The Fire Fighters

DIRECTOR: Jacques Jaccard

CAST: Jack Daugherty, Helen Ferguson, Wilbur McGaugh, Lafe McKee, Albert Hart

RELEASE DATE: 17 Jan. 1927 RELEASING COMPANY: Universal

CHAPTER TITLES:

1. For Life And Liberty
2. Paths of Peril
3. The Crimson Terror
4. Out Of The Past
5. The False Alarm
6. Fighting Fate
7. Plunge of Peril
8. Face To Face
9. Wanted For Murder
10. The Reckoning

The Golden Stallion

DIRECTOR: Harry Webb

CAST: Maurice "Lefty" Flynn, Joe Bonomo, White Fury (horse), Molly Malone, Joseph Swickard, Burr McIntosh

RELEASE DATE: 15 Jan. 1927 (SR) RELEASING COMPANY: Mascot Pictures Corporation

CHAPTER TITLES: 10 episodes

Hawk of The Hills

DIRECTOR: Spencer G. Bennet

CAST: Allene Ray, Walter Miller, Frank Lackteen, Paul Panzer, Wally Oettel, Jack Pratt, Jack Ganzhorn, Parks Jones, Fred Dana, Evangeline Russell, George Magrill, Chief White-Horse

RELEASE DATE: 28 August 1927 RELEASING COMPANY: Pathé

CHAPTER TITLES:

1. The Outlaws
2. In The Talons of The Hawk
3. Heroes In Blue
4. The Attack
5. The Danger Trail
6. The Death Menace of Lost Canyon
7. Demons of The Darkness
8. Doomed to The Arrows
9. The House of Horror
10. The Triumph of Law and Love

Heroes of The Wild

DIRECTOR: Harry Webb

CAST: Jack Hoxie, Joe Bonomo, Tornado (dog), White Fury (horse)

RELEASE DATE: 1 Nov. 1927 (SR)

RELEASING COMPANY: Mascot Pictures Corporation

CHAPTER TITLES:

1. Heroes of The Wild
2. Sword To Sword
3. The Plunge of Peril
4. The Slide of Life
5. The Trap of Death
6. The Flaming Fiend
7. The Clutching Hand
8. The Broken Cable
9. The Fatal Hour
10. The Crown of The Incas

Isle of Sunken Gold

DIRECTOR: Harry Webb

CAST: Anita Stewart, Duke Kahanamoku

RELEASE DATE: 1 Sept. 1927 (SR)

RELEASING COMPANY: Mascot Pictures Corporation

CHAPTER TITLES:

1. Isle of Sunken Gold
2. Trapped In Mid-Air
3. Engulfed by The Sea
4. The Volcano's Pit
5. The Hulk of Death
6. The Prey of Sharks
7. Fire of Revenge
8. The Battle of Canoes
9. Trapped by The Ape
10. The Devil Ape's Secret

🎞 King of The Jungle

DIRECTOR: Webster Cullison

CAST: Elmo Lincoln, Sally Long, Gordon Standing, George Kotsonaros, Arthur Morrison, Cliff Bowes, Virginia True Boardman

RELEASE DATE: July 1927 (SR) RELEASING COMPANY: Rayart

CHAPTER TITLES:

1. A Great Tragedy
2. The Elephant Avenger
3. Battling For Her Life
4. Into The Lion's Jaws
5. The Striped Terror
6. Gripped by The Death Vice
7. The Slinking Demons
8. The Giant Ape Strikes
9. No Escape
10. The Death Trap

🎞 The Mansion of Mystery

DIRECTOR: Robert J. Horner

CAST: William Barrymore, Teddy Reavis

RELEASE DATE: Nov. 1927 (SR) RELEASING COMPANY: Capitol Production Exporting Company

CHAPTER TITLES: 10 chapters

🎞 The Masked Menace

DIRECTOR: Arch B. Heath

CAST: Larry Kent, Jean Arthur, Tom Holding, Laura Alberta, John F. Hamilton, Gus De Weil, Agnes Dome

RELEASE DATE: 6 Nov. 1927 RELEASING COMPANY: Pathé

CHAPTER TITLES:

1. Against Odds
2. An Unknown Assassin
3. The Enemy Strikes
4. A Half-Wit's Fury

5. An Attack At Midnight
6. Checkmate
7. By Hook or Crook

8. Still Face Shows His Hand
9. The Last Stand
10. The Menace Unmasked

✆ *Melting Millions*

DIRECTOR: Spencer G. Bennet

CAST: Allene Ray, Walter Miller, E. H. Calvert, Frank Lackteen, William N. Bailey, John J. Richardson, Bob Burns, Ernie Adams, John Cossar, William Van Dyke, Richard C. Travers, Ann Gladman, Eugenia Gilbert, Albert Roccardi

RELEASE DATE: 10 April 1927   RELEASING COMPANY: Pathé

CHAPTER TITLES:

1. A Shot In The Dark
2. Perilous Waters
3. The Fatal Attack
4. The Heiress of Craghaven
5. The Hidden Harbor

6. A Strange Voyage
7. The Mysterious Prisoner
8. The Imposter
9. The Spy
10. Exposed

✆ *On Guard*

DIRECTOR: Arch B. Heath

CAST: Cullen Landis, Muriel Kingston, Louise Du Pre, Walter P. Lewis, Tom Blake, Hal Forde, Edward Burns, Jack Bardette, Gus De Weil, Tom Poland

RELEASE DATE: 30 Jan. 1927   RELEASING COMPANY: Pathé

CHAPTER TITLES:

1. Enemies Within
2. Deception
3. Silent Evidence
4. The Sinister Warning
5. False Orders

6. Stolen Papers
7. Hidden Watchers
8. The Counterplot
9. The Air Battle
10. Foiled

✆ *Perils of The Jungle*

DIRECTOR: Jack Nelson

CAST: Eugenia Gilbert, Frank Merrill, Bobby Nelson, Milburn Moranti, Albert J. Smith, Will Herman, Walter Maly, Harry Belmore

RELEASE DATE: July 1927 (SR)

RELEASING COMPANY: Weiss Brothers Artclass

CHAPTER TITLES:

1. Jungle Trails (3 reels)
2. The Jungle King
3. The Elephant's Revenge
4. At The Lion's Mercy
5. The Sting of Death
6. The Trail of Blood
7. The Feast of Vengeance
8. The Leopard's Trap
9. The Gorilla's Bride
10. The Tiger's Den

The Return of The Riddle Rider

DIRECTOR: Robert F. Hill

CAST: William Desmond, Lola Todd, Grace Cunard, Tom London, Henry Barrows, Scotty Mattraw, Lewis Dayton, Norbert Myles, Howard Davies

RELEASE DATE: 8 March 1927

RELEASING COMPANY: Universal

CHAPTER TITLES:

1. The Riddle Rider Rides Again
2. A Day of Terror
3. Not A Chance
4. The Hold-Up
5. The River of Flame
6. The Trap
7. The Crooked Deal
8. The Rock Slide
9. The Silencer
10. Vengeance

The Scarlet Brand

DIRECTOR: Neal Hart

CAST: Neal Hart

RELEASE DATE: 1927

RELEASING COMPANY: New-Cal Film Corporation

CHAPTER TITLES:

1. Wheels of Death
2. Thundering Hoofs

3. Waters of Doom
4. The Battle in The Clouds
5. Fatal Bullets
6. Millions At Stake
7. Desert Fury
8. Pledge of Hate
9. The Devil's Stampede
10. The End of The Trail

🌀 Trail of The Tiger

DIRECTOR: Henry McRae

CAST: Jack Daugherty, Frances Teague, Jack Mower

RELEASE DATE: 7 Nov. 1927   RELEASING COMPANY: Universal

CHAPTER TITLES:

1. The Mystic Mountebanks
2. The Trap of Terror
3. The Shaggy Monster
4. The Tiger Strikes
5. Flaming Fury
6. The Tiger's Lair
7. The Hour of Fear
8. The Flight of Terror
9. Buried Alive
10. The Reckoning

🌀 Whispering Smith Rides

DIRECTOR: Ray Taylor

CAST: Wallace MacDonald, Rose Blossom, J. P. McGowan, Clarke Comstock, Henry Herbert, W. M. McCormick

RELEASE DATE: 6 June 1927   RELEASING COMPANY: Universal

CHAPTER TITLES:

1. Lawless Men
2. Caught In The Crash
3. Trapped
4. The Ambush
5. Railroad Gold
6. The Interrupted Wedding
7. A Coward of Conscience
8. The Bandit's Bargain
9. The Trail of Sacrifice
10. A Call of The Heart

1928

🌀 The Chinatown Mystery

DIRECTOR: J. P. McGowan

CAST: Joe Bonomo, Ruth Hiatt, Francis Ford, Al Baffert

RELEASE DATE: 1 Sept. 1928 (SR)   RELEASING COMPANY: Syndicate Pictures

CHAPTER TITLES:

1. The Chinatown Mystery
2. The Clutching Claw
3. The Devil's Dice
4. The Mysterious 13
5. Galloping Fury
6. The Depth of Danger
7. The Invisible Hand
8. The Wreck
9. Broken Jade
10. The Thirteenth Hour

Eagle of The Night

DIRECTOR: Jimmie Fulton

CAST: Frank Clarke, Shirley Palmer, Joseph Swickard, Max Hawley, Earl Metcalfe, Roy Wilson, Jack Richardson, Maurice Costello

RELEASE DATE: 21 Oct. 1928   RELEASING COMPANY: Pathé

CHAPTER TITLES:

1. The Death Plunge
2. Snatched Into Space
3. Trapped in The Flames
4. Dead Wings
5. The Brink of Eternity
6. The Fangs of The Wolf
7. The Sky Hitcher
8. The March of Death
9. Headlong to Earth
10. No Man's Land

Haunted Island

DIRECTOR: Robert F. Hill

CAST: Jack Daugherty, Helen Foster, Al Ferguson, Grace Cunard, Myrtis Grinley, Carl Miller, Scotty Mattraw, John T. Prince

RELEASE DATE: 26 March 1928   RELEASING COMPANY: Universal

CHAPTER TITLES:

1. A Night of Fear
2. The Phantom Raider
3. A Trail of Terror
4. The Haunted Room

5. Buried Alive
6. A Race With Death
7. Fires of Fury
8. The Treasure Trap
9. Unmasked
10. Uncut Diamonds

⑤ *The Man Without A Face*

DIRECTOR: Spencer G. Bennet

CAST: Allene Ray, Walter Miller, E. H. Calvert, Sojin, Jeanette Loff

RELEASE DATE: 15 Jan. 1928 RELEASING COMPANY: Pathé

CHAPTER TITLES:

1. A Perilous Mission
2. The Barrage
3. The Death Shell
4. The Abduction
5. The Mark of Crime
6. The Road of Peril
7. The Master Strikes
8. The Crime Craft
9. A Mysterious Visitor
10. Unmasked

⑤ *Mark of The Frog*

DIRECTOR: Arch B. Heath

CAST: Donald Reed, Margaret Morris, George Harcourt, Gus De Weil, Frank Lackteen, Tony Hughes, Frank B. Miller, Helen Greene, Ed Roseman, Sidney Paxton, Morgan Jones, William Willis

RELEASE DATE: 25 March 1928 RELEASING COMPANY: Pathé

CHAPTER TITLES:

1. The Gas Attack
2. Decoyed
3. The Jail Delivery
4. Triple Vengeance
5. The Enemy Within
6. Cross Fire
7. Framed
8. A Life At Stake
9. A Race With Death
10. Paying The Penalty

⑤ *The Mysterious Airman*

DIRECTOR: Harry Revier

CAST: Walter Miller, Eugenia Gilbert

RELEASE DATE: 1 June 1928 (SR)   RELEASING COMPANY: Weiss Brothers Artclass

CHAPTER TITLES: 10 chapters

The Mystery Rider

DIRECTOR: Jack Nelson

CAST: William Desmond, Derelys Perdue, Sid Saylor, Walter Shumway, Tom London, Bud Osborne, Red Basset, Ben Corbett

RELEASE DATE: 25 Nov. 1928   RELEASING COMPANY: Universal

CHAPTER TITLES:

1. The Clutching Claw
2. Trapped
3. The Stampede
4. Hands Up
5. Buried Alive
6. The Fatal Shot
7. Hurled Through Space
8. Unmasked
9. Doomed
10. The End of The Trail

Pirates of The Pines

DIRECTOR: J. C. Cook

CAST: George O'Hara

RELEASE DATE: 1 Sept. 1928 (SR)   RELEASING COMPANY: Goodart

CHAPTER TITLES:

1. Death's Marathon
2. The Swirling Waters
3. The Ice Flood
4. Wages of Sin
5. Burning Barriers
6. Hands of Fate
7. Danger Ahead
8. Flaming Masts
9. Hurled Through Space
10. The Duel in Mid-Air

Police Reporter

DIRECTOR: Jack Nelson

CAST: Walter Miller, Eugenia Gilbert

RELEASE DATE: 1 March 1928 (SR) RELEASING COMPANY: Weiss Brothers Artclass

CHAPTER TITLES: 10 chapters

The Scarlet Arrow

DIRECTOR: Ray Taylor

CAST: Francis X. Bushman, Jr., Bess Flowers, Hazel Keener, Al Ferguson, Aileen Goodwin, Clarke Comstock

RELEASE DATE: 4 June 1928 RELEASING COMPANY: Universal

CHAPTER TITLES:

1. Flames of Courage
2. Thundering Death
3. Desperate Men
4. Wild Bullets
5. The Cave of Hazard
6. Plunge of Peril
7. Fires of Vengeance
8. Call of the Northland
9. Guardians of The North
10. Held By The Law

Tarzan, The Mighty

DIRECTOR: Jack Nelson

CAST: Frank Merrill, Natalie Kingston, Al Ferguson, Robert Nelson, Lorimer Johnston

RELEASE DATE: 13 August 1928 RELEASING COMPANY: Universal

CHAPTER TITLES:

1. The Terror of Tarzan
2. The Love Cry
3. The Call of The Jungle
4. The Lion's Leap
5. Flames of Hate
6. The Fiery Pit
7. The Leopard's Lair
8. The Jungle Traitor
9. Lost In The Jungle
10. Jaws of Death
11. A Thief In The Night
12. The Enemy of Tarzan
13. Perilous Paths
14. Facing Death
15. The Reckoning

𝔖 The Terrible People

DIRECTOR: Spencer G. Bennet

CAST: Allene Ray, Walter Miller, Wilfred North, Fred Vroom, Tom Holding, Larry Steers, Mary Foy, Alice McCormack, Allen Craven

RELEASE DATE: 5 August 1928   RELEASING COMPANY: Pathé

CHAPTER TITLES:

1. The Penalty
2. Disaster
3. The Claws of Death
4. Hidden Enemies
5. The Disastrous Rescue
6. The House of Peril
7. In The Enemy's Hands
8. The Dread Professor
9. The Death Trap
10. The Capture

𝔖 The Tiger's Shadow

DIRECTOR: Spencer G. Bennet

CAST: Gladys McConnell, Hugh Allan

RELEASE DATE: 23 Dec. 1928   RELEASING COMPANY: Pathé

CHAPTER TITLES:

1. The Storm Breaks
2. The Tiger's Mark
3. The Secret Mission
4. The Danger Trail
5. The Gas Chamber
6. Behind The Clock
7. The Tiger's Claw
8. Prisoners in The Sky
9. A Desperate Chance
10. The Sky Clears

𝔖 The Vanishing Rider

DIRECTOR: Ray Taylor

CAST: William Desmond, Ethlyne Clair, Bud Osborne, Nelson McDowell

RELEASE DATE: 16 Jan. 1928   RELEASING COMPANY: Universal

CHAPTER TITLES:

1. The Road Agent
2. Trapped

3. A Fight For Life
4. Brother Against Brother
5. The Wings of Fury
6. The False Message
7. The Waters of Death
8. The Bargain of Fear
9. The Last Stand
10. Vengeance

The Vanishing West

DIRECTOR: Richard Thorpe

CAST: Jack Daugherty, Leo Maloney, Yakima Canute, Jack Perrin, William Fairbanks, Eileen Sedgwick, Fred Church, Mickey Bennett, Helen Gibson

RELEASE DATE: 15 Oct. 1928 (SR)

RELEASING COMPANY: Mascot Pictures Corporation

CHAPTER TITLES: 10 episodes

Vultures of The Sea

DIRECTOR: Richard Thorpe

CAST: Johnnie Walker, Shirley Mason, Tom Santschi, Boris Karloff, Frank Hagney, John Carpenter, George Magrill, Joe Bennett

RELEASE DATE: 1 August 1928 (SR)

RELEASING COMPANY: Mascot Pictures Corporation

CHAPTER TITLES:

1. The Hell Ship
2. Cast Adrift
3. Driven To Port
4. Scum of The Seas
5. The Harbor of Danger
6. The Stolen Ship
7. At The Mercy of The Flames
8. The Fight For Possession
9. The Traitor
10. The End of The Quest

The Yellow Cameo

DIRECTOR: Spencer G. Bennet

CAST: Allene Ray, Ed Hearn, Cyclone (dog), Noble Johnson, Tom London, Maurice Klein, Ed Snyder, Frank Redman

RELEASE DATE: 3 June 1928   RELEASING COMPANY: Pathé

CHAPTER TITLES:

1. The Train Robbery
2. The Mystery Man
3. The Race For Life
4. In The Path of Doom
5. The Signal Tower

6. The Tower of Death
7. Fangs of Fury
8. The Devil's Cauldron
9. The Underworld Peril
10. The Lost Treasure

1929

✆ *The Ace of Scotland Yard*

DIRECTOR: Ray Taylor

CAST: Crauford Kent, Florence Allen, Grace Cunard, Monty Montague, Herbert Prior

RELEASE DATE: 30 Sept. 1929   RELEASING COMPANY: Universal (Released in 2 versions, silent and sound, the latter with synchronized musical score, sound effects, and dialogue)

CHAPTER TITLES:

1. The Fatal Circlet
2. A Cry In The Night
3. The Dungeon of Doom
4. The Depths of Limehouse
5. Menace of The Mummy

6. Dead or Alive
7. Shadows of Fear
8. The Baited Trap
9. A Battle of Wits
10. The Final Judgment

✆ *The Black Book*

DIRECTORS: Spencer G. Bennet, Thomas L. Storey

CAST: Allene Ray, Walter Miller, Frank Lackteen, Paul Panzer, Marie Mosquini, Edith London, Willie Fung, Edward Cecil, John Webb Dillon, Evan Pearson, Clay de Roy

RELEASE DATE: 21 July 1929   RELEASING COMPANY: Pathé

CHAPTER TITLES:

1. The Secret of the Vault
2. The Death Rail
3. A Shot in The Night
4. The Danger Sign
5. The Flaming Trap
6. The Black Dam
7. The Fatal Hour
8. The Mystery Mill
9. The Assassin Strikes
10. Out of The Shadows

The Diamond Master

DIRECTOR: Jack Nelson

CAST: Hayden Stevenson, Louise Lorraine, Al Hart, Monty Montague, Louis Stern, Walter Maly

RELEASE DATE: 3 Feb. 1929 RELEASING COMPANY: Universal

CHAPTER TITLES:

1. The Secret of The Night
2. The Diamond of Death
3. The Tunnel of Terror
4. Trapped
5. The Diamond Machine
6. The Wolf Pack
7. The Death Trap
8. Into The Flames
9. The Last Stand
10. The Reckoning

The Fatal Warning

DIRECTOR: Richard Thorpe

CAST: Helen Costello, Ralph Graves, George Periolat, Phillip Smalley, Lloyd Whitlock, Boris Karloff, Sid Crossley, Thomas Lingham, Symona Boniface

RELEASE DATE: 15 Feb. 1929 (SR) RELEASING COMPANY: Mascot Pictures Corporation

CHAPTER TITLES:

1. The Fatal Warning
2. The Phantom Flyer
3. The Crash of Doom
4. The Pit of Death
5. Menacing Fingers
6. Into Thin Air
7. The House of Horror
8. Fatal Fumes
9. By Whose Hand
10. Unmasked

A Final Reckoning

DIRECTOR: Ray Taylor

CAST: Newton House, Louise Lorraine, Jay Wilsey, Edmund Cobb

RELEASE DATE: 15 April 1929 RELEASING COMPANY: Universal

CHAPTER TITLES:

1. A Treacherous Friend
2. The Man Trap
3. Trapped
4. Face To Face
5. Ambushed
6. Unmasked
7. In Wolf's Clothing
8. An Attack in The Dark
9. A Ride For Life
10. The Blast of Death
11. The Living Dead
12. The Reward

The Fire Detective

DIRECTORS: Spencer G. Bennet, Thomas L. Storey

CAST: Gladys McConnell, Hugh Allan, Leo Maloney, John Cossar, Frank Lackteen, Larry Steers

RELEASE DATE: 3 March 1929 RELEASING COMPANY: Pathé

CHAPTER TITLES:

1. The Arson Trail
2. The Pit of Darkness
3. The Hidden Hand
4. The Convict Strikes
5. On Flaming Waters
6. The Man of Mystery
7. The Ape Man
8. Back From Death
9. Menace of The Past
10. The Flame of Love

King of The Kongo

DIRECTOR: Richard Thorpe

CAST: Jacqueline Logan, Walter Miller, Richard Tucker, Boris Karloff

RELEASE DATE: 20 August 1929 (SR) RELEASING COMPANY: Mascot Pictures Corporation (Released in 2 versions, silent

and sound, the latter with synchronized musical score, sound
effects, and dialogue)

CHAPTER TITLES:

1. Into The Unknown
2. Terrors of The Jungle
3. The Temple of Beasts
4. Gorilla Warfare
5. Danger in The Dark
6. The Fight At The Lion's Pit
7. The Fatal Moment
8. Sentenced To Death
9. Desperate Chances
10. Jungle Justice

Pirate of Panama

DIRECTOR: Ray Taylor

CAST: Jay Wilsey, Natalie Kingston

RELEASE DATE: 8 July 1929   RELEASING COMPANY: Universal

CHAPTER TITLES:

1. Pirate Gold
2. Mutiny
3. The Treasure Chest
4. The Pirates' Secret
5. Vengeance
6. Trapped By The Tide
7. The Shadow of Death
8. The Menacing Swamp
9. The Signal of Hope
10. Two Lives For One
11. The Price of Greed
12. The Greatest Treasure

Queen of The Northwoods

DIRECTORS: Spencer G. Bennet, Thomas L. Storey

CAST: Ethlyne Clair, Walter Miller

RELEASE DATE: 12 May 1929   RELEASING COMPANY: Pathé

CHAPTER TITLES:

1. The Wolf Devil's Challenge
2. A Bottomless Grave
3. Devil Worshipers
4. Wings of Death
5. The Wolf Devil Strikes
6. The Leap of Death
7. The Flaming Peril
8. Brand of The Beast
9. Trapped By The Fiend
10. The Den of Evil

Tarzan, The Tiger

DIRECTOR: Henry McRae

CAST: Frank Merrill, Natalie Kingston, Al Ferguson

RELEASE DATE: 9 Dec. 1929 RELEASING COMPANY: Universal

CHAPTER TITLES:

1. Call of The Jungle
2. The Road to Opar
3. The Altar of The Flaming God
4. The Vengeance of La
5. Condemned to Death
6. Tantor, The Terror
7. In Deadly Peril
8. Loop of Death
9. Flight of Werper
10. Prisoner of The Apes
11. The Jaws of Death
12. The Jewels of Opar
13. A Human Sacrifice
14. Tarzan's Rage
15. Tarzan's Triumph

1930

The Indians Are Coming

DIRECTOR: Henry McRae

CAST: Allene Ray, Tim McCoy, Edmund Cobb, Francis Ford, Wilbur McGaugh, Bud Osborne, Charles Royal

RELEASE DATE: 10 Oct. 1930 RELEASING COMPANY: Universal (Released in 2 versions, silent and sound)

CHAPTER TITLES:

1. Pals In Buckskin
2. A Call To Arms
3. A Furnace of Fear
4. The Red Terror
5. The Circle of Death
6. Hate's Harvest
7. Hostages of Fear
8. The Dagger Duel
9. The Blast of Death
10. Redskins Vengeance
11. Frontiers Aflame
12. The Trail's End

The Jade Box

DIRECTOR: Ray Taylor

CAST: Jack Perrin, Eileen Sedgwick, Monroe Salisbury, Francis Ford

RELEASE DATE: 24 March 1930

RELEASING COMPANY: Universal (Released in 2 versions, silent and sound, the latter with synchronized musical score, sound effects, and dialogue)

CHAPTER TITLES:

1. The Jade of Jeopardy!
2. Buried Alive!
3. The Shadow Man
4. The Fatal Prophecy
5. The Unseen Death
6. The Haunting Shadow
7. The Guilty Man
8. The Grip of Death
9. Out of The Shadows
10. The Atonement

The Lightning Express

DIRECTOR: Henry McRae

CAST: Lane Chandler, Louise Lorraine, Floyd Criswell, Jim Pierce, Robert Kelly

RELEASE DATE: 2 June 1930

RELEASING COMPANY: Universal (Released in 2 versions, silent and sound, the latter with synchronized musical score, sound effects, and dialogue)

CHAPTER TITLES:

1. A Shot In The Dark
2. A Scream of Terror
3. Dangerous Rails
4. The Death Trap
5. Tower of Terror
6. A Call For Help
7. The Runaway Freight
8. The Show Down
9. The Secret Survey
10. Cleared Tracks

⑤ *Terry of The Times*

DIRECTOR: Henry McRae

CAST: Reed Howes, Lotus Thompson, Sheldon Lewis, John Oscar, William Hayes, Mary Grant, Norman Thom, Kingsley Benedict

RELEASE DATE: 11 August 1930   RELEASING COMPANY: Universal (Released in 2 versions, silent and sound, the latter with synchronized musical score, sound effects, but no dialogue)

CHAPTER TITLES:

1. The Mystic Mendicants
2. The Fatal 30!
3. Death's Highway
4. Eyes of Evil
5. Prowlers of The Night

6. The Stolen Bride
7. A Doorway of Death
8. A Trail of Trickery
9. Caught In The Net
10. A Race For Love

INDEX OF NAMES

INDEX OF TITLES

GENERAL INDEX

A

Allgood Picture Corporation: 89
American Film Manufacturing
Company: 4, 31, 38–39, 86
Animated Weekly: 10
Arrow Film Company: 16, 72, 77,
95, 101, 104, 111–13, 130
Associated Photoplays Corpora-
tion: 26
Astra: 26, 58, 66

B

Balboa: 35, 58
Biograph: 4, 21, 124
Bulls Eye Film Corporation: 79
Burston Films: 73, 78, 96

C

California Studios: 129
Canyon Pictures: 85
Capital Film Company: 26
Celebrated Players Film Cor-
poration: 79
Chicago Tribune: 7–8, 15
Cinema Chats: 73
Consolidated Film Industries: 140
Crystal Film Company: 10

D

Davis Distributing Division: 122,
129–30
Dell Henderson Productions: 113

E

Edison Company: 4–5, 17, 19, 53
Essanay Film Manufacturing
Company: 45, 55
Export-Import Film Company:
102

F

"Fame and Fortune Contest": 114
Famous Players: 39
Film Booking Office (F.B.O.):
111, 138–39
Film Daily: 102
Fine Arts: 39, 131
First National: 77, 129
Fox: v, 76, 78, 82
Frohman Amusement Corpora-
tion: 83

G

General Film Company: 61
Goldwyn: 77
Goodwill Pictures of California:
130

291

Rayart: 113, 122, 137
Reliance: 4, 33
Republic Pictures Corporation:
140

S

Sawyer-Lubin: 114
Select Films: 83
Selig Polyscope Company: 6, 52,
103
Serial Film Company: 40
Serial Producing Company: 55
Serials: songs from, 9, 33, 66, 147;
audience tastes, 59–60, 75–76;
stories made into, 124–25, 128,
143, 145, 149, 151; silent-sound,
147–48, 150–52
SLK Serial Corporation: 66, 68
Star Serial Corporation: 99
Syndicate Pictures: 141

T

Thanhouser: 4, 15
Triangle: 68

U

Unicorn Film Service Corporation:
47–48
United Artists: 77
Universal: v, 4, 10, 19–21, 23, 25–
26, 31, 35, 39–40, 55, 63, 68, 70,
76–78, 86–87, 98–101, 103, 109–
13, 117–18, 120, 122, 126, 129,
135, 139–40, 144–45, 149,
150–51

V

Vitagraph: v, xvi, 4, 16, 32–33, 51–
52, 63–64, 70, 82, 95, 110, 112
Vital Exchanges: 122, 129–30

W

Warner Brothers: 78, 88, 96,
101–102
Weiss Brothers Artclass: 97, 137,
141
Weiss Brothers–Numa Picture
Corporation: 97
Western Pictures Corporation: 114
Wharton Studio: 27, 44–45, 61, 82

Continued Next Week has been printed on paper designed for an effective life of at least three hundred years. The book has been planned for maximum comfort in reading and handling. The type is eleven-point Old Style No. 7, set on the Linotype with two points of spacing between lines. This face is transitional and has more "modern" than "old style" characteristics. As a letter form, it is without pretension or notable distinction, but its pragmatic sanction has always been its excellent readability for people in all walks of life.

UNIVERSITY OF OKLAHOMA PRESS

NORMAN